THE SMILING LAND

THE
SMILING

LAND

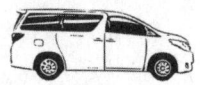

All Around the Circle in My Newfoundland and Labrador

ALAN DOYLE

DOUBLEDAY CANADA

PUBLISHED IN 2025 BY DOUBLEDAY CANADA

Doubleday Canada, an imprint of Penguin Random House Canada Limited, 320 Front Street West, Suite 1400, Toronto, Ontario, M5V 3B6, Canada penguinrandomhouse.ca

Doubleday Canada and colophon are registered trademarks of Penguin Random House LLC.

The authorized representative in the EU for product safety and compliance is Penguin Random House Ireland, Morrison Chambers, 32 Nassau Street, Dublin, D02 YH68, Ireland, https://eu-contact.penguin.ie

Library and Archives Canada Cataloguing in Publication
Title: The smiling land : all around the circle in my Newfoundland and Labrador / Alan Doyle.
Names: Doyle, Alan, 1969- author
Identifiers: Canadiana (print) 20250153734 | Canadiana (ebook) 20250153742 | ISBN 9780385694414 (hardcover) | ISBN 9780385694421 (EPUB)
Subjects: LCSH: Doyle, Alan, 1969-—Homes and haunts. | LCSH: Newfoundland and Labrador—Description and travel. | LCSH: Curiosities and wonders—Newfoundland and Labrador. | LCSH: Newfoundland and Labrador—Miscellanea. | LCGFT: Travel writing.
Classification: LCC FC2167.6 .D69 2025 | DDC 917.1804/5—dc23

Cover design by Kelly Hill
Cover photograph: David Howells
Map and chapter opener illustrations: Adobe Stock
Book design and map by Kelly Hill
Interior photos courtesy of the author
Typeset by Terra Page

Printed in Canada

10 9 8 7 6 5 4 3 2

Penguin
Random House
DOUBLEDAY CANADA

For the people of Newfoundland and Labrador,
who never cease to amaze and delight me.

CONTENTS

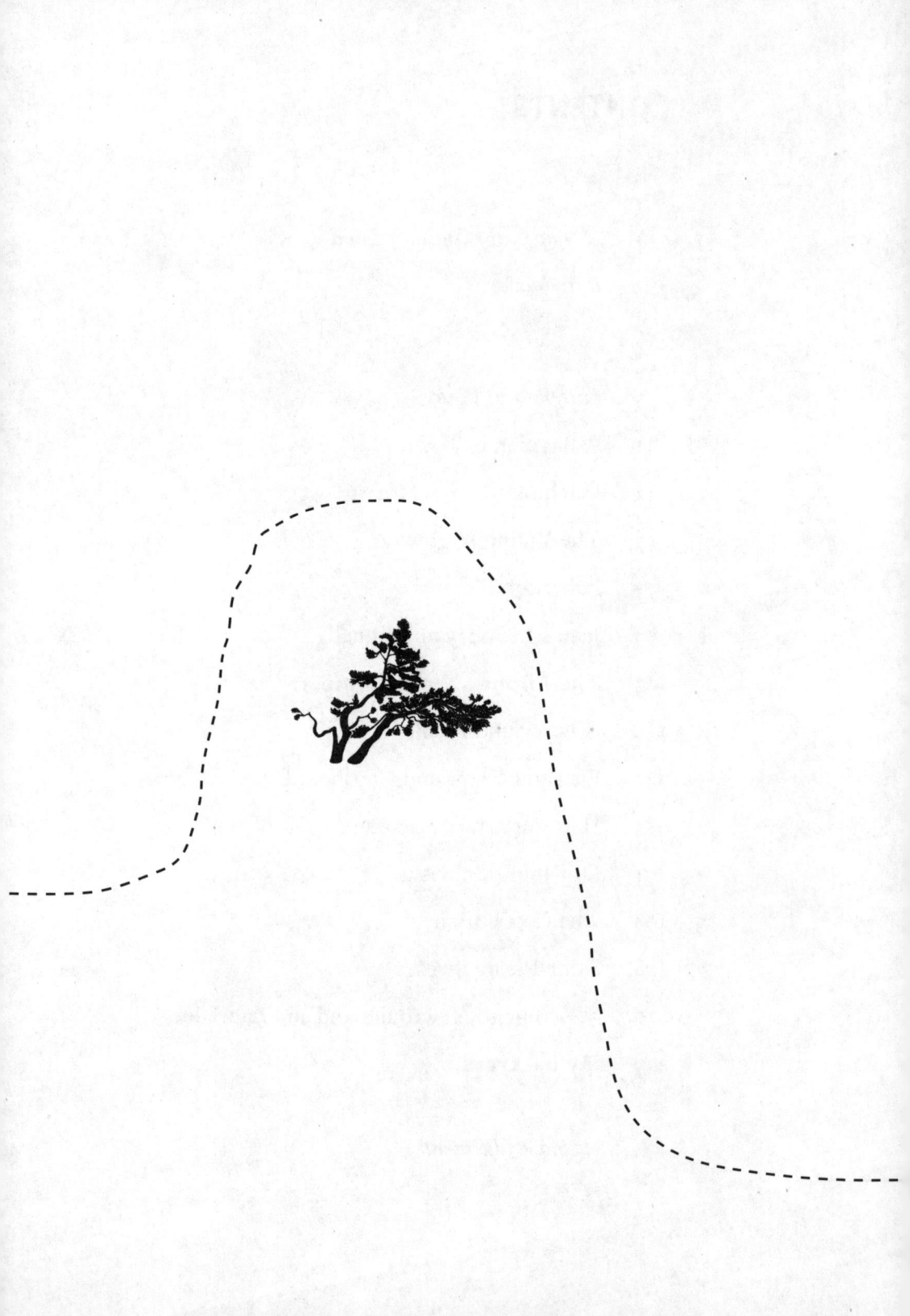

LABRADOR PENINSULA

QUEBEC

Battle Harbour

Red Bay

L'Anse aux Meadows

Point Amour

Blanc-Sablon

St. Anthony

St. Barbe

Port au Choix

GREAT
NORTHERN
PENINSULA

Cow Head

GROS MORNE
NATIONAL PARK

Western Brook Pond

Norris Point

The Tablelands

Deer Lake

Green Bay

Twillingate

FOGO ISLAND

Moreton's Harbour

Farewell

Lewisporte

CENTRAL

Gander

PORT AU PORT
PENINSULA

Corner
Brook

Gambo

Bonavista

Stephenville

Terra Nova

Port Rexton

Trinity

Come By Chance

Harbour Grace

St. John's

Rose Blanche

Dildo

Channel-Port
aux Basques

Petty Harbour

Witless Bay

BURIN
PENINSULA

Ferryland

SAINT-PIERRE
AND MIQUELON

FORTUNE BAY

Marystown

Salt Pond

Bread
and
Cheese

Fortune

Trepassey

Saint-Pierre

Newfoundland
Labrador
Welcome

TRINITY BAY

CONCEPTION BAY

THE SMILING LAND

INTRODUCTION

The Smiling Land.

It is an odd nickname for a rock in the middle of the cold North Atlantic Ocean. Sir Cavendish Boyle coined it when, as governor of Newfoundland, he penned a poem about this place. A poem that would become the beloved ode or national anthem of this dominion and province.

It's such a bright and cheerful title. What was he thinking, I wonder?

You'd be hard pressed to think he called it such because of the weather. This is a rock that is often cloaked in fog when it isn't beaten by wind and water of biblical proportion, or smothered in a winter storm bad enough to be globally called "Snowmageddon."

And you'd have to suspend your logic more than just a little to imagine that the economic prosperity of the place made it, and everybody in it, grin . . . ever. Suffice it to say, we've never been known for our riches and wealth. In recent times, we fist-pump any years we are not named Canada's poorest province, and in not-so-recent times, at the end of the nineteenth century, our national banks completely crashed.

And you'd have to be completely off your head to think Newfoundland's political stability made the Smiling Land a good moniker for the place. Nope. In less than a century, this place has been an independent British dominion, a colony with a British-controlled commissioned government, the easternmost province of Canada, and almost a part of the United States.

From Britain's oldest colony to Canada's newest province. And that was just in my parents' childhood.

So, the Smiling Land might be an unlikely name—but I love it. It makes me smile. And just about everything in this place does.

I am a Newfoundlander. I was born in Newfoundland and live here still. I have never actually lived anywhere else. And what's even more notable is that it has never even occurred to me to do so. Despite having the good fortune to travel and experience dozens of the greatest places in the world, and despite being lucky enough to have the means to live almost anywhere, I still choose to live here, at home, in Newfoundland and Labrador.

I am often asked why.

I have struggled to articulate a specific and practical answer to this question. I mean, most folks around North America would reply with something like "I live where I live because it is where I work." Well, I almost never work here. Others might say something like "I live where I live because it is convenient." Well, as a fella who does the bulk of his work two to four time zones from my house, I can tell you this is not the case for me. Still more people might offer, "I live where I live because the weather is so awesome all the time." See my note about Snowmageddons.

I suppose I don't offer a practical answer when asked why I live here because I just don't have one.

Most others who do what I do for a living move to a more central location, like Toronto or Chicago, where they likely get away with flying less than 120 times a year, with a hundred or more of those flights taking well over three hours apiece. Others go to the heartbeat of the entertainment industry, in places like Nashville or Los Angeles, to be close to the action instead of being far, far removed from it. Still more take the elite opportunity to afford themselves a life in cherished and glamorous places like London, New York, or Paris. But not me. I was born in the St. John's area and have lived in that same place for fifty-five years and counting.

I've somehow convinced myself that I have the best of both worlds. The world at home and the world abroad. I once described this ideal situation as "Always going somewhere. Always coming home."

Again, why?

In the absence of a simple and practical answer, I often resort to existential responses like "This is where I belong" and "I feel like I am supposed to be here." These answers are genuine, if not specific. Maybe I shouldn't try to answer with anything but the one thought that comes to me whenever I'm asked why I live here.

I love it.

I wonder if it still smiles as it did for Sir Cavendish over a century ago.

Events like the tragic 1992 cod moratorium, which in the stroke of a government pen destroyed a centuries-old economy, and the dawn of international connectivity have changed so much of this place. Isolated fishing towns are not isolated anymore, and they don't fish like they used to, if at all. I've long wondered how this has affected life along our coast. Is this a place in transition?

Life here had been one thing. Was it becoming something else? It makes me want to discover and rediscover my own backyard.

So, I decided to set out around Newfoundland and Labrador and see what surprises me. I persuaded my wife, Joanne—and even our eighteen-year-old son, Henry—to join me on parts of the journey as I revisited some places and explored others I've always wanted to see. And I've documented each trip in the chapters you are about to read. Interspersed, I'll tell you about my long love affair with St. John's, the only home I've known or wanted to know since I was a teenager. We won't go everywhere in this glorious province, as we should save a few spots for a lifetime of trips, but let's head to a bunch together. In each case, I'll take you along and show you what I see, as well as offer some commentary about the many, many peculiarities of this wonderful, whacky place I call home.

I bet there'll be surprises for you and me both. Maybe we'll discover what time it is in southern Labrador. Maybe we'll find pirates in Harbour Grace. And maybe, just maybe, we'll figure out why Sir Cavendish was so charmed by the place.

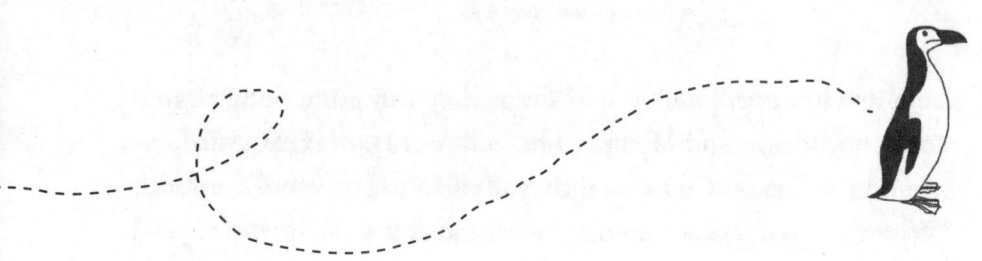

FAREWELL TO FOGO

F arewell.

Odd way to start a book, I know. But here we are. Approaching a line of cars and trucks awaiting a ferry in Farewell, Newfoundland and Labrador. I have my well-worn computer on my lap as I look over the dash through the bug-beaten windshield of our road-weary Honda Odyssey minivan, which my wife, Joanne, has captained some four-hundred-plus kilometres northwest of our home in St. John's. Through the glass, I can see a car ferry stubbornly plugging its way towards us through the cold, cold North Atlantic, which today—and I suspect most days—is about as tranquil and inviting as you would ever expect it to be in a place called "Goodbye."

This is one of the many times in my life I've been made truly aware of how remote the various parts of my home province are. I often imagine a scenario in which some family in Chicago get offered a trip to Newfoundland and are excited to do it, but have no idea how far off the beaten track they'll be going. I picture them driving north and east as far as they can go, well past New York and Boston and Maine, even well past Halifax. Somewhere around the Canso Causeway, they could be forgiven for asking, "Where the frig are we going?" Imagine that same crowd finally arriving in North Sydney and being told they need to get on a ferry. Again, they could be forgiven for asking for specifics.

"Oh, is this a long ferry?" they might inquire.

And the toll operator might say, "Well, this is the shorter of the two ferries."

"Ah, good, so quite short then," the Chicago dad might say with a sigh of relief. A relief that will be short-lived when the toll operator continues:

"Yes, my son, this one is only about eight hours when it's not windy, but it is always windy here, so more likely about twelve hours. But that's still only about half as long as the other one, so yes b'y this is the short one, for sure."

As they sail away from the shore and find themselves bobbing in the Gulf of St. Lawrence, they surely could not be blamed for asking, again, "Where the frig are we going?"

Imagine that same family getting off a ferry ride longer than an average day's work in Port aux Basques and kissing the solid ground beneath them, and asking the missus at the gas station for directions to Fogo Island and discovering they still had over six hundred kilometres to drive to get to where I am sitting right now. I can picture Dad fuelling the car for the tenth time on this trip, somewhere around Badger, and one of the kids yelling out the window, "No, seriously, where in the frig are we going?"

I giggle as I picture the faces in that car as if they were right behind us now, absolutely astonished that they still have one more not-at-all-insignificant ferry ride ahead of them. And that ferry is heading out—and I mean *straight* out—to the wild and windy ocean.

"Where the frig are we going, indeed?"

I must have said it out loud, as Joanne responded with an energetic "Out there. Way out there."

"Loves it." I feel a breeze as the driver's-side window opens to the wind off the water.

"Nice calm day for a crossing!" offers the happy fella in the ferry toll booth, and his smile tells me he believes it. As we pull ahead to take our spot in line, I note that his optimistic attitude is not just refreshing and sprightly, as many have come to expect from Newfoundlanders, but is quite likely a completely necessary survival trait. "Wonderful drop of rain," my grandmother used to say as she hurried to get the clothes off the line. This scenario here today is as good an example of this provincial compulsion as any, I guess.

I am excited to head back to Fogo Island, but it would be misleading to suggest that the whitecaps on the grey water look anything like the welcoming seas of the wonderfully shot provincial tourism commercials. I love those idyllic portrayals of rolling green hills and home-knit sweaters riding a gentle breeze on a Cape Broyle clothesline as a cute red-haired kid runs to Nan's bright yellow clapboard saltbox house, the smoke from its chimney drifting straight as an arrow up to the cloudless blue sky. But that's not what I see out over the dash today. I can totally understand why that family from Chicago might find it cold and windy here, and the thought of sailing over those whitecaps a hardship. But I'm with the toll booth fella. Compared to what it could be, this is indeed a calm day for a crossing, and it for sure is a very pleasant place to get rolling.

So, why start with Farewell? I have decided our journey around this province should begin here for a few reasons.

One is that this could very well be seen as the place where the province itself got started. This area is about as close as you can get to the Old Country and is indeed in the discussion about the earliest settlements in the New World. It is well known that the most easterly point in North America is Cape Spear. But here's a fun fact that is perhaps more significant: Pick a settlement on the west coast of Ireland, like Dingle, and draw a line on Google Earth across the Atlantic to a settlement in Newfoundland. You'll see that it is 3,035 kilometres to Cape Spear, but only 3,034 to Tilting, on Fogo Island. Splitting hairs, arguably, but the point is a good one, I figure. When fishermen left Ireland to sail to the New World, one of the closest and best-suited spots for them to touch ground was here on Fogo Island. Even before them, the Indigenous Beothuk frequented this area for fish and seals and birds. All this to say, this group of islands has been ground zero for ocean-based communities and industries for centuries.

Another good reason to start here is the fact that Farewell leads to the spot where, for many people living in other parts of Canada and beyond, a curiosity about this island and province started in the most formative years of their lives.

This was likely the first place you ever heard spoken about, or sung about, in Newfoundland and Labrador. We are headed "all around the circle," or as many of you may remember from your elementary school songbooks, *Fogo, Twillingate, Moreton's Harbour / All around the circle*. This lyric from the famed folk song "I'se the B'y" made its way into practically every school choir and singalong repertoire, thanks to a publication by Edith Fowke and Richard Johnston known simply as *Folk Songs of Canada*, published in the mid-1950s. If you were in school in Canada between 1955 and 1975 and you knew one fact about Newfoundland, it was probably that there were three places called Fogo, Twillingate, and Moreton's Harbour, and that the route between them likely looked like a circle on the map.

As a folksinger I am charmed, by the way, that I live in a place where songs lead the way and are often perfect ways for visitors to learn our story. I have often said, "If you want to learn about Newfoundland and Labrador, just listen to twenty folk songs from here and you'll get a pretty good picture." That makes me feel lucky as a singer, for sure.

The ferry pushes into the specially made ramp, and as we roll onto the ship, I admire the size and modernity of this marvel on the sea. I shamefully confess I'm still not sure how things made of metal can float at all. As a fella with an arts degree, this feat of engineering is a miracle to me. And as the hydraulic ramp lowers, the precision with which it mates the ferry with the wharf looks like magic, too. As a fella who can barely parallel-park a compact car, I am head-scratcher impressed with the way the captain dances this vessel the size of three office buildings over swells and in the face of gales into a parking spot with hardly a few inches for error.

I am always fascinated by the docking of massive modern ships like ferries and cruise liners, but the final brushstroke of the process always makes me grin. These giant vessels, with their GPS and autopilot and sonar and radar and all kinds of side thrusters and God knows what other technology, these vessels still send a sailor over to the side, and he tosses a rope to someone on the wharf, and a dock worker ties it on, the same way they have done for thousands and thousands of years. All this futuristic engineering and technology, moored by a rope. Not even a cool, high-tech rope. A plain and simple rope.

"They still haven't topped the idea of just tying her on with a rope, have they? No magnets or mechanical or electrical holder-on-ers, just an old-fashioned fella with an old-fashioned rope."

I look to my naval architect wife, who often giggles at my artistic observations.

"Don't fix it if it ain't broke, Alan, b'y." Joanne puts the van in gear, and a clang beneath the wheels announces we have left the mainland of Newfoundland and are indeed aboard the ferry. I have been on Fogo Island before, but never completed the trifecta of Fogo, Twillingate, and Moreton's Harbour. So, off we go. All around the circle.

I wish I could tell you the ocean looks welcoming as we push away from the Farewell Wharf, but to be perfectly honest, these waters look more ominous than anything else. Again, this is not the blue, sunlit water of the well-shot tourism commercials, with the smooth voice whispering, "Newfoundland and Labrador. Come play with us," or something like that. This is the ocean of my childhood. Dangerous, but hopefully merciful, and maybe even generous and accommodating if you are really lucky. It was to be travelled upon for sustenance and hard labour only. I was taught at an early age to respect, if not full-on fear, the North Atlantic.

"The open water is for working and dying. That's it," an old skipper who lived close by used to profess over his Sunday morning drink at our kitchen table. The Doyles in the fishing hamlet of Petty Harbour were the odd ones out, as almost all of my dad's brothers followed in my grandfather's footsteps and were not at all fishermen. Rather, many of them worked for what was known as the Light and Power, and a few of them directly in a small hydroelectric plant known as The Powerhouse.

So, while it is true I grew up in a tiny fishing village and spent my young summers running around on the wharves, I spent very little time on the actual ocean. I had few opportunities to do anything but watch boats go out empty and hopefully come back full as quickly as possible. By contrast, I remember my first-ever morning in downtown Vancouver and seeing the Pacific Coast for the first time. As dawn lit the peaceful waters of English Bay, I barely recognized it as an ocean.

"I've seen ponds with bigger lops on them," I reported on a phone call home.

The apex of my confusion was when a man gently paddled by me on his way to sea in what I would come to learn was a sea kayak. I wondered what kind of commercial fishing he could be doing in such a small boat. It took me a few minutes to realize I was seeing something I had not witnessed even one time in my life growing up in a busy little fishing town. I had seen hundreds of boats come and go to and from the open ocean, but on that morning, on a wharf on Granville Island in Vancouver, I was watching someone go onto the ocean recreationally for the very first time. Here today, in my mid-fifties, aboard a vessel on the waters headed straight out into the swells, I can barely believe anyone would ever do it unless they absolutely had to.

I make my way up to the top deck and nip outside to watch the ferry pull away from the wharf and bid farewell to Farewell. Leaving a big island to head to a smaller one, and passing a few even smaller ones on the way. Fogo is one of a few islands around here. Others include Change Islands—three small islands, one town—which has a few hundred full-time residents, and Funk Island, which was used as a fishing and hunting station through the centuries. I suspect many of these islands were used for cutting wood or for a multitude of other reasons, but Fogo was, and remains, the centrepiece and is the biggest offshore island around Newfoundland.

Fogo Island was mapped and noted as early as 1529 and was most likely named by Portuguese fishing crews, as *fogo* means "fire" in Portuguese, though some argue it really comes from *fog*. Let's go with Portuguese fire. Way cooler. The proximity to the Old Country and the wealth of resources of fish and seals made Fogo an extremely popular summer work camp for the very earliest of European settlers. It has been used as a fishing station since the early 1600s, as this was one of the main stops on the codfish highway for a couple of hundred years. As I stand on this ferry heading further and further out on the Atlantic, it becomes easier to imagine why people settled out here.

While this place is far from everything and everyone who travels North America by car, or train, or helicopter, or plane, I remind myself that, for centuries, it was ideally located for European ships in the cod hunt. In those days, Fogo Island made all the sense in the world. But since the decline of the codfish world, places like this have had to pivot and pave a new way forward. And that leads us to the main reason why I wanted to set out from here.

If part of the motivation for our journey around this home of mine is to celebrate the history, observe the present, and help imagine the future of this place, there is nowhere better to start than on Fogo Island. For this place has been rolling with the punches and paving a new path forward for centuries.

I have a love-hate relationship with ferries. I suppose it stems from being a lifelong island dweller and having depended on them for practically everything in life. The guitar you hoped to get is in a courier truck on the ferry. The concert at the stadium is cancelled because the band is stranded on the ferry in North Sydney in high winds. This frustration was amplified later in life when I started touring in bands and lobby calls were always obnoxiously early because "We have to line up for the ferry to

Vancouver Island." And then "You can't sleep in the van or bus while the ferry is moving," etc. So, I always get a bad taste in my mouth whenever I see a ferry on the travel schedule.

But the second I board a ferry, my attitude shifts, and I am delighted to be on the water no matter what the weather. I would venture to say that island folks like us get our sea legs early and, hopefully, hang onto them. I recall a ferry ride during a Great Big Sea video shoot from the island of Cozumel, Mexico, to the mainland in Playa del Carmen. We GBS lads had had a long night of celebrating in the heat the night before, and the seas were not friendly for the crossing the morning after. Tourists and locals, one after the other, all started looking green around the gills as we headed out from the dock. One person yakked in a bag in the seating area, and the inevitable chain reaction kick-started, and within minutes almost everyone was chucking. Everyone except the three Newfoundlanders, of course. Even in deep morning-after mode, we didn't mind the bobbing and weaving at all.

Today, luckily for me and all aboard, the seas that appeared ominous have calmed considerably . . . or maybe *I* have. Either way, the ride is quite pleasant as the ferry slips past a few smaller islands en route to Fogo Island.

After a brief stop for a single truck and a single walk-on passenger at Change Islands, the ferry turns ever north out to sea, and after rounding yet another smaller uninhabited island cuts hard to the east. The full view of Fogo rises out of the water and is instantly impressive in size. It is about twenty-five kilometres long and fourteen kilometres wide, making it a little longer and a lot wider than the island of Manhattan. It is very easy to imagine how early settlers and sailors would be curious about what might be ashore here.

As we approach the ferry dock, I consult an older map I've been carrying and notice far more place names than I would have thought existed on this island. The island is home to ten communities, but most Newfoundlanders will tell you there are four main towns on Fogo Island: Seldom, Fogo, Tilting, and one of my favourite names in the province, Joe Batt's Arm.

I do love the reaction of mainlanders when they hear of the whackiest place names from around the province. Lots of Arms and other body parts. Lots of Herring Necks and Devil's Heads. Dildo, the inspiration for much snickering, has been made famous by Jimmy Kimmel on American TV. I love to add the fact that directly across from our Dildo is a place called Spread Eagle. Others in that vein include Leading Tickles, Blow Me Down, and Conception Bay. I've always favoured Come by Chance, as it just sounds like good luck, and there's a small town on the south coast called Push Through, which I can only imagine harbours the toughest people on earth.

An announcement that we are docking sends us down to the vehicle deck, and in minutes we roll onto Fogo Island. I barely have time to explain to Joanne that I've been writing about Newfoundland place names when we pass what has to be in the running for the loneliest place name on earth.

Seldom Come By.

It even looks sad by itself on the page like that. Locals would later tell me this place was named for being busy, as in "the boats seldom come by without stopping in." I am relieved to hear this, but a lonely-sounding name is still a lonely-sounding name. No wonder they mostly refer to it as just Seldom these days, though I'm not sure that's much more optimistic.

We drive across Fogo Island, which takes us ever up from the Seldom side through some wooded areas to what feels like a plateau in the middle, then quicky down again, bound for the town of Fogo. I ask Jo to stop for a sec and I jump out to take a photo or two from high above this place, which appears as fantastical as ever and could easily be the setting for the next *Lord of the Rings* or *Game of Thrones*. Whoever first called Newfoundland "The Rock" could very well have been standing where I am, looking over Fogo. It would be unfair to say there's not a tree to be seen, because from where I am standing, I can see six. Everything else is hard rock, with a thin layer of topsoil or grass or moss here and there. These houses I see are undeniably perched on bedrock just inches from the sea, with little or no protection from the wide-open ocean's gales. It somehow simultaneously looks like a place that could be swept away at any moment, while appearing solid as the rocks it sits upon.

"Every house in this place must have salt water sprayed on it at least once a week." I slide my selfie-taking iPhone back into my jacket pocket and nip back into the minivan.

To survey Fogo is to look over a place built with one thing in mind: access to the ocean. And it is taken to extremes here. Not only are these few dozen rough-side-out clapboard houses built in a very exposed area, but they seem to be concentrated around the narrowest piece of land in sight. The town of Fogo has been settled since 1697 and is effectively built around an isthmus that connects the mainland of Fogo Island with a smaller island. A short but definite bridge connects them and feels to me, here today, like the centre of town, and confirms for me that the original settlers, and everyone since, had the greatest ocean views on a nice day and even better ones on a stormy one.

As we drive through town, Fogo looks busy for a place with less than a thousand people, and there are quite a few signs for Airbnbs and tourism accommodations. With excellent boat excursions and brilliant hikes on the Fogo Head and Lion's Den Trails, I'm sure tourism plays an ever-growing role in the local economy, but make no mistake: this place was built for the fishery. I look up, way up, as the minivan stops on a gravel parking lot. One glance and I know for certain that we have reached the very thing I wanted to see.

Dominating the view above the ocean is Brimstone Head. If the town of Fogo itself was *Lord of the Rings*-y, Brimstone Head makes it positively film-ready. This grey, bone-rock monolith rises up and up and up again out of the edge of town and reaches to the clouds, with one narrow footpath leading to a peak that somehow looks equally inviting and treacherous at the same time. It's like a prehistoric giant whale had just breached and been turned to stone by Medusa's glance, its massive head and torso in mid-air for all eternity. It might not stand out if it were in the Rockies or the Alps, but next to this tiny sea-level town, Brimstone Head might as well be Mount Everest.

It is a daunting climb, but you absolutely got to do it, so I turn my back on the town and head straight towards the summit and the outer edge facing the sea. As I make my way up the winding, ever-rising path, I am reminded of a fun fact. There are still quite a few folks kicking around that swear the world is flat. You know the gang, the Flat Earth Society. They figure the Earth has four corners. And according to the Flat Earth crowd, Brimstone Head on Fogo Island is indeed one of those corners.

Now, I am no scientist. I have a Bachelor of Arts and I've been playing in bands for thirty-plus years. So, what do I know about the shape of planets, really? I've heard very convincing arguments by learned people who tell me definitively that the Earth is round, and with apologies to the Flat Earthers, I tend to believe the scientists when it comes to outer-space-type stuff. Truth be told, I never doubted the scientists for a second.

Till now.

As I reach the plateau of Brimstone Head, I honestly wonder if I have dismissed the Flat Earth crowd prematurely. I grab onto the rail of the observation platform and peer over the side, straight down into the cold, windy North Atlantic. A fall from here would end a god. I face the gale, look as far off as I can see on this day, and what I can see is . . . well, nothing. Just water and wind and the whitecaps where those two meet.

"If the Earth did have four corners, this would definitely be one of them," I say to Joanne when I make it back to the mini-van. I'm soaked to the skin, looking like a man who has very recently started doubting much that he thought he ever knew. We start to roll, and I make one more observation with Brimstone Head filling the rear-view mirror: "That hill of granite towers over the town like the Grinch's mountain over Whoville." I am grateful the coffee in the travel mug is still warm as we head to Joe Batt's Arm.

The edges of Fogo Island are dotted with cool, interesting communities, and the middle is no man's land. There is almost no sign of human habitation along the road from one town to the next, as I suppose none of these towns were ever meant to be connected by car or train. While this might be no man's land, it is great land for caribou. We spot a half dozen of them along the low-lying brush, no doubt feasting on the many wild berries and shrubs that cover this place.

Where one singer fella sees very little, a caribou sees lots.

Just as I become convinced that we won't see a house till we hit Joe Batt's Arm, we all of a sudden come to an intersection that has tons of stuff. Right in the middle of the island, not particularly close to any community, there is a junction with a school, a clinic, a drug store, a hockey rink, and amongst other things, the detachment for the police. I can only imagine that having all these facilities in one town or another would tip the scales, so they did the most cooperative thing they could think of and put everything in the middle, where all hands could access them equally.

Cooperation. If there's one thing that connects the towns on this island, it is cooperation. It is the superpower of this place, and has been for a very, very long time.

But more about that after we get to Joe Batt's . . . or J'Bat's, or the JBA, as the locals call it.

A tiny town with at least two nicknames. God, I love Newfoundland.

The name Joe Batt's Arm often puzzles mainlanders and almost never puzzles Newfoundlanders. Someone from Mississauga might wonder why someone's baseball bat or body part warrants naming a town after it, while we Newfoundlanders just know at first glance that this is an arm of the bay named for a fella called Joe whose last name was clearly Batt. We are nothing if not totally sensible people. Sometimes.

In the middle of the northern shore, Fogo takes a sharp turn inland and opens up for what is known as Shoal Bay, and as we roll to its far end we come to the start of the next settlement, which is really a collection of settlements that decided to get along and survive. Barr'd Islands and Joe Batt's Arm were once distinct towns but then became one. As a matter of fact, all the towns on Fogo Island are now administered as one. In an astonishing act of good sense, this place accomplished the impossible and amalgamated all eleven towns in 2011.

That is just one of the more recent examples in the history of Fogo Island's long-established policy of rolling with the punches and paving a better path forward. These people have been organizing and holding fast since they defeated Premier Smallwood's attempts to resettle the place not long after Confederation with Canada. Before that, the Fishermen's Protective Union started in 1911, and in the '60s they formed the Shipbuilders Co-operative. Scholars have been coming here for decades to study what has come to be called the Fogo Process, which has made this place a model for rural collaboration.

Even the destruction of the sealing industry in the 1970s and the infamous cod moratorium of the early '90s could not flatten this place, as these folks have once again conjured up an incredible economy based on adventure and ecotourism. In a most fascinating way, this place shows us its future by shining a light on its past. The centre of this revitalization comes into view as we round the turn into Joe Batt's Arm.

The Fogo Island Inn looks unlikely at first glance, and after a good stare or two it seems simply impossible. Its silhouette, with its fish flake–inspired stanchions, is familiar, but its enormous scale makes me blink and rub my eyes, despite the fact that I've seen it a few times before today. This twenty-nine-room five-star inn is perched on the bare rocks, inches from the crashing Atlantic ocean on the edge of Joe Batt's Arm. It dwarfs any other building in sight despite being several hundred metres away from any neighbour.

We use the term "awesome" a lot around here. Perhaps too much. But I am confident using it to describe the Fogo Island Inn. To look upon it gives me a sense of awe and surprise that can only come when something is so beautiful and unexpected that one can't help but wonder how someone ever thought of it, much less actually built it. You immediately assume your eyes are playing tricks on you and that you can't actually be seeing what you think you are seeing. I remember walking through a crowd of people in Barcelona, and the Sagrada Familia rising up before me, and feeling a tear well in my eyes as I stood below it. That building and the Fogo Island Inn are the only two ever to have given me this involuntary reaction. They both seem beyond human capability to me. So, yes, the Fogo Island Inn is awesome.

"Positively alien," I said to Joanne as we stood together in Spain, and I say the same thing here as we pass Barr'd Islands.

As well as for the writing of this book, I am here to participate in a weekend in support of Shorefast, a social enterprise focusing on building economic and cultural resilience on Fogo Island. I am to play a concert with some local musicians in one of the many historic buildings that this organization has preserved and restored. Shorefast and the inn are all part of the incredible vision of one incredible Fogo Islander. If the decades and generations of holding fast and thinking outside of the box could possibly produce an Olympian-level hold-faster and out-of-the-box thinker, that prodigy would be Zita Cobb.

Zita is as Fogo Island as it gets. Her bio proudly claims her as an eighth-generation Fogo Islander who was born in the late 1950s into a house where she had no running water or electricity, but did have six brothers. Her Fogo survivalist traits served her well at a young age as she battled and beat tuberculosis, a disease that sadly bested many Newfoundlanders at that time. Zita forged ahead and graduated high school on Fogo Island and university in Ottawa.

After an impressive early career she eventually made her way to an Ottawa company called JDS Fitel, which later merged with another outfit called Uniphase to form JDS Uniphase. Based in

California, this company made and sold fancy technical stuff for optical communications. It quickly boomed, and not long after the merger, Zita exercised stock options worth lots and lots and lots of money. She then donated lots and lots and lots of it to start the Shorefast Foundation and eventually build the inn, which opened in 2013 and has been running successfully ever since.

It is an architectural marvel conceived by Zita and Newfoundland-born architect Todd Saunders. People fly from all over the globe to see and visit this place.

David Letterman, Gwyneth Paltrow, and I have stayed there.

(Sorry, I just wanted to type that sentence once in my life.)

As we round the corner on the main road through the JBA, we pass a few of the buildings the Shorefast Foundation has taken under its wing. The SUF (Society of United Fishermen) Hall is in the fleet, and amongst other acquisitions stands the former St. John the Evangelist Church, where I'll be playing tomorrow night. A quick look around the harbour shows that Joe Batt's Arm has an unlikely number of public buildings for what, even in its heyday, would have been hundreds, certainly not thousands of people. The harbour ahead is wider than your average rural Newfoundland community. Practically its entire perimeter is lined with wharves or boat launches, small marinas or fishing stages. Even for a Petty Harbour fella like myself, it is worth a trip to Fogo just to see how this place has made a living and a life as a part of the ocean around it.

"I was brought up near the water. These people were brought up *in* it."

Joanne nods in response, as I'm sure she's weary of my yammering and just wants to get to the inn after a long day of driving. I'd been looking hard to the right for a few moments and had not realized we'd turned onto the road out to the inn. In those few seconds, the inn went from being an anomaly far out on the rocks to an undeniably real and present wonder of modern architecture. We finally stop the minivan and have reached our destination. And what a destination it is.

I should say at this point that I have been lucky enough to stay at the inn a few times, but you don't need to stay here to enjoy much of Fogo. There are quite a few options for other visitor accommodations on the island, for almost any budget. You can book a tour of the inn or reserve a table for dinner in the lobby restaurant. Whether you stay for a week, or just pop in for a tour and lunch, you will experience the most sophisticated and contemporary treatment of the most simple and traditional things.

The first thing you see when you walk into this modern marvel is a wood stove. Not a fancy new kind of ski lodge Scandinavian open fireplace . . . a simple wood stove. And next to it, a locally made wooden rocking chair with a home-knit blanket draped over the back. I am amazed as ever that Zita and Todd have made this five-star place out of things that me and people from my parents' generation would have taken for granted their whole lives.

Just about every time you sit on a chair, wrap up in a quilt, lean on a bar, or rest your glasses on a nightstand, you are in contact with something locally made from local materials. The gourmet food often features fish and game caught locally, vegetables and herbs from local gardens and root cellars, and even mosses, plants, and berries that grow wild on the island.

The dining room is walled with floor-to-ceiling glass overlooking the rocks and waves.

"The windows are gently kissed by the saltwater spray on a calm day, and slapped by the waves on the odd rough one," our server says as he offers us a teeny white loaf and molasses butter. As we study our menus, I can see this entire place is a celebration of all that has sustained these people and a clear reminder that it is, or at least should be, these same things that will carry us forward.

We ditch our stuff in a room with another wood stove, more locally made wooden furniture, and a bed covered in a magnificent patchwork quilt, all of which sits in front of more floor-to-ceiling windows so you can look upon the blue-and-white sky and ocean and, quite perfectly, nothing else.

It would be easy to just flop off and read, or write a book, but we have got a couple of stops to make before our evening event.

The actual town of Joe Batt's Arm has several highlights, including small art galleries and craft shops, but my favourite by far is Joe Batt's Point Trail. This hike reaches past Joe Batt's Arm South, which to my eye always appears more west of the JBA, but what the frig do I know? And to confuse you more, Dear Reader, it goes due north.

This easy, flat coastal trail offers an arresting view of the inn across the harbour. The point of land we are walking on extends further out into the ocean than the site of the inn, so you can look back in on it in a way that's impossible to do from the other side. The inn sits so close to the ocean that you can't see its magnificent northern facade without getting washed into open ocean. But from this side, on this sunny day, this one glance at something so impossibly impressive is worth the trip to Fogo.

This trail also allows for a good look at one of the six artist studios that the Shorefast Foundation commissioned Todd Saunders to imagine, design, and install on various parts of the Island. These buildings, as well as being just friggin' cool things to look at, are designed to be inspirational artist workspaces. In one, you might find a musician writing and recording songs, and in another a painter might have a few easels wet with fresh paint.

Like the inn, these structures are fascinatingly familiar and foreign at the same time. The Long Studio, which sits before me now, is a long and narrow structure, its shape and inspiration instantly recognizable. The roofline is simple, like a local shed; the cladding rough-sawed wood, like the houses in town; the concrete supports, like the stanchions of the inn, taken directly from a fishing flake. Yet, in a single glance, it is easy to see that this building, though inspired by this place, is not at all *of* this place. It is like a lot of stuff around here, yet there is nothing like it. And I suppose that dichotomy is the charm of many of the aspects of the Shorefast Foundation, and why any hungry traveller absolutely must come here.

Or you could just come for the auk statue, which is the third reason I love this trail. A few kilometres out on the Joe Batt's Point trail stands a human-size bronze statue of an auk—or great auk, as they are more commonly known. These flightless birds once inhabited Fogo and Funk Islands, feeding off the plentiful fish and crustaceans in the area. They were beautiful black-and-white birds that, to a novice birder like me, look like the progeny of a large seagull and a penguin. They were decent, family-minded creatures, too, whose couples mated for life and co-parented their young even after they hatched. They must have been a delightful sight, slowly and clumsily puttering around these rocks and cliffs. I can just picture them in their black-and-white coats like a thousand bird-butlers waiting for you to ask for tea. There was just one problem with these auks.

They were delicious.

These birds grew to well over two feet tall and plumped themselves up on seafood till they were ten or eleven pounds, like a decent Christmas turkey, only stuffed with fresh lobster and kept fresh in cold salt water. They were easy to catch, too. Perhaps a little too easy, as they became scarce by the mid-nineteenth century, here as well as in their other habitats in northern places like Greenland and Iceland and parts of Scandinavia. By 1850 or so, they were all gone. Victims of their own tastiness, I figure. My mom can make decent gravy from a frozen rock. I can only imagine the gravy she could have made from a fresh auk.

In any case, I wish we had jumped on the Save the Auk bandwagon a century or two earlier, as I would love to see a flock here today. Even so, this human-size statue is a quite impressive substitute. Created by American sculptor Todd McGrain, this wonderful cast-bronze work of art is so hefty, it had to be airlifted in place by helicopter. I am told that as the chopper laid it in place, a local fella shouted, "Ah, look. The first and last flight of the great auk."

God, I love Newfoundland.

But this statue is a very solid reminder that precious things are precious. And that we human crowd are best served when we live within the natural world we are given. On behalf of all humanity, I wink a far-too-late apology to the auk, and we make our way back to the minivan for a dance around the most Irish place in the world.

Tilting is often called the most Irish place on Earth outside of Ireland. It was occupied originally by the French, who called it Tilken, and many suspect the present name is a result of mispronunciation by the Irish who effectively settled the place by the early 1700s. The culture that came with those early settlers remained isolated and intact for hundreds of years and earned Tilting its famous place in the Irish diaspora. Ideally located for cod fishing in the summer and sealing in the winter, Tilting was the perfect spot to make a living off the sea.

As we roll over the hill in the trusty minivan, the treasure of Tilting becomes immediately obvious. In stark contrast to the town of Fogo, this deep and reaching harbour is protected by a narrow entrance to the open sea, which itself is guarded by Pigeon Island. It must have just looked like the perfect place to set up shop. And many of those shops, or sheds or stages, are still here today.

Whereas other towns and communities have saved and preserved the finest churches, community halls, and houses, this place has preserved and celebrated all the small but essential working buildings used in the fishing and sealing industries that made this place what it is. Many flakes and stages and salting and drying areas are all as they would have been for hundreds of years. It is easy to picture this place bustling with activity. Quintals of fish being lifted over there, and wheelbarrows of vegetables being pushed into that root cellar over there.

There's a lot to see and do in Tilting. The hiking trails in and out of it are magnificent, especially the one to Oliver's Cove. Newer places like Winds and Waves Artisans' Guild make for yet another chance to experience how these people continue to work together and support an economy today and tomorrow. And if you want to venture into the deep past, the Lane House was built a very, very long time ago, with some claiming as early as the 1700s. It's no wonder this place is a National Historic Site of Canada.

It should be hard to pick a favourite stop in Tilting, as there are so many good ones, but I confess it isn't hard for me. I'm a sucker for a good time, and you'd be hard pressed to find a better one than singing a song in Foley's Shed.

"That's the place!" I spot Foley's Shed near a turn in the road. It appears innocent enough, like a normal shed or collection of joined sheds, but I know it has magic powers. "You go in there and start singing, and the door disappears behind you. It's almost impossible to leave."

I went there later on a Saturday night, on a previous visit to Fogo, and somehow my "short, one-drink visit" took around four hours to complete. Daylight shone like God's flashlight by the time I found the exit. Owned by Phil and Maureen Foley, this place has played host to many parties, and they are just legendary. If you are looking for holdovers from the Irish tradition, this shed is a holy shrine. Amongst a million pub artifacts, hanging in a prominent spot high on the wall is an Irish goatskin drum decorated with a shamrock that announces the place as Foley's Bar. When I arrived there, the party was in full swing, with accordions and whistles and guitars a-blazing while merry voices rang out Irish and Newfoundland folk songs loud enough to shake the place. I was handed a beer and a guitar at the same time and joined mid-verse. By the time I looked up, four hours had passed.

"What's the occasion?" I asked a fellow singer between choruses, and expected the announcement of a special event. I suppose I got one as he shouted:

"It's Saturday!"

Joanne speeds up the van, no doubt worried that I might jump for it, and I probably would if I didn't have a gig in a few hours back in the JBA.

My community concert is only part of the weekend festivities on Fogo Island. Back at the inn, two new friends from Toronto, Afrim from the Cheese Boutique and Franco from Charlie's Burgers, are offering a very special combo of cheese and food with a wine pairing, and I suppose I am doing a song pairing, too. When these types of highly curated elements of food and drink are matched up with the hikes and talks and workshops given by learned local people, it makes for a weekend visit that is world-class but distinctly local and unique to this part of the world. Afrim knows what Belgian cheese goes with the white homemade rolls of Joe Batt's Arm. Franco knows what German white wine goes with the salt cod of Fogo. And I know that the folk song "A Boat Like Gideon Brown" is about a trap skiff just down the road, and that song goes with everything. It's fancy, but very authentically Fogo fancy.

In the evening, we leave the inn and head to the massive church on the main road. A small town with a massive church. It is a phenomenon we'll no doubt encounter time and time again as we make our way around the rural parts of this province. As a matter of fact, a more likely scenario is a small town with *a few* massive churches. It is a remarkable feature of any trip, almost anywhere in rural Newfoundland. You arrive in a town with a few dozen houses that could hold, at most, a few hundred people. And there amongst them are two or three or four large churches that between them could hold thousands. One could be forgiven for regularly asking, "Who were these churches built for?" or, "Were there ever enough people to fill these massive buildings?"

Well, one thing is for sure, this wooden beauty is certainly packed tonight. A few amazing local players offer great songs and tunes on guitars and accordions, and I'm quickly reminded that I am from a place where the bar for the average singer is incredibly high. Cape Breton has fiddlers. Nashville has guitar players. New Orleans has brass players. Newfoundland has singers. Lots of them. Singing is part of the language here. And a big part of the recording of history. Songs are important around here. And that's why I'm stoked and a bit nervous to sing one song in particular tonight.

"Laying Down to Perish," from my 2015 album *So Let's Go*, was written shortly after my first-ever visit to Fogo around 2012.

On that trip, I noticed an artifact in a museum that I recognized as a gaff—a long, wooden-handled tool with a hook at the end used by fishermen and sealers. The lady working there explained it was called the Laying Down to Perish Gaff, and went on to tell me the most incredible story.

In April of 1917, four men left Fogo Island and walked out onto the sea ice to hunt. The fog rolled in and the wind shifted not long after, and those men became stranded. They must have known they were never going to make it home, because one of them took the gaff and carved their names, dates, and a message into the wooden handle. Back on shore, the families and friends were desperate to find their loved ones, but they were lost forever. Weeks later, this very gaff—belonging to one Joseph Jacobs, who'd died on the ice along with the other three, including two of his brothers—washed ashore in Moreton's Harbour. The words it bore shook this area to the very bone:

Down . . . Perish . . . April 11

A message from the dying men to their families.

I was flattened. I had never heard this story of selflessness. On a day that must have been painful and terrifying, those men thought of their families first. They had to get a message to them, and they did. It still chills me to this day to picture the various scenes of those poor men on the ice, the desperation of the families ashore, and finally the astonishment of receiving word from their loved ones, even from an icy grave.

It was one of only a handful of times I was truly inspired to write a song. I wrote the whole thing on a piece of cardboard at a gas station stop the next day, and it remains one of the songs I'm most proud to sing. But tonight is my first time ever singing it in public on Fogo Island, and I am quite nervous about it. I wonder why, as I stand on the side of the stage, waiting for my introduction to finish. I have confidently sung this song hundreds of times in dozens of cities around the globe. Yet, I suppose there is only one home for this song, and it is here. And here I am, a visitor to Fogo, singing one of their own stories, and a most tragic and deeply personal one, back to them. I hope it goes well as I take the stage and sing.

Living isn't easy
Dying isn't hard
When the hungriest days of Winter
Plays her wicked cards

I'll not be called a quitter
For I choose to take a knee
'Cause the ice won't e'er be broken
Not by no man
Not by me

Laying down to perish
And God knows where I'll go
Laying down to perish
I just wanted you to know

The rest goes by in a blur and the next thing I see is a standing crowd of people applauding. It comes with great relief when many tell me how glad they are that I put the story to song and that this tale of selflessness in the face of tragedy has made its way off Fogo and to many other places beyond. It is even more satisfying to think that I might, just might, have added to the list of songs that would help a visitor learn about Newfoundland

and Labrador. Again, songs are important around here. So, this moment is an especially humbling one for me.

I finish the show and make my way back to the inn for a night of great company and cheer. In the morning, the sun fills the room as it dances magically off a sea that looks a little less ominous than it could. We make our way back across the island through the junction, and I make a point to at least wave to the Seldom Come By area to make it feel a little less lonely. The ferry is waiting and we roll on.

I head to the outside deck and watch Fogo slip behind another island as we make our way back to the shore. I think about how much we packed into this very short trip and how it all adds up to a must-see destination. A must-have experience. The people here have made a future that doesn't just build on their past traditions, but insists that those very traditions are indeed the future.

Before we head back to St. John's, I figure we have to complete the All Around the Circle quest, so we also pop into both Twillingate and Moreton's Harbour, and spend the better part of two days exploring the many former islands that are now connected by bridges and causeways. Highly recommended. Twillingate, in particular, is another incredible town built not by the sea, but in it. Driving around finds you in a spot or two where you are sure you are looking up at the ocean.

As the ferry docks, I conclude that Fogo Island is far from everywhere, and that is a very good thing.

And I can't wait for the next chance to say Hello to Farewell.

A Bayman in Town

S t. John's. The City of Legends. The Oldest City in North America . . . with the oldest street and most easterly point and site of the first transatlantic wireless signal and so on and so on. St. John's has more subtitles than a foreign film festival. More claims than a coat check. And no one likes to shout them and brag about his city quite as much as I do. I love the place and have called it home since my later teens, and for my entire adult life. I can't imagine writing a book about travelling around this province without including the coolest capital city. See? Another subtitle. St. John's has got dozens of them.

Since I started this journey of a book, I've been wondering what to do about St. John's. How could I honestly lead you, Dear Reader, around St. John's on a mission of discovery, when in fact I have lived here for almost forty years.

Wow. Forty years. I have been living in this city for four decades. I was still a teen when I started hitchhiking here on a near-daily basis from my hometown of Petty Harbour.

Maybe that's a good place to start.

I was born a Bayman and not a Townie. That is to say, I was born in a town around the bay, and not in the city of St. John's, which most of us call Town. Confused? Understandable. The great Townie-versus-Bayman distinction is really our provincial way of distinguishing between urban and rural lifestyles. This whole deal has been made more confusing by the fact that Town is mostly made up of Baymen, like me, who moved to the city. I have spent more time living in Town than around the bay, but was born in the bay. So, am I a new hybrid Newfoundlander? One who likes espresso, but owns a chainsaw? I couldn't say.

Petty Harbour is not part of St. John's, but is actually surrounded by it. It wasn't when I was a kid, but since then, the city has expanded to include the suburb of Kilbride and the farming town of The Goulds, as well as the tiny town of Blackhead, on the road that leads to Cape Spear. So, these days, yes, Petty Harbour is surrounded by—and, in fact, is very close to—St. John's.

But it was not when I was a kid. Sure, the distance to Water Street in St. John's from the bridge in Petty Harbour is the same as it ever was, but in the late 1970s, opportunities for me to get to the city were irregular at best. It took close to an hour on a bus to get to the city from my house, and we didn't have a car. Or much else, in retrospect.

Any readers of my earlier books know that it came as a great surprise to me in my mid-twenties to learn that I was poor when I was a kid. I honestly had no idea. We had no car or cable TV. We never went on holidays. We really didn't have modern plumbing and a shower till I was almost a teen. But I was well fed and warm and safe and loved. And we had a piano and a guitar and an accordion. So, I always thank and praise my folks for having their priorities exactly right.

All of this to say, St. John's was not easily accessible to me. Getting to it and from it was a puzzle to be solved.

My love for this place started before I ever lived here. I loved my time in a fishing town of five hundred people as a kid, but by the time my mid-teens came around, I was eager for new sights and sounds and to meet girls that weren't my first or second cousins. And by all reports, St. John's had all that, and more. It was like there was a Narnia just on the other side of the hills of Shea Heights, which was known back then as The Brow and was infamous for being a sketchy place to walk late at night. I just had to figure a way to climb the mountain, and climb it again on the way home.

By the time I was eighteen, I knew I wanted to move to the city, but it would not be in the cards for another year or so. Me and my lifelong pal Freddie both wanted out. (Oh, by the way, I have changed a few names in this book . . . to protect the likes of Freddie and myself!) We wanted to go where the cooler gals and guys in their twenties headed on Friday nights. We'd heard them tell tales of cool bars that stayed open till 3 a.m., filled with hot babes from the city. They spoke of this place as a mecca for the young and wild and free. Freddie and I wanted to be all three of those things, but there was a problem. We had no car. We needed a ride to George Street.

George Street started as a back alley for thirsty sailors and wharf workers who were just too dirty to come in the front door. The front door, as anyone familiar with St. John's would know, would be on Water Street, which claims to be the oldest commercial street in North America. When gents and ladies from the upper class of St. John's dressed up in their finest to make their way to the fancy shops on Water Street, it would have been completely unbecoming for them to have to mingle with unwashed crew who'd been at sea for weeks and months, building up a thirst for rum and a hunger for God knows what else. But the businesses on Water Street, eager to collect the money that was burning holes in the lonely sailors' pockets, didn't turn the riff-raff away. Rather, they sent them around back to the alley, where they'd sell and serve them whatever they wanted.

That alley became a street. George Street. Our Bourbon Street of iniquity. It all led to another St. John's boast: "More drinking establishments per square foot than any other street in the world." Me and Freddie wanted in. We wanted to get there early evening, which was challenging in the pre-Uber world, though doable with a modest amount of effort. But then we needed to get home, which required significantly more ingenuity. But young fellas are resourceful.

At the end of the night, when the go-home lights came on, Freddie and I would pool our money and see if we had enough cash to get some food and have twenty dollars or so for a taxi in case we could find one willing to take us to Petty Harbour. I cannot recall a single night when we had enough for both.

As he counted the crumpled bills and loose change, Freddie would slur, "It's cab home and wake up the house making toasted bologna sandwiches, or eat like a king in Town and hope to hitch a ride." Unless the snow or wind or rain or all three were bad, we regularly decided to eat like kings and roll the dice on hitching a ride.

Freddie and I would walk the length of Water Street, and Water Street West, to the farthest edge of downtown, to start the precarious task of hitching a ride home to Petty Harbour over the hills of The Brow, all while dreaming of a way for us to not have to choose between late-night food and transport. It had always been one or the other. But as Petty Harbour dogs do,

Freddie found a shortcut. A hack, if you will. And he found it at Power's Take Out.

Power's Take Out sat on that farthest edge, before St. John's gave way to The Brow, then Blackhead, Cape Spear, Maddox Cove, and eventually Petty Harbour, some twenty-plus kilometres later. It was a single-storey wooden building with faded red clapboard, and a single large window featuring a hand-painted, grease-stained poster that read *"Fresh" Fish and Chips*. I think they meant for the quotation marks to emphasize just how fresh the fish was, when in fact they just made you wonder if it was exactly the opposite of fresh. Atop the must-be-leaky roof was affixed a long rectangular box containing a white plastic sign with simple black lettering. The three sections of lights that backlit the words *Power's Take Out* through the semi-translucent plastic never worked simultaneously. At least one or two of the three sections was dark, often resulting in the foreboding announcement of *Out* as you walked in through the weathered front door onto the broken linoleum tiles.

Power's—offering large pieces of deep-fried cod sitting on a mountain of fries shrouded in dressing (turkey stuffing) and drowned in brown turkey gravy—served us well as a regular fortifying stop before braving the hitchhike home to Petty Harbour. On a few occasions, we even lucked into a few Petty Harbour folks in there who were driving and offered us a ride. But those occasions were rare. Most times, it was chips and gravy and get your thumb out.

Freddie's hack was inspired when Power's started doing something that was unheard of in Petty Harbour: home delivery. In this day and age of Skip the Dishes and Uber Eats and DoorDash, it may be difficult to imagine a time when you could not easily get hot food delivered to your door at a moment's notice. In the mid-'80s, no one could just push a button or hit a favourite on their handheld device and get cashless, contactless delivery, but they could phone a takeout or pizza joint. Petty Harbour's small population could not really sustain an in-town restaurant, and it was so far from any neighbouring town that it made little sense to run a vehicle out there. But Power's serviced The Brow area for free and offered a five-dollar charge to deliver to Petty Harbour. It was a thing.

"It's a miracle!" Freddie insisted. "Dial a few phone numbers and a hot fish and chips shows up at your door! Jesus, you haven't got to go to the grocery store to get the food. You haven't got to cook the food. You can stay in your pyjamas and goddamned slippers and a fee and chee shows up!"

Petty Harbour people flooded the phone lines. It was like Santa Claus had made himself available 365 days a year for five dollars a trip.

Admittedly, there was a flaw in the concept of delivering food to home addresses in Petty Harbour. There were no home addresses in Petty Harbour. You read that correctly. There were no street names or house numbers anywhere. Locals had names or nicknames for generally-agreed-upon roads, paths, and areas, but that was little or no help to a delivery driver in the dark.

Call-in orders would have asked Power's to send fish and chips to "the red house by the red plant" or "last spot up the Cribbies with the light over the door" or "blue place by the new bridge—not the old one, but the new one." It was challenging, and ultimately proved so inefficient that the service came to an end. But for a few glorious months, the drivers persisted.

Here comes the hack. Fish and chips was about seven dollars an order, and delivery was five dollars. Freddie quickly did the math. "So, we can pay twenty dollars to Gulliver's for a ride home.

Or pay twenty dollars to Power's for a ride home and two fish and chips?!"

I was not totally sure what he was talking about. But I was sure Freddie's plan was either genius or dubious, and I was eager to find out which. Either way, we were about to test-run it for the first time.

We'd just had a great night on George Street and started our walk along Water Street West.

"Stop here." Freddie was acting with military precision, speaking in short, stunted sentences like a drill sergeant issues orders to the troops.

"Quarter!" He sharply extended his hand as he stepped into a telephone booth.

The door closed behind him so I could not fully hear what he was saying, but I did recognize that he punched in the numbers for Power's as I squinted through the cracked and graffitied fading plexiglass. I heard a polite hello and something about two fish and chips and something about "the white house by the new bridge." The only other thing I heard was "Oh, Max is on tonight, is he? Grand!" Freddie offered a polite goodbye and stepped confidently back out on to the Water Street West sidewalk. He continued with the marching orders.

"Onwards!" A man on a mission. I could barely keep up and was out of breath by the time Power's was upon us.

Under the glow of the "Power's Out" sign, I put my hand to the handle of the plywood door.

"Halt." Freddie might have been taking this military role a hair too far, but what was I to do? I halted and he whispered: "Patience, now."

"Freddie, I have no idea what—" But a single Freddie finger in the air told me to be silent. He kept it in the air as he studied the cook and who we assumed to be the delivery driver through the window past the "Fresh" sign.

"Hold . . ." Was Freddie impersonating Braveheart? I was about to ask, but his finger shot up again.

This dance went on for another five or six minutes till Freddie stepped back from the window and pointed at a rusty Honda Civic parked on the street. "Game on" was all he said as he strode towards the Civic like a man who'd just been handed an Oscar.

I stood beside him nervously because, well, what else was I supposed to do? I was completely complicit, so I might as well be in it. The door swung open and a moustached man who looked to be in his late forties walked with purpose towards his car. Freddie's voice rang out, but it was not his army general voice that spoke. Rather, the voice that sung across the small parking lot was more like a mattress salesman.

"Max, my good man! Off to perfect little Petty Harbour again. Great stuff."

"Yeah . . . who are you guys?" Max was confused. So was I.

"We are the fellas with an offer no wise man could refuse. And we know you are a wise man, Max. We've seen you make your way around Petty Harbour, not one bit put off by the lack of street signs or addresses. You are practically a celebrity in the Harbour. Knows your way through Maddox Cove and up the Cribbies, down the South Side, Skinners Hill, the works of it. You are no fool, Max, and everyone in Petty Harbour knows it and we knows it, too, don't we, Alan?"

As noted above, what was I supposed to do? "Yeah, you are the man, Max." Freddie flashed me a glance that said, "Reel it in."

Max opened the car door. "What are you on about? Could you step away from the car, please, I got a delivery to make."

"Yes, of course!" Freddie slid to the side like Fred Astaire. "And it is that very delivery that is at the heart of the offer a wise man like yourself wants to hear about in detail."

Max rested his forearm on the roof as Freddie continued.

"I believe that double order of fish and chips is bound for the white house by the new bridge in Petty Harbour. Is that correct?"

"Yeah, so what?" Max was getting impatient.

"Well, I have good news for you. Me and Alan here will surely be at the white house by the new bridge in Petty Harbour. If you just let us slide into your back seat, you'll find us waiting for you at your destination."

"Look, I am not supposed to let people in the delivery car. I'll get in trouble." Max looked tired now.

"But if you deliver the food as planned, I can assure there'll be no one there to meet and pay you."

A silence hung in the night . . . till Freddie broke it: "A dilemma, for sure, but one with an easy fix at no extra cost to you.

"Think about your choices, Max, like the wise fella we know you to be."

Freddie held a single digit in the air. "Option one: You go back in there and tell Mr. Power that you just wasted two perfectly good fish and chips and got no money in exchange. He's not going to be one bit happy with this."

Freddie added a second digit. "Option two: You let Alan and me slip into your back seat, and upon arrival at the white house by the new bridge, we give you the fourteen dollars for the fee and chee, five dollars for delivery, and the remaining dollar from this twenty-dollar bill as a tip. You return to a happy Mr. Power with his cash and a bit extra for your trouble.

"A wise man like you—"

"If I lets ye in, will he shut the f—k up?" Max rubbed his head in frustration as he eyeballed me.

"Yes, of course!" Freddie pushed me in the back. "Nothing better than a quiet night drive over The Brow to Petty Harbour. Just you and the stars pulling you south. No one yammering on . . ."

Freddie talked the whole way through The Brow and beyond.

We sat on the new bridge, home in Petty Harbour, as Max's taillights disappeared around the corner, Freddie and I passing vinegar and salt packs back and forth. My heart raced from the con, but Freddie seemed calm as a clock as he tasted the first bites.

"Fish is fresh, too."

He never batted an eye till I said with certainty:

"We are moving to St. John's."

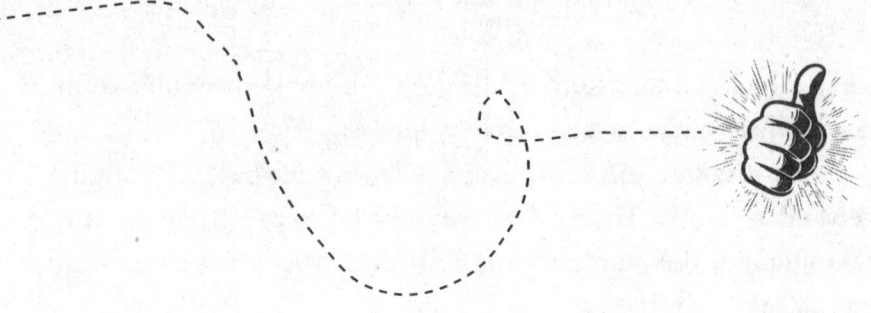

HITCHING TO GROS MORNE

"The first time I ever came to Gros Morne National Park, I hitchhiked almost seven hundred kilometres from home." With the Tablelands looming ominously over us, I probably should have checked myself before I spoke so matter-of-factly.

"You hitchhiked?! Mom says that's not safe!" Henry is nothing if not cautious, and I quickly underplay the whole deal.

"Oh, this was years ago, bud."

"Was it safe back then?" Henry leans forward in the back seat, eager for the truth, so I figure I have to give it to him.

"No, bud. No it wasn't."

I was barely nineteen when I stood on the edge of the Trans-Canada Highway just outside St. John's with my thumb out, hoping to catch a ride for seven hundred kilometres or so. My brother, Bernie, an engineering student, was on a winter work term in the park, and being curious as I am, I wanted to check it out. I had considered taking the bus, and I may have told my parents I was doing just that, but when I investigated that option and learned it would take over twelve hours to cross the island, I guess I just couldn't spare that much time in 1988. The choice between a safe, warm, and secure twelve-hour ride and a risky, completely unknown, potentially life-altering eight-hour one was an easy one for young me to make.

Within ten minutes, I hitched a ride to Goobies (yes, that's a real place) about 150 kilometres west of St. John's with a very chatty fella in a pickup truck who was headed to Marystown. I peed and got a Pepsi in the Big Stop and started strolling along the two-lane highway towards Clarenville. I assumed my hitching luck would be the same and I'd be in a warm westward vehicle in no time.

I was wrong.

I walked the next eight or nine kilometres. It was just about to rain when I saw the exit for Hodge's Cove up ahead. There was a convenience store there, and figured I might have to go in and wait for the bus, but just as I hit the parking lot, a transport truck came up from the Hodge's Cove area.

A happy-looking fella not much older than me hung his head out the window. "Where you going?"

"Gros Morne!" I yelled back hoping that was the right answer. Apparently, it was, as he smiled.

"I'll get you to Deer Lake if you talks a lot and keep me awake."

Now, that was deal I could take with confidence. A free 450-kilometre ride and all I had to do was talk!

I shouted back with enthusiasm. "Talk?! It takes me four and a half hours to say hello!"

By the time the happy fella I came to know as Dwayne dropped me in Deer Lake, we had covered our family histories, what was right and wrong about Newfoundland joining Canada, and the indisputable fact that the Habs would win the Cup.

As we pulled into the Deer Lake Irving station, he pointed to a white shuttle van.

"See that little one there? I bet it is going to Rocky Harbour, and they'll let anyone on for a few bucks."

I was pulling out a crisp five-dollar bill as I ran over while my knapsack bounced on my back. A wink and a nod later, I had my ride to the park.

I'd love to tell you about how entranced I was by the hills and valleys and the splendour of it all, but truth be told, I sat between two heavy-set fellas who had just flown from Fort McMurray. The heat off them, combined with the pillowy nature of their coats, made things all too comfortable for a fella who'd been on the go as long as me. I fell sound asleep before we crossed the overpass outside the Irving, and they woke me up in the parking lot of the Ocean View Hotel in Rocky Harbour.

"I got dropped off right there, Henry." I notice my son's jaw almost hitting the floor as he fully realizes how far I had hitchhiked.

"I'm not doing that," he says quickly.

"No, you're not," his mom says quicker as we pull into our accommodations for the evening. I am keenly aware that the three of us might need some time and space apart, having driven some six-hundred-plus kilometres today, so I decide to head down to the water for a walk.

I have been coming to Gros Morne National Park regularly since that first hitchhike ride, and am delighted to be showing it to our son and seeing it through his eyes. Over the years, I've come here to visit my brother, play at music awards, camp in tents, sleep on couches, and stay in the best of accommodations. I have sung and read at writers' festivals and led groups of pals on trips of a lifetime. The pull of this place is ongoing.

This national park and UNESCO World Heritage Site is the largest park on the island and is best known for its mountains and coastal walks, as well as its incredible geological elements, which bring scientists and sightseers from all around the world. It is easily one of the biggest tourist attractions in the province, with over a quarter million visitors each summer. That's more than ten times the amount of people living here in and around the park full time. The park wraps around the arms of Bonne Bay and contains a dozen or more towns like Birchy Head and Shoal Brook, but there are really three main towns in the park: Rocky Harbour, Woody Point, and our family destination tonight, Norris Point.

Rocky Harbour has hosted me several times for events, and of course before that I hitchhiked to my brother's de facto frat house while he was on his engineering work term. Woody Point is famous for its writers' festival, where Stephen Brunt and the rest of the organizers have the good sense to put authors together with songwriters. I've been there many times as both, and loved it every time. I drop my family at the hotel and head to the wharf in Norris Point to take a few pictures before the sun fully sets. Of the three main towns in the park, Norris Point is the one in which I've spent the least amount of time. But as I walk along the wharf here at dusk, dwarfed by the enormous Tablelands still aglow in the setting sun, I wonder if I haven't been missing the best of the three.

There is activity here that one would expect, like tourists with every kind of photography equipment known to man, trying to get that one perfect shot of the sun on the hills, as well as fishermen coming and going with nets and pots stacked to the sky. But there is also an unexpected flurry of academic activity here, as marine biology students from all over the globe flock to study and stay at the Bonne Bay Marine Station right on the wharf in Norris Point. This education and research facility also features a small interactive aquarium, which gives a great up-close look at the local ocean ecology. I can only imagine how exciting it must be to get one of the treasured berths to live here and study the ocean literally from the wharf in Gros Morne.

We have an excellent supper at Chanterelles restaurant, and me and my family crash hard after a long day crossing the province. I wake early in the a.m. and try not to wake the gang as I head out on a solo mission.

The park has a couple of dozen cool places to hike, like Trout River, Green Gardens, Lomond River, and many more. But I'll just tell you about three of my favourites. Two I visited in the past, and one I'll venture into this morning.

The first time I climbed Gros Morne, I was as hungover as a person can get. I was twenty-four years old and at that stage in life when tomorrow's consequences of tonight's activity never entered the discussion. Certainly not at midnight, while opening a second bottle of rum on a campsite picnic table while me and a few others sang John Mellencamp songs. Surely, climbing a hill over eight hundred metres high at 8 a.m. is no reason to stop drinking and singing at 3 a.m.?

I remember being shaken awake that morning by the others, who were in no better shape than me. Despite our swollen heads, we had to stick to our early hike plans, as there was weather coming in the afternoon that would make the ascent difficult and dangerous. So, off we went with, as my brother Bernie says, "heads like paint cans."

The biggest challenge of climbing Gros Morne hungover isn't the climb at all. Rather, it is the walk into the base of the hill. Even with a ripping head, I mentally prepared myself for a steep ascent, but was not at all ready to walk almost five kilometres to get to it. I've returned to climb Gros Morne a couple of times since, and can tell you that walking towards it on a perfectly beaten path through ponds and marshes is actually delightful. But it did not feel as such with a half-bottle of Old Sam still coursing through my youthful veins.

When we finally made it to the base of the mountain, we faced the one truly challenging part of this whole deal. It's what the guidebook calls a "steep boulder gully"—but I called a "friggin' rock slide"—stretching into the clouds for a half a kilometre.

"This is the way up?!" I involuntarily put one hand to my forehead and the other on my stomach just to check how ill I really was. Not that it mattered. We were doing it, and thirty seconds later, me and my sick-as-dogs pals were scrambling up over loose rocks and boulders that inevitably moved and fell behind each climber. As I was the slowest, I had to climb while dodging rocks the size of baseballs and some the size of footballs.

I suspected I would die. Then it got worse. I suspected I wouldn't.

But then I could see the light over the summit. I was going to live through this after all. In just under an hour of scrambling, we made it. We had crested the second-highest mountain on the island and were strolling to the famous photo location high above Western Brook Pond. We did what most do and took the standard photo. Shot from behind us as we faced the fjord below. Arms raised in celebration.

I was feeling good. Victorious, even. Not only had I climbed the hill, I had defeated the hangover. I was superhuman. Nothing could faze me. We made our way around the top trail and started our long descent. My head was clearing and I was moving pretty good. Then, from behind me, came the sound of fast-approaching footsteps. They seemed out of place in such a rugged environment, not because they weren't solid and paced for speed, but because they featured the unmistakable repetitive flapping sound of flip-flops.

I turned to see what manner of young, prime-of-life beast could possibly be up here in Jimmy Buffett footwear, but I need not have turned at all, as the beast in question blew past me like I was standing still.

"Excuse me, young chap!" His British accent was distracting, but nowhere near as distracting as the tufts of snow-white hair popping out over his ears and waving up over his otherwise pink bald head.

The beast in flip-flops was seventy years old if he was a day. I stood up a bit straighter and tried to speak, but I likely gasped more than talked.

"Hey . . . ahem . . . hey." I lifted my hand weakly as he looked over his shoulder and shouted.

"It's going to rain this afternoon, so I did this walk a couple of times this morning. Lovely, isn't it? Cheerio!"

Then he disappeared around a turn in the rock face and I never saw him again. I wondered if I had hallucinated, but the others reported seeing an iron-man senior citizen as well.

Bested by a man older than my grandfather. So much for my victory lap on Gros Morne Mountain.

I have hiked the Tablelands a few times. My favourite time being one fall not so long ago when I had a special group of pals in tow.

"The Tablelands is where two really different bits of the planet smashed together and they just stayed there. Like, right next to each other, even though they look like they shouldn't be anywhere near each other." My bus full of musical theatre friends didn't look confident, and I suppose in retrospect they shouldn't have. I elected myself the tour guide for a visit here in the fall of 2022 in the middle of a touring run for our *Tell Tale Harbour* musical on a day off in Corner Brook. My castmates were excited for the trip, and happy for me to show them the park and some of its wonders, but we all learned quickly that I am possibly the worst fella on earth to describe the scientific theories around plate tectonics.

I was quick to confess to it. "Okay, I don't know much about continental drifts, but I friggin' knows about a cold plate and a beer in the Legion!" All hands were very confident about those two facts.

We had all been working on and performing *Tell Tale Harbour* for about fourteen weeks at this point. There's a scene in the show where the town's folk bamboozle a come-from-away while dancing with cold plates in the Legion. Legions, of course are clubs for and by military service folks who often use them as town halls and bars and darts leagues and fundraising places and all kinds of fun. I explained to the non-Newfoundlanders in the show that a "cold plate" is a legendary culinary feature of garden parties and Legion fundraisers where cold turkey and ham slices are paired with potato salad and a fluffy white dinner bun. I promised the gang that when we got to Newfoundland, I'd take them to an actual Legion for an actual cold plate, and true to my word, we boarded a bus in Corner Brook, bound for Gros Morne National Park.

Even the crowd from out west, who were well used to the Rockies, were impressed by the drive up and down the hills and valleys that lead into Woody Point. We dumped some folks in the town to putter, while others bolted for the main Gros Morne Mountain and the rest of us headed for the Tablelands.

A year and a bit later, and I still wouldn't describe the first sights of this geological wonder much differently. The Tablelands is where two really different bits of the planet smashed together and then just stayed there.

A narrow strip of asphalt runs along a valley between two massive hills that start right down next to the road and reach up to the clouds on either side. That's probably not all that notable in itself, but here's the deal. The hills on the right and left of the road look absolutely foreign to each other. They are not slightly different; they are *completely* different. The hill to the right is covered in green trees, moss, and vegetation. It looks much like the rest of the hills on the way here. But the hill to the left, the Tablelands itself, looks like a desert moonscape. Alien orange rock with not so much as a bush growing in barren patches kilometres high and long.

"It is like the middle of Australia smashed into the west coast of Ireland!" one of my cast mates shouted from the back of the bus. I could feel my scientific credibility growing. To walk on this barren rock that stretches as far as you can see in one direction while looking just metres behind you at a lush green landscape that goes as far as you can see in the other direction is jarring and quite humbling in the oddest way. You can't help but feel that massive forces bigger than all of us put together were at play to bring these two unlikely bedmates together here in the park. All the human energy and labour ever exerted, combined with all the technology we've developed over thousands of years, could not accomplish this natural wonder.

We follow the trail and boardwalk up through the orange rocks and occasionally turn back to see the incredible views gained with every new height. This walk is as otherworldly as anyone can imagine, and completely singular. There simply isn't another one like it on Earth.

I turn back on the path and shout to the gang trailing behind: "Like I said, I don't know much about plate tectonics theory or the debates around it, but I figure if you were trying to prove it to anyone, you would just bring them here to the Tablelands."

When we'd all finished our various hikes and walks, we met as scheduled at the Legion in Woody Point, where local ladies had prepared cold plates for us. I sat and watched as my friends who knew nothing of this place were charmed by the hospitality they were shown, astonished by the sheer wonder of the park, and were finally able to delight in a cold plate at the Legion, like they had been talking about for months. It was as full-circle a satisfying moment as I've ever had. I'll never forget it.

We sang for our supper and rolled back to our hotel in contented silence.

The Tablelands, Gros Morne Mountain, and Western Brook Pond are must-dos when visiting the park. I wish I had time for all three today, but I have to pick one.

Undeniably, the shining star of the park, and perhaps all Newfoundland and Labrador, is not really the mountain that gives the place its name; rather, it is Western Brook Pond. If you have seen three tourism photos of Newfoundland, you have likely seen, in no particular order, a whale breaching at Cape Spear, a Newfoundland dog at Signal Hill, and a hiker, having victoriously crested Gros Morne, peering satisfied over Western Brook Pond. You climb one to get to look down over the other. No trip to the park is complete without a visit. So, I make my way to the parking spot off the highway and head in.

It occurs to me that we here in our province might be overly humble about our bodies of water. Western Brook Pond is huge. It is sixteen kilometres long, and seventy metres deep at one spot. This pond would be called at least a lake, and maybe even a fjord, anywhere else. What we call a gully would surely be a pond in Ontario. And a pool here might be a lagoon in California. We can be modest about the oddest things.

The three-kilometre walk from the parking lot to the wharf at Western Brook Pond winds through the woods. It's longer than you might want, but I figure it serves as a perfect buffer between the real world behind you and the magical experience you are about to have. It's like a pleasant purgatory to prepare you for the fjord's golden gates.

Western Brook Pond is yet another UNESCO World Heritage Site in our province and is impossibly impressive and full of surprises. The first one being that it is not on the ocean, where most would think to find fjords, though apparently it used to be. I am no geologist, as must be very clear by now, but a little reading tells me that glaciers carved this big cut in the escarpment, and when they melted, the land bounced back and cut the remaining fjord off from the salt water. The result is nothing short of mind-blowing. Cliffs over half a kilometre high surround this massive body of water. The large tour boat on the dock is dwarfed by rocks and water. It is all so epic that, as I approach, I assume Frodo and the Orcs from *Lord of the Rings* will be doing battle around me any second.

After a peek into the Dock Side Café, I board the boat operated by BonTours, a company that has been operating here in the

park since the mid-1970s and is still showing people a great time.
BonTours does everything from boat tours here on Western
Brook Pond, and in Bonne Bay itself, to running a water taxi from
Norris Point to Woody Point and offering guided hikes and marine
explorations. They also run my favourite night out in the park: the
Anchors Aweigh show, a subject I'll be returning to a bit later.

You can see this area on foot from the wharf, or high above
from the back of Gros Morne. But this boat tour is the way to
go. It is a disconnect from everything around you as you float
into the impossible. It's only fitting that on this boat, my feet
rest on the gangboard and don't touch the ground. Because what
your eyes see is otherworldly. The hills, the birds, the waterfalls.
The sheer scale of being surrounded by what feels prehistoric,
yet recent. Like the Earth has moved for you, and not too long
ago. Like the actual smash of the glaciers happened last summer
and the trees only just grew back. As we reach the far point of
the pond, there comes a most humbling feeling: bobbing in a
boat that feels miniature under a huge waterfall and a cliff face
created by this colossal earthly event.

Perhaps the following tells it clearly. And I offer it as humbly
and gratefully as possible, given that it is undeniably a First World
rock-and-roll story.

Flight delays once resulted in me being late landing in Bergen,
Norway, for an event on the southwestern coast of the country.
The organizers of the event were worried I would not make it
in time by winding road, so they sent a helicopter. I could not
believe my luck. On a bright and sunny Scandinavian day, I
boarded a chopper at the airport in Bergen and flew out over the
mighty fjords of Norway. Dozens of them. Green meadows in
the sky rolling to steep cliff faces, and crystal-clear waterfalls
diving down to the blue ocean. Below the sun, above the puffins

and whales, peering straight out at the top of a waterfall. I was literally flying across the most famous fjords in the world, and all I quietly could think was, *This is almost as cool as Western Brook Pond.*

I finish the boat trip and walk back to the van, and rejoin the family as we head for a meal at Neddies Harbour, a short drive from downtown Norris Point. Still glowing from great meals at Java Jack's and Chanterelles earlier in our visit, we were hoping for three out of three at the Black Spruce. We were not disappointed, by the food or the view. This is a gem of a place nestled in the Neddies Harbour Inn, and the harbour and the hills are on display in every window.

"The fish is amazing," I mumble between happy mouthfuls.

Joanne nods, as the food is too good to waste time talking too much. But the food is not the only reason for coming here. I am looking forward to a chat with Annette and Wayne Parsons. Annette is one of the heartbeats of this place, and Wayne has been the heartbeat of the Newfoundland music scene for as long as I can remember.

Annette and her business partners converted this building from its previous incarnation as a seniors home to a beautiful hotel and restaurant. Which, I have to say, sounds impossible to me, as so often with our aging population, the exact opposite is happening in our rural towns. Hotels and restaurants are shut down and converted to apartments for seniors. But Annette instantly strikes me as the type of person who sees very little as impossible. She also runs a local coffee shop and has her capable hands and mind into God knows how many other pies in the area.

I am always a bit geeked out when I get a chance to speak with Wayne. He is a legend of the music and entertainment world in

Newfoundland. I first saw him in an incredible country band called Uncle Harry's Bar Band. Me and my Petty Harbour friend Dave were barely old enough to get into bars when we'd drive to the edge of St. John's in a car borrowed from Dave's brother and line up to watch them play. Uncle Harry's Bar Band mixed Newfoundland traditional music and country, Wayne leading the way with his great singing voice and incredible stagecraft. In the noisiest of dance bars, he could hold the crowd in his palm and keep them in stitches when they were not jammed on the dance floor.

Since then, Wayne has been involved with BonTours in the park, doing everything from tours on the bay and pond to leading groups to hiking trails. As good a guide as I am sure he is, I am happy to say he has not left the performance stage. Along with another legend of the Newfoundland music scene, Reg Williams, Wayne now fronts Anchors Aweigh, a musical comedy show I mentioned earlier that plays regularly in a dedicated venue in the Ocean View Hotel in Rocky Harbour. It is as good a night out as you can get. I've seen them a few times over the years, and I am always blown away by Wayne's ability to charm the pants off a crowd while teeing up his amazing musical castmates, like Reg with his accordion-playing and dry humour. They sell out the show in advance, and let me put it to you this way: if you want to go see them in the summer, you better hope someone gets you a ticket for a Christmas present. It is a great night out. Thank me later.

We wake with time left for one more adventure. There are several excellent touring groups in the park. Having had an amazing trip yesterday with BonTours on the fjord, we are bound for a boat trip with Gros Morne Adventures. Rob and his gang run kayaks and Zodiacs all over Bonne Bay, and as Henry has taken a surprising shine to casting a rod and reel, I've asked Rob to take us cod fishing.

Fishing gear aboard, myself, Joanne, and Henry head off with Rob, and as soon as we leave the dock, the trip is worth ten times the fee. We are floating in Bonne Bay, surrounded by huge green hills on three sides, while on the fourth, the impossible Tablelands just dominates the sky. We stop and wet a few lines in the middle of the bay between Norris Point and Woody Point. These two towns are nearly an hour apart by road, but just a hop, skip, and a jump by boat.

We get a few nibbles and even catch three or four decent-size codfish. It's been just a perfect morning on the bay to end a perfect trip to the park.

"What's that?" Henry points to a ripple in the water that leads to a few more, and he calls it before we do. "That's dolphins!"

So, here we are, with fresh cod for supper still flopping around the boat, floating under a mountain from another planet, accompanied by a school of dolphins. One of them pushes just ahead of the boat and rises up almost completely out of the water.

"That guy wants to lead the way home," I say, hoping the poignancy of such a remark will win the day and leave a lasting impression in this perfect family memory. But Henry one-ups me perfectly.

"Nah, he's just hitchhiking."

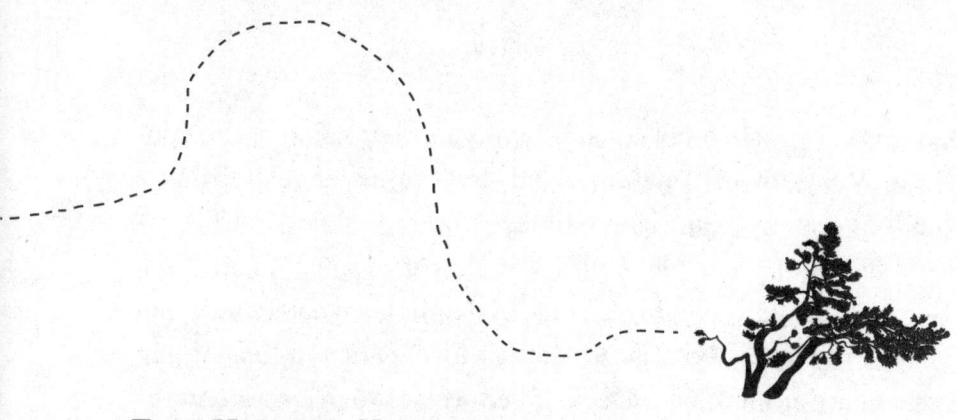

THE VIKING HIGHWAY

"Let's go find some Vikings."

Henry is stoked to learn that the "toughest guys in history" made this place a home.

I smile as the Honda Odyssey heads north of Cow Head and give myself a mental high five. I do this every time I travel on new ground. Any time I get somewhere I have never been before. It always feels like such a victory. I realized early on that one of the great benefits of being in a successful band was the opportunity to travel. I suspect the possibility of getting to see the province, or the country, or the world was, and still is, one of the biggest reasons a life as a touring musician has always appealed to me.

Perhaps my hunger for it came from growing up in a small fishing town with steep hills on three sides and the cold Atlantic on the other. For much of my young life, the closest town was a five-kilometre walk away. My family had very little money, and exactly no expendable income, so we never travelled to central or western Newfoundland, and certainly not out of province. We occasionally visited my cousins on my mother's side of the family in Marystown, Newfoundland, but we never really took a family vacation. Not a single time.

I did not fly in a plane till I was almost twenty. When Great Big Sea started travelling around Atlantic Canada, I could not believe my luck. We'd go to Halifax for weeks at a time, doing residencies at the Lower Deck. Then we got to drive around the Maritimes to places like Yarmouth, Truro, Sydney, Charlottetown, Summerside, Souris, Fredericton, Moncton, Saint John, and Bathurst. The highways and the back roads. I loved them all. A different bed every night! It was literally a dream come true.

The GBS boys would often describe me as the perfect touring machine. Like a robot specially built for the job. I loved the gigs, but most musicians do. Most, however, do not love travelling 250 days a year and sleeping in a van or a bus or a strange hotel room every night. I loved that almost as much as I loved the gigs. I still love it. Getting to see so much of the world out of a van or tour bus window remains one of the greatest privileges in my lucky life.

As I type here today, I have been to every province in Canada and two of the three territories. I've played in every US state except Hawaii and Wyoming. I've so gratefully played in Australia, England, Wales, Scotland, France, Ireland, Germany, Denmark, Sweden, Hungary, Austria, Slovakia, Belgium, and Poland. There may be more. Oh yeah, Iceland.

And I make it a point to get out and see the towns I play in. I always have. I have never been the type to roll into the back of a club or theatre or rink and just hang there till showtime. I know lots of musicians who do it that way, but it's not for me. Seems a shame to miss such an opportunity. Also, as a front guy for a travelling band, I have found that walking around the town in the afternoons gave me something to talk about onstage that night between songs. As a young concert fan, I was always chuffed when the visiting band mentioned some local bar or restaurant from the stage. Made me feel like they'd actually been in my backyard and liked it.

I dreamed of travelling and seeing new places when I was young, and the thrill of laying eyes on a new town or feet on new ground thrills me to this day. So, as the minivan turns north from Cow Head, I grin my fresh-ground grin.

I've successfully convinced my family to stick with me on this leg of the trip. We had such fun in the park that we might as well roll on together. Joanne is driving the two Doyles in her life: myself and our son, Henry. Joanne is quiet and sensible. Me and Henry are neither of those things. We are loud and scattered. A friend once pointed out that Joanne lives with ADHD. I thought they meant to suggest Joanne suffers from attention-deficit/ hyperactivity disorder, but what they were really referring to was me and my son.

Alan Doyle. Henry Doyle. ADHD.

Hey look, a squirrel . . . what was I saying? Oh yeah.

The Northern Peninsula is the large, really large, piece of land that reaches north towards Labrador. By any global standards, it is vast, stretching up for almost three hundred kilometres, and across it's nearly a hundred kilometres at its widest point. At 17,500 square kilometres, it is well over three times the size of Prince Edward Island. And our party of three are about to drive from Gros Morne National Park as far as you can go on this massive stretch of land to the very tip of Newfoundland.

As we've started back east in St. John's and hope to end back there, this minivan will have travelled well over three thousand kilometres by the time this trip is over.

Newfoundlanders are used to drives like this. We live on the sixteenth-biggest island in the world. We are also used to travelling long, uninhabited distances between towns and cities. As me and my family roll north with the enormous mountains on one side and the vast Atlantic on the other, it is easy to feel very small, and two facts become unmistakably clear: we have a lot of land here in the province, and we have very few people living on it.

By way of comparison, Newfoundland and Labrador is over 405,000 square kilometres, with about 520,000 people living in it, while Germany covers 357,000 square kilometres and has a population of 83 million. New York City, which covers less than 800 square kilometres, packs in 16 times as many people as Newfoundland and Labrador.

The drive begins just as we exit Gros Morne National Park, and we quickly pass fishing towns like Parsons Pond and Daniel's Harbour along the coast.

That's what makes this drive so special. It is most certainly a coastal highway, which is more rare than you might imagine, with open ocean on the left and a mountain range to the right.

"Why are the trees bent over?" Henry points to a stretch of growth that runs just to the right of the van and only a few metres from the smooth, weathered, rocky beach to our left.

"That's the tuck," I say, with a little more excitement than anyone was expecting.

Henry looks to his mom for a more sensible answer. He is smart to do so.

"Dad means 'tuckamore,' Henry." She points to a set of short deciduous trees that reach out in front of us along a long, nearly barren stretch for several kilometres ahead. They are all very obviously and conspicuously leaning to one side.

A quick look at an online dictionary defines *tuckamore* as "a spruce tree bent and entangled by winds on the coastal shores of Newfoundland." Imagine a spruce tree about a foot and a half tall, so determined to survive in the brutal winds ripping in off the ocean, that it has mutated. These short and stubborn coastal trees have needles and branches only on their inland side.

"It looks like the wind blew all the branches over to one side and tipped it over," says Henry, pointing, as we roll ever north with the spray from the ocean splashing the driver's side while the passenger's side is still dwarfed by the mountain range slowly turning inland away from us.

As well as short and one-sided, these trees are unmistakably bent over. I don't mean to suggest they are broken in any way. Quite the contrary. They look invincible. Like giant rubber bonsai trees that have withstood everything winter and wind had to throw at them. They are the embodiment of that proverb about trees that bend in the wind. They have adapted to grow *along* the ground, rather than up from it.

Tuckamore magic goes even further, though. The trees that grow in the worst of coastal and windy locations bond together to form a kind of mini-forest that is unique to this area. Sheep and anyone short enough would take shelter under the low, impenetrable forest ceiling. The trees rely on each other for strength and protection. Together, they can survive living on a frozen rock in the ocean. Without each other, they would so likely perish.

They adapt, work together, and do just fine.

"Strong and stubborn. Like Newfoundlanders." I figure my son will think I'm cool for making such a solid point, but he looks less than impressed with my analogy and goes back to studying the trees.

About halfway up the Northern Peninsula, we pass through River of Ponds, which is among my favourite place names in the province, en route to a scheduled stop in Port au Choix, a town of fewer than a thousand people. I have never been here, and I expect a quaint and quiet little fishing village, but I quickly learn that my preconceived notions are misguided. We've come to see a couple of significant historical sites, but I'm embarrassed to say I hadn't realized how vibrant the present is here. This is a bustling hub of a town.

"This spot is on wheels," I exclaim as we pass a busy shipyard in Port Saunders on the way to a harbour near-filled with offshore fishing boats in Port au Choix. Forklifts and trucks come and go as the wharves are teeming with activity.

So, the people here seem to be doing well. And as we are about to learn, they've been doing well for a very, very long time. The Canadian government's website describes the area as "the cross-roads of 6,000 years of human history."

This place has a lot going on that I hadn't known about. Start with the name. Like many, I assumed it to be of French origin and meaning "Port of Choice," but it's actually derived from a Basque term meaning "Little Port." The Basques fished here along with other European nations back as far as the 1500s. But the Basques, English, and French were newcomers compared to the long line of Indigenous peoples who are thought to have been here since 1200 BC. That's a long time for a place to be rocking, but Port au Choix is still on the go.

Our first stop in our journey into the past brings us to the French Rooms Cultural Centre.

And bread oven.

"Did we just come here because there's a bread oven?" Henry knows the truth.

This charming little museum explains much of the local French history. It comes as no surprise to learn that the French fought with the English here—and, well, everywhere else—for a very long time. Following one unsuccessful battle with the English, the French likely worried they'd be kicked out of this area for good. But they managed a few lines in the treaty that allowed them to continue to fish out of Newfoundland from spring to fall, but not to build any permanent dwellings. So, as they were not allowed to build permanent houses, they assembled temporary camps. And in places like Port au Choix, the French built open-air wood-fired bread ovens to feed themselves during their summer fishing stays.

Here at the cultural centre, they have recreated one of the ovens: an open-sided dome of foraged stones. Once a day, the guides make traditional French dough and serve the resulting hot rolls with butter and jams made from local berries. I devour two with familiar jams so quickly, I need a third to learn about a jam I'd never heard of.

The two I *had* heard of were blueberry, which probably needs no introduction, and bakeapple, which probably does.

Though Newfoundlanders and southern Labradorians like to lay claim to bakeapples, they can be found in a few places in the northern world. These translucent peach clusters about the size of a small raspberry are simply delicious. They are known elsewhere by names like cloudberry, salmonberry, or yellowberry, but we refer to them as bakeapples, and in true Newfoundland form, no one is quite sure why. The leading suggestion is that it's a corruption of the French *baie qu'appelle*.

Call it whatever you like. Bakeapple jam on a hot roll is to die for. As is the jam from the berry I'd never heard of. Well, I vaguely recognize the term *squashberry*, as I think several berries around the world are locally called such. But I had no idea we had something called a squashberry in my home province. These sweet, cranberry-shaped and -coloured berries are new to me, and I'll be looking for them from now on.

After we spend some time wandering the small museum and displays, we make our way back to the minivan, and Henry can't help himself from speaking first.

"Yeah, Dad just came for the bread." He is correct.

I could have sat around that bread oven and ate rolls and jam for another few hours, but another date with the past awaits. A past far more distant than the days of the French or the English or the Basques.

After a wonderful stroll on the Phillip's Garden Trail, we head to the Port au Choix National Historic Site. This archaeological landmark's attractions include the Point Riche Lighthouse, which I learn was completed in 1871 by the Canadian government to help steamships navigate their way from the Gulf of St. Lawrence through the Strait of Belle Isle on their way to Europe. I find this odd, as Confederation with Canada was still seventy-five years away. But I suppose it only makes sense that the Canadians would have noted the benefits of owning this rock in the ocean quite some time before they actually acquired it.

"Dad!" Henry points to low, shrub-covered land covered in mist drifting in off the sea. "Is that moose?"

Henry is almost right. There, grazing on the misty berries and shrubs, is a small herd of caribou. The closest of them not much more than a hundred metres from where we stand. They peacefully munch on whatever they can find and seem completely unfazed by the dozen or so admiring humans with cameras and iPhones.

The rain has started pelting, so it's a perfect time to take shelter in the interpretation centre for the National Historic Site. This delightful little space has a lot to say, but the most amazing story told here explains just how long this area has been home to thriving humans. Burial sites found in the 1960s and '70s led to one of the most significant archaeological finds in North American history: European, Maritime Archaic, Groswater Paleoeskimo, and Dorset Paleosekimo peoples, had all spent time fishing, hunting, sealing, and living here for over fifty centuries. It's an incredible stat to consider, by North American standards especially.

I say a thank you to the excellent staff, who are more than just informed but incredibly welcoming and engaging. I had two phone numbers and three invites to supper before we left to head out into the mist to make our way very north.

"Got a bit damp," I scoff as we prep for another long leg of driving.

"Sure would love a good americano," I continue with a false hopefulness, while Townie cynicism makes me think the chances of getting good coffee in this neck of the woods are—

"Is that a Jumping Bean truck?" Joanne interrupts my jabs as she spots the trailer by the side of the road, emblazoned with the logo of one of my favourite coffee shops in St. John's.

We can't believe our Townie eyes. Like a mirage in the desert that turns out to actually be a pond, here is a trailer selling super high-end coffee in Port au Choix. We stop, I walk up to the window, and as I'm greeted by a lovely woman, I ask her the dumbest Townie question ever.

"Are you selling Jumping Bean coffee here?"

Her eyebrows raise. She points to the logo in two-foot-high letters and politely says, "Yeah. What would you like?"

Two americanos and a few baked treats later, we are riding a caffeine buzz as we hit the highway.

I summarize the past couple of hours with delight: "So, this place has a shipyard, a shrimp plant, dozens of offshore boats, a French bread oven, an amazing walking trail, a lighthouse, a caribou herd, ancient civilizations, and a coffee truck. Port au Choix rocks. And it has for an extremely long time."

We sip our coffees and head ever north towards our destination, St. Anthony.

"Holy frig. We still got over two hundred kilometres to go."

I don't have the words out of my mouth when Henry states, "Newfoundland is too big." He might be right again.

We pass through Eddies Cove West, Bird Cove, Blue Cove, Deadman's Cove, Nameless Cove, and Green Island Cove, and I cannot help but notice an odd fact. None of these places actually look like coves. They are fishing stops on the open ocean, as far as this Petty Harbour fella is concerned. Where I come from, coves are tucked away in cliffs and islands, where they are protected from the sea and the worst elements. I am struck by how exposed these places are. I cannot imagine what a winter storm must be like here.

"They must be as tough as the tuck," I say, pointing to a boat full of strapping fellas headed out to face the gale.

Within a hundred kilometres of St. Anthony, we encounter the start of a roadside attraction that continues as far as we can see. Stacks of neatly piled firewood line the highway. I mean *a lot* of firewood. Some junked and split, and some left in eight-foot lengths.

Twenty minutes later, we are still driving at a hundred kilometres an hour past the continuous pile of firewood. We're also now passing the sleighs, or komatiks, they must use to haul this wood by Ski-Doo in winter. Dozens of them for the next hour. When we finally reach St. Anthony, my friend Steve is there to greet us. First thing I say is, "There must be enough firewood on this road to power the space shuttle." I shake his hand and jump from our van to his truck.

"Twice as much as that," says Steve with a laugh.

He's going to show me the area. He knows it well. Steve has lived in St. Anthony for a while and has spent much of his adult life guiding folks on whale-watching tours, salmon fishing expeditions, and hunts for large game. We met a few years back on an expedition ship that circumnavigated the island of Newfoundland. Over that ten-day period, we were both on the host team, me as a singer and cultural guide, while Steve knows the wilds of this province like the back of his hand.

As we approached the Labrador coast on that trip, I told the guests, "One of us sings songs and the other knows how to protect us all from polar bears. Don't get us mixed up, for Jesus' sake."

I confess I have often quietly giggled at the notion of polar bears cresting the hills coming towards us and me trying to protect our group with a sea shanty.

We drive around St. Anthony, which, unlike the places we've whipped past a while ago, is very much a protected harbour or cove, but isn't called either. This is very much a hub town. With a population of almost 2,500, it is easily the biggest on the peninsula and holds about 25 or 30 percent of the entire population of this massive piece of land. Like Port au Choix, the main industry here is the fishery, with boats and a plant, but this is also the service town for most things on the Northern Peninsula.

It has the largest high school on the peninsula, marine support facilities, and a small but cool group of shops, like the ever-present (in rural Newfoundland and Labrador) Riff's, as well as restaurants to support the locals and a decent tourism industry. But one name dominates the signage of St. Anthony.

I see his name on the visitor centre and the historical society. The local health-care region bears his name, as does a hotel on the main drag. His house is a museum. His name, of course, is Dr. Wilfred Grenfell.

Sir Wilfred Grenfell was a prominent medical missionary who dedicated his life to improving health-care services in rural and remote areas of Newfoundland and Labrador. Born in England in 1865, Grenfell moved to Newfoundland in 1892 to work as a physician in the impoverished fishing communities along the coast. Grenfell's work focused on providing medical care, education, and social services to the people living in these isolated areas. He established hospitals, including the one that bears his name here, as well as nursing stations and dispensaries, and trained local people to become health-care workers.

There are many stories of Grenfell's adventures while travelling up and down this coast, but I'll tell you one just so you get a sense of how dangerous and difficult delivering medical services to this area must have been.

One day in the winter of 1908, Grenfell set out from St. Anthony on dogsled to provide emergency medical assistance to a patient some one hundred kilometres south. He decided to cut across a frozen bay, but halfway across, he and eight of his beloved dogs ran into trouble as the sled sank beneath the ice and one of the dogs drowned. Soaking and surely bound to freeze to death overnight, Grenfell did what the dog lover in him would find unthinkable. He stabbed and skinned three of his dogs. He made a crude tent of their furs and bones, and he and the other dogs crawled inside. In the morning, they were rescued and carried ashore.

You might be tough, but perhaps you are not kill-and-sleep-inside-your-dogs tough. Oh, and he operated on—and cured—the patient, too.

Grenfell's legacy continued long after his death in 1940, as the health-care system he established in Newfoundland and Labrador still benefits communities to this day. His tireless work and humanitarian efforts have left an indelible mark on the region, and he is remembered as a true hero and champion for those in need.

Steve drives me out of St. Anthony, even further north to some of the most beautiful places we've seen on this trip. Saint Lunaire-Griquet is as close to a pair of picture-perfect-postcard fishing communities as you'll ever see. They look charming as the small boats reflect off the still water in the beaming northern sun. Quirpon and Quirpon Island are just as beautiful, and we take to a walking trail through the green meadows that line the sloped hills to the beaches.

"Now, it's not like this in February." Steve does his best to slow to my speed as we crest a hill and chat with a fella who's walking with his two dogs.

"Hello, nice day. Where are you from?" Like I said, Steve has been a tour guide of sorts most of his adult life, and his passion for chatting with people is infectious.

We learn that this retired gent is from Connecticut and up here for the summer with his wife and their four-legged companions. I ask if this is his first time.

"No," he giggles, "this is my twentieth summer here. We rent a house or a trailer to escape the New York heat and noise.

We left home one day in June to drive north, and well, this is as far as we could drive."

I reflect to myself that we northern island folks tend to regard our isolation and moderate weather as shortcomings. We sometimes forget that there are loads of people longing for this life. Longing to escape the bustle and the ever-sweltering urban centres of North America and beyond. Okay, maybe not in February, but my instinct tells me our summer and fall days of being sparsely populated and remote are numbered.

Back on the wharf, I spot a buoy made from a white plastic Javex bottle. I know Steve is a man of the water, so I mention, "That's not your first time seeing one of those?"

He laughs. "No, b'y. Leave it to us Newfoundlanders to reuse something for any reason other than the one intended."

"We were recyclers before it was cool," I add as we jump in the truck to head back to St. Anthony. Along the way, we list all the things our parents were tickled to reuse.

"Javex bottles for buoys and bailers!" says Steve as we roll.

"Plastic butter tubs! Nan never threw out a single one!" I add, "Newfoundland is the only place in the world where Tupperware never stood a chance."

Then, one after the other, we just shout them out as they occur to us.

"Old deep-freeze for roadside garbage box!"

"Old tires for front lawn flower beds!"

"Mayonnaise jars with the metal tops screwed up under the shelf in the shed!"

"Tobacco tins for nails!"

"Broke-off hockey stick handles for hooks and gaffs!"

"Grey fish boxes for . . . everything!"

This conversation continues later when Steve asks us all up to his place for a fire. He and his family have a lovely spot on the hill, and we head there after a few craft beers and supper at the RagnaRöck Brewery in town.

At Steve's house, he uncovers a metal firepit contraption that looks unusual, yet perfectly made for providing a safe, contained, well-ventilated outdoor fire. I watch him skillfully place paper and kindling in the perforated container, and within seconds there's a welcoming blaze.

"Steve, where did you get this rig?" I am on my hands and knees, trying to find the logo or brand name of whoever makes such a perfect firepit.

"That's a clothes washer tub." Steve seems puzzled I would even ask.

"A what?" I am still on my hands and knees when Steve adds a log or two.

"A washer tub. From an old clothes washer."

I laugh and brush off my knees. "Steve, how is it this did not come up today? We spent an hour talking about recycled and reused stuff, and the washer-tub firepit never crossed your mind?"

Steve doesn't break stride, and keeps loading logs.

"No sir, sure, you don't throw out clothes washer tubs. Everybody knows that."

We have a grand night, and as we are leaving, Steve says, "I'll be in Town next week. I'll drop off a washer tub on your step." I get in the van knowing he will, too.

Joanne and Henry and I have some more St. Anthony–area fun, especially around Fishing Point, where walking trails surround a very cool lighthouse, gift shop, and café. Seabirds and whales fight for attention as a massive Carnival cruise ship heads out to sea.

We have one more spot to visit in this Great Northern Peninsula Trip. You could say we have saved the best for last. We are to visit one of the most significant archaeological findings in human history. I'm serious. It's a few kilometres up the road in L'Anse aux Meadows.

I ask Joanne and Henry to humour me just before we enter the official site. They are annoyed because I want them to follow me up on the steep rocks next to the path.

"That's not the site, Dad . . . why are we going up there?" Henry is skeptical, but I insist.

When we crest the rocks and are at the top of the hill, I point across the ocean strait to a point of land in the distance.

"Look!" My excitement is not immediately shared by my eighteen-year-old.

"What?!" Henry is about to turn around.

"That is the mainland of Canada and North America! This is one of the only areas on the island of Newfoundland where you can see anyplace else. Over there, on that same piece of land, are Vancouver and Miami and Mexico City."

"Yeah, cool. You said there were Viking swords up here?" Henry heads off to the site and Jo shrugs as if to say, "He'll realize how cool that is someday . . . we hope."

We enter L'Anse aux Meadows National Historic Site, which is also a UNESCO World Heritage Site. I don't think it's an exaggeration to say that the discovery made here is one of the most significant in the world. There are not many places you can walk amongst artifacts and remnants of buildings that rewrote history. But that is exactly what happened here.

This is the site where it was proven undeniably that Christopher Columbus was not the first European to cross the ocean and land in North America. Not, as it turns out, by a long, long shot. And by long, long shot, I mean half a millennium.

Last century, Norwegian scholars Helge and Anne Stine Ingstad had spent half a lifetime studying the writings of the Norse people known commonly as Vikings. These writings seemed to suggest that the Norse had settled in North America some five hundred years before our pal Christopher was even born. Scholars wondered if this home away from home—called "Vinland"—might be in Massachusetts, but no evidence to support this claim could be found.

This scholarly power couple believed northern Newfoundland was a possible site of Vinland, and to test their theory, they travelled north of St. Anthony. What transpired next was nothing short of incredible.

Helge and Anne Stine arrived in L'Anse aux Meadows town in 1960 in pursuit of this crazy, far-fetched scholarly notion that they and others had been investigating for years in the hallowed halls of libraries and archives of northern Europe. They walked into town and immediately met a local fella named George Decker. Our fella George was kind and curious and greeted them friendly and asked what brought them to town.

I imagine the conversation went something like this:

"We are from Norway and we are here—well, this may sound outrageous, but we suspect the claim about Columbus to be false and . . . well, we have been researching the possibility of a Norse settlement in this area and—"

George would've interrupted them and matter-of-factly said: "Oh yeah. Over here." The couple must have been gobsmacked as George casually continued. "Probably what we calls this old Indian spot over here is what you're looking for. These bumps in the meadow used to be their houses, see."

And with that, Helge and Anne Stine were led to a site that was the living answer to the mystery they and others had spent years investigating. Soon after, artifacts and dwellings unearthed there proved that this was indeed the Vinland spoken of in the Norse writings and that Christopher Columbus had been a distant second in the race to find the New World.

I giggle as I watch my wife and son walk ahead of me. What I wouldn't give for a time machine to stand on the side of the road in 1960 and witness the look on Helge's and Anne Stine's faces.

The site is incredible, and the recreations are wonderfully done, right down to the costumed guides. We learn that the Norse likely inhabited this place for a couple of dozen years, caught fish and whales, and then moved on to wherever was next.

In other words, the Vikings just couldn't hack it here, while my ancestors surely stayed.

"So, they got cold and left . . . and we stuck it out?!" Henry looks equally as proud of himself as he is disappointed in the "toughest guys in the world."

I wonder if I should adjust to my earlier thought about the tuck for future chats. "The people here are like the tuckamore trees. Tough. Malleable. They adapt and survive and stay . . . not like the Norse crowd, who shagged off when it got windy."

That's the polite version. When I get a few too many drinks in and the subject comes up, I might rudely and dismissively over-simplify with "Ha! Vikings! Bunch of wimps!"

LABRADOR TIME

"To the Big Land!"

I am excited. Way too excited for my sleepy teenage son, who we have dragged from bed at 7 a.m.

"How big is it?" mumbles Henry as he sleepwalks his way into the back of the van.

I can't help but think about what a good question this is as we make our way back across the tip of Newfoundland, bound for St. Barbe. This is a narrow part of Newfoundland, and yet the drive still takes us almost two hours. I ask out loud, "How can this be the small land?"

I don't know it yet, but we are about to find the answers to both questions.

We roll the Honda Odyssey minivan onto the ferry in St. Barbe to leave Newfoundland for Labrador—"But first we go to Quebec for about ninety seconds."

My announcement to my family is met with the confusion the situation deserves. The ferry between Newfoundland and

Labrador, you see, doesn't actually go from Newfoundland to Labrador. For some reason, this ferry lands a few hundred metres from the Newfoundland and Labrador border in a Quebec town called Blanc-Sablon. As far as I can tell, there had been a pre-existing ferry-friendly wharf in Blanc-Sablon, so it made sense to land our intra-provincial ferry in another province—but just barely in another province.

So, we are headed to Labrador, which is part of the province of Newfoundland . . . well, it used to be. Now, it is part of the province of Newfoundland *and Labrador*. Labrador used to be part of this province the way Cape Breton is in Nova Scotia or Vancouver Island is in British Columbia, but in 2001 the name was officially changed and the Big Land became part of the title. Lots of people thought this was an excellent step to recognize the incredible contribution the people and resources of Labrador have made to the province. Lots thought we just made an unwieldy name for ourselves.

Whatever one might think of the renaming, it has undeniably made telling people what I am and where I am from a clumsier task. It used to be easy. I am a Newfoundlander from Newfoundland. But in making such a statement these days, I run the risk of sounding exclusionary or dismissive, as folks might assume I'm clinging to our old provincial name and not adopting the new one. But here's how I explain and defend my nomenclature choices: I am from the Canadian province of Newfoundland and Labrador, but I can't be a Newfoundlander and Labradorian, because that would mean I was from two places. So, here's my disclaimer: when I say I am a Newfoundlander from Newfoundland, I am referring to the island rather than the province. I am a Newfoundlander from the Canadian province of Newfoundland and Labrador. Does that work? I hope so.

As we approach Quebec, I can't help but think of all the arguments and disputes there have been between our two provinces.

The biggest stone-in-shoe here at home is the deal between us and Quebec over a hydroelectric dam at Churchill Falls, Labrador. The billion-dollar facility was built in 1970, on our turf but with Quebec money. It is an engineering marvel and is by all measures a huge success story. That is, by all measures except the sour deal our province signed for ongoing royalty rates for the power. I'll keep the math simple for you and just say that the rates negotiated when the thing opened in the early 1970s would stay the same until around halfway through the next century, with no increase for market value or inflation or anything like that. Many Newfoundlanders and Labradorians of my parents' and grandparents' eras have felt completely hosed by the deal, and it remains perceived as a blunder for our leaders of the time, giving rise to a provincial feeling that we got taken advantage of by the slippery Quebec crowd.

Some would suggest that lingering feelings from the Churchill Falls hydro deal led to the more recent Meech Lake racket. Canadians of my vintage and older will remember that in the late 1980s there were proposed amendments to the Canadian Constitution that, among other things, declared Quebec to be a "distinct society." The prime minister and most of the provincial premiers were all for it, but guess who put his hand up and opposed such a distinction? Our premier, that's who. And Newfoundlanders and Labradorians loved him for it.

But the oldest racket between the two archnemeses would have to be over the actual border between us. The eastern coast of Labrador has been fished by the same gang who've fished the coast of Newfoundland for centuries and has been part of the entity known as Newfoundland since the mid-1700s. But the western border that tells us all where Labrador ends and Quebec begins has been the source of a massive racket for a long, long time. And some real stubborn folks consider the fight still ongoing. To this day, the odd Quebec politician looking to get a few fists pumping publishes a map of his province with the border where he thinks it should be, and not where it actually is. You can imagine the eye-rolling when our crowd sees a map where more than half of Labrador—and a quarter of our whole province—is under the Quebec banner.

Most agree that the racket was settled with the decision of the Judicial Committee of the Privy Council in 1927 in London and that the debate about the border did, in fact, end then. The crux of the successful argument had much to do with the definition of the word *coast*, and how it should not be defined as just "by the ocean," but also where the watershed line reaches further inland. And by further inland, they meant only about 750 kilometres.

So, maybe we can all understand why some try to keep the argument rolling, but officially speaking, it is over. At the risk of oversimplifying history, allow me to suggest that we in this dominion, colony, wannabe republic, or province do not always come out on the winning side of court decisions such as this. But the successful petition for the western Labrador border remains one of the biggest victories in the history of this place. I can't help but think we got a big W there over twenty years before we ever joined Canada.

So, while many folks take one glance at the Canadian map and figure it makes little sense that the Lab West area does not belong to Quebec, I—and dare I say, everyone from my province— am happy to tell them it doesn't. Officially, the border runs from just ahead of where this ferry docks, on the eastern side of

Blanc-Sablon, some 3,500 kilometres north, making it easily the biggest provincial boundary in Canada.

If they have had a hard time figuring out the border issue here, it also seems they had a hard time deciding what time of day it is. As we approach Blanc-Sablon, I check the time on my iPhone. We left St. Barbe on schedule at 10:30, and should be landing an hour and forty-five minutes later, at 12:15. So, I'm confused to see that my phone thinks it is still just barely past 10:40. A few minutes later, as we roll off the boat into the province of Quebec, I realize we have switched to Eastern time, ninety minutes earlier than Newfoundland time, which means in a matter of a kilometre or so, we will likely switch back.

"Hey bud, look at your phone!" That's a statement I rarely need to make to our eighteen-year-old. "Your clock is about to do something very strange."

We both look, and we both shout, "Whoa!" as our phones flip from 11:00 to 12:30. Driving around North America, I have watched the clocks flip an hour hundreds of times. Cross Alberta into BC, and it flips an hour. Same thing happens between Nevada and Utah, and loads of other places, including somewhere in the Chunnel between the UK and continental Europe. On low-flying airplanes and aboard the ferry, I've seen the clock jump thirty minutes between Newfoundland and Nova Scotia many times. But, I think this is the only occasion I have had to watch it leap *ninety* minutes.

All of the province of Quebec—sensibly, I might add—is on Eastern time. Our province has two time zones, which is far less sensible. For about fifty of my fifty-five years on this planet I thought all of the island of Newfoundland was on one time zone, while all of Labrador was on another. That would be the most sensible way to divide it, if we have to, which apparently we do. But what's the fun in being sensible? There is a sliver of Labrador on the southeast tip that operates on Newfoundland time. And it happens to be one of the two parts that border Quebec. So, in one stride you can lose ninety minutes of your day as you walk from noon to 1:30. But not to worry, take the same stride later, and you can step from suppertime at 6:30 right back into happy hour at only 5 p.m.

As we cross under the "Welcome to Newfoundland and Labrador" sign, I offer, "It's like we never left." Henry groans a groan he reserves for Dad jokes.

Our first stop is in Point Amour, with its magnificent nineteenth-century lighthouse. I'm quite frankly surprised at how magnificent the meadowland is, too, as it rolls as green and pristine as a golf course from the highway to the sea.

"It's like we are on the emerald rolling seaside hills in Ireland," I say romantically.

To which Joanne replies, "Yeah, come in February and see if you still think that."

My wife has spent much more time than I in Labrador, and I suspect she is right on the money as ever, because while the land all around is lush and green, there is barely a tree or bush to be seen. I can only imagine the winter winds out on this exposed point.

The lighthouse quicky rises up from the meadows. At thirty-three metres, it is the highest lighthouse in the province and the second-highest in the country. (The tallest one is in Gaspé. See my earlier comments about competitions and rackets between Quebec and Newfoundland and Labrador.) It is as impressive as this area is beautiful on what I assume to be a rare windless day.

As we approach, signage makes a second bragging point: "World's First Foghorn."

Turns out Canada had steam-driven alarms for foggy days from the mid-1800s, but the first lighthouse to use a compressed-air foghorn that emits the sound that drifts across northern coastal towns was right here.

Not to get finicky on the facts of the claim of the Point Amour gang, but sources say this compressed-air foghorn was originally situated in Cape Ray and moved to Point Amour. Perhaps I am splitting hairs, and there's no need to clarify if this horn lived somewhere else first. I don't blame them for stretching the truth here, if indeed they did. After Great Big Sea returned from a few European festivals, I told everyone we were "really big in Poland." I'll let you decide how big we actually were.

So, I am happy to join the Point Amour gang and repeat that this indeed is the WORLD'S FIRST FOGHORN.

Henry has been reading along with me and asks a simple question: "How do they know?" I look to him and he clarifies.

"How do they know they were first?"

This is one of those parenting moments when your kid asks for very straightforward information and it stings a little when you can't immediately give a straight answer. So, I do what I assume most dads do. I make something up.

"I think I heard a fella one time say something about an International Foghorn Organization that verifies the time and date of each new foghorn."

I can see his forehead wrinkle. I know this kid, and he's not buying it. He looks to his mom.

"Dad doesn't know, does he?"

Before she can answer, I point to the thirty-three-metre-high light and enthusiastically offer: "Let's climb the stairs!"

Luckily, they follow me up to the light tower and I convince myself I still look somewhat knowledgeable to my son.

The view from the top is breathtaking on this beautiful day. We can easily see across the strait, back to the Northern Peninsula, and the sky and ocean are clear and calm. The location and conditions are perfect for seeing all there is to see around the lighthouse. And that is, well, practically nothing.

We can see as far as the curvature of the Earth will let us in most directions. Only the hills between us and the ferry terminal back in Blanc-Sablon harbour block our view of nothing. Beautiful nothing. There isn't a boat on the water or a car on the road. There are no buildings other than those directly beneath us, servicing the lighthouse and the museum. The Wyatt family who ran this place for around a hundred years must have been excellent at solitaire. I somehow find it peaceful and unsettling at the same time. The view from the top of Point Amour Lighthouse is a perfect reminder that we have just entered the Big Land and we are about to feel really, really small.

As we drive east across the southeastern corner of Labrador, we are charmed by industrious and busy towns for the first fifty kilometres or so. Forteau, L'Anse-au-Loup, and L'Anse-au-Clair, along with a few others, are all bustling little places on this perfect, calm, sunny August day. All the way over the mighty Pinware River into East St. Modeste, there is enough distraction to keep us from realizing where we are and how unlikely it is for us to be here, driving a domestic vehicle across this incredibly remote part of the world.

But then there comes a most unsettling stretch of about thirty kilometres before we reach Red Bay. There are no towns to charm us and I am immediately struck by the near impossibility of this road. This is a paved highway that doesn't present itself as one, that was once a route for local drivers to get from town to town, or before that, a beaten trail for horse and cart, or a walking path before that. This pavement looks very recent and very out of place. We are driving through a beautiful but barren tundra, and this road is the only man-made thing I can see ahead or behind us. There is not a house, a shop, a building, a quarry, a woods road— or woods, for that matter. There isn't a pole with a wire on it. I have not seen so much as a cellphone tower in a long, long time.

With the exception of a rare encounter with another vehicle, which is almost always rigged with extra gear for off-road survival, we are alone on a raised bed of crushed rock that splits this northern barren expanse. A ribbon of asphalt dropped where it looks like it never should have been dropped.

"This is like some road an army built to get to the secret space station launch site in Alaska or something." I scan to find even a short bush on this beautiful rocky terrain when Henry notes, "This is like a road in a *Star Wars* movie."

The rocks look prehistoric. It feels like we are driving to the edge of the Earth. I simply cannot guess how much money, time, and labour went into building and paving this road. How did they get the machinery and supplies in here? How long did it take? And how in God's name do they possibly keep this road open in the winter? There isn't a tree, let alone a forest or a hill, to break the wind. The snowdrifts must be as wild as they are high.

I can picture the shot in a feature film. A lonely snowplow operator pushing through this even lonelier highway as the dim early-morning light shines across an endless field of white. As the drone camera pulls out and up, we see the plow shoving the snow aside as it feebly bucks through the remnants of a winter storm. As the camera rises further again, we realize the futility of the stubborn little plow. The second it pushes the white snow away, revealing the black asphalt, the stiff Labrador wind blows the snow right back behind it. Like it was never there.

As beautiful as this place is, its vastness is unnerving. I am relieved to see the welcome signs for Red Bay.

Arriving in Red Bay for me is a bit like a lifelong hockey fan finally making it to Maple Leaf Gardens. I spent many of my formative teenage years behind the desk and walking the halls of the provincial museum. I had just turned sixteen when I got a summer job learning about and talking about Newfoundland and Labrador. All my previous summer jobs had been knee-deep in fish or crab guts or lugging sods across farm fields, so I was stoked to spend a summer with clean clothes on. What I didn't know was how much I'd come to love showing off the exhibits, and how that would lead me to a love of the story of this place. My fascination and passion for Newfoundland and Labrador just blossomed.

One of the coolest exhibits was about Red Bay, Labrador, which for almost a century was the whaling capital of the world. The Basques came from southern France and northern Spain from around the middle of the sixteenth century till the end of the eighteenth and found whales in such abundance that they established not just a landing site for the hunt, but an entire processing operation as well. Some estimates figure over a thousand sailors at a time planted here in the summers to hunt whales and melt down the blubber to sell to the ever-expanding global market for the oil.

I bet I told the story of this place hundreds of times at the museum. How the Basques from small beginnings quickly built up an industry. How they built processing buildings with roofing techniques and tiles from Spain. How they brought and left massive kettles and tools for the dissecting and melting of the whale flesh. And my favourite part, concerning a Basque galleon, the *San Juan*, which sank in the waters off Red Bay during a storm in 1565. Underwater archaeologists found it, and a smaller rowboat known as a *txalupa*, preserved in near-perfect condition in the cold, salty waters between Red Bay and Saddle Island. I spent hours imagining the sight of these distinctly European wooden vessels sunk deep in the frigid waters of Labrador.

The whole place just sounded so badass and international to me. A thousand dark and dirty fellas yelling in foreign languages, rolling barrel after barrel all over the wharf, and under a pile of steam and smoke from roaring fires and massive boiling kettles. I loved the thought of it. A tourist once noted that he understood the name Red Bay came from the fact that the bay was filled with blood from so many whales. While I knew this to be an incorrect and gruesome suggestion, I chose not to correct him because the whole bloody bay deal sounded so wickedly pirate and old school. Why kill that story with something as foolish as the truth that it was named for the red cliffs in the area? Where's the fun in that?

As I type, I am grinning at the memory of how much I loved to say *txalupa*, and brag about the bay being listed as one of the most significant underwater archaeological sites in the world. Imagine how I would have glowed to know it would become a UNESCO World Heritage Site in 2013.

I was a self-proclaimed member of a Red Bay fan club I had invented in my mind some thirty years ago. So, finally getting to see all this in person is like arriving on the set of a movie that I have been watching since my teens. I hop excitedly into the local museum like a 1980s groupie getting backstage at an Aerosmith concert. I run from artifact to artifact till I finally get to one of the excavated boats, and you knows I shouted *"Txalupa!"* a bit too loudly.

Red Bay has a whole lot else to offer a visitor, including amazing seafood at the local restaurant called, what else, Whalers, and an incredible walking trail in Tracey Hill. Almost seven hundred steps take you up one of the hills, where you're treated to picturesque views of the town and the strait. The whole deal makes for a delightful stop. I wish we had more time to hang, but we have a boat to catch another hour or so away in Mary's Harbour.

We turn the minivan north and head back onto the impossible road. I said that this road felt unsettling while we were travelling east to Red Bay, and that was with the ocean on the passenger side most of the way. Well, after Red Bay, the ocean view disappears mostly, and we are headed due north into more beautiful nothingness. If possible, this leg of the drive is even more intimidating and ominous. I must repeat, it really feels like this average domestic minivan has no business on this sci-fi highway. I wonder if it was built as a runway for a spaceship. Like we are driving off the planet in the year 2099 to avoid the millennium crash or something. It is awesome, in every sense of the word.

We take the exit for Mary's Harbour, and a shift occurs instantly. We have been driving on a near-futuristic escape highway for a few hundred kilometres, and the moment we turn off, I instantly feel the rumble of dirt and gravel under the tires. In a second we go from a road I'd never imagined to a road I remember all too well. I had never seen a highway like the one we have been on, but I know exactly what it feels like to swerve to avoid a muddy pothole in the dirt. I grab the interior handle on the minivan door so I don't fall over into Joanne's lap.

In my mind, we have gone from my future to my past. I'm back on the dirt roads of my childhood in Petty Harbour.

"Feels like another time jump, but way more than ninety minutes this time!" I say aloud. And even I have no idea how true that statement will turn out to be.

In a moment, in the tiny but bustling town of Mary's Harbour, I am eleven years old again, back in Petty Harbour. Fishing boats coming and going. Forklifts buzzing. Two fish plants clearly at peak processing capacity. This place is on the go. I want to linger in it for nostalgia, but another boat is waiting for us. A boat that will take us to one of the most magical places in Labrador or anywhere else. After decades of hearing about it and reading about it and longing to see it, I am finally headed for Battle Harbour.

Battle Harbour is a town and fishing station on Battle Island, about fifteen kilometres out from Mary's Harbour in the North Atlantic off the southeast coast of Labrador. If that sentence makes it sound remote and isolated, that's because Battle Harbour is both of those things. If that sentence makes it sound like a difficult or uncomfortable place to spend a few days, I apologize. Because Battle Harbour is neither of those things.

European people have been living and working here since as far back as 1770, and Indigenous people long before that. It was once known as the salt fish capital of the world and is still often referred to as the capital of Labrador. Grenfell himself built one of the first hospitals in Labrador here in the 1890s. All this to say, Battle Harbour had been a going commercial concern for well over two centuries until the dreaded cod moratorium of the 1990s. At that point the owners of the station donated all its commercial buildings to the Battle Harbour Historic Trust, which operates just about all the dwellings on the island as an inn and resort. It is one of the most impossible scenarios for luxury and high-end accommodations imaginable, and I've been dying to see it for a long, long time.

The moment we round the head of the bay, we are engulfed in a fog so thick that I am convinced a special effects department is responsible for executing this moment perfectly. My notions of time travel and of being headed to a magical place could not be more piqued if we were headed through the mist to Hogwarts.

"I can barely see the end of the boat," says Henry, wiping the water from his travel-weary face. It feels like a week ago we woke up in St. Anthony and drove to the ferry. But that was just this morning. We push along to the sounds of the engine and the bow breaking the water and the sight of nothing but endless white cloud, broken only by one curious seagull who looks terribly disappointed to find that this boat is carrying three jacketed humans and not a load of fish to be gutted.

It would be very easy to get uneasy here. I take a moment to pinpoint where I am in the universe. This is well past the middle of nowhere. Most would consider Newfoundland to be remote, or at least far-flung (to be kind), and St. John's to be well up there and out there on the map. I just left a point of land that is around a thousand kilometres northwest of St. John's. I am in a small boat that started pushing out to sea into dense fog, and we have gone over fifteen kilometres into the abyss. If my family wanted to kill me and drop the body where it would never be found, this would be a good spot.

And then, with a wisp of wind, the white fog is dented by a red horizontal line. Then a blue vertical one. It confuses the eyes the way a magic trick should. I rub them, but won't close them, as I'm afraid I'll miss a hint of what's to come. One instant, there is nothing; then, as if on cue with the height of a percussionist's cymbal swell, there is a town.

An impossible town that is somehow possible.

A place out of place.

As we slip into a narrow channel between two islands, we see a collection of white houses with perfectly painted red or blue trim. The exact horizontal lines of well-kept clapboard and shingled roofs as straight as a carpenter's line appear almost ridiculous against the round and irregular moss-covered rocks and hills still drenched in foggy mist. One perfect house after the other, connected by an impeccable wooden boardwalk you could traverse in dance shoes, lead up the hill to a church so quaint and untarnished that you'd swear it was built last weekend. A wooden church stands tall at the crest of the hill. All these wonderful houses and sheds flowing so easily down to the main wharf, where my eyes can't believe what they see. I have to swear.

"Jesus, there's a downtown."

The buildings and facilities used for generations in the Labrador fishing industry line the wharf. They are in perfect condition. The main commercial buildings on the wharf stretch up three stories, all with preserved and painted white clapboard with red doors and trimmed windows. Same can be said for the weigh houses for weighing the fish, the wet rooms for salting and curing, the dry rooms for storing the finished product. All this industry surrounded by the generations-old infrastructure that a bustling little town would need. A slipway and a wooden storage barn. A flour store and a twine loft. A cooperage and a gear shed. All impossibly preserved. Not recreated, but preserved.

The general store halfway up the path appears to be the centre of all the activity, as it no doubt has been for ages. The entire scene is nothing short of mind-boggling. This is not a fragile, well-kept museum piece, but a group of buildings that stand as solid and proud as they have done for decades. Looks like the place was in full function yesterday and will be again tomorrow.

Like we have arrived on the day of the garden party in the middle of a busy fishing season rather than a hundred years since some of these various facilities were built.

I have never seen anything like it, and I guarantee you haven't, either. There's nothing like it. Anywhere in this province or any other. This is the greatest act of preservation I've ever seen in a rural place. I've seen the great churches of Europe, with every stone restored in cities like Cologne or Lyon. I've sung in opera houses and theatres in urban Italy and France with histories stretching back to the Roman Empire. But this is not just an act of preservation in a very rural place. This is an act of preservation fifteen kilometres out in the ocean from a very rural place. It is astounding. The mere sight of it from the water on a cold, damp, foggy day is well worth the journey.

Our boat reaches the wharf and the welcoming committee is eager to help us ashore.

Peter Bull greets me the second I step onto the wharf, as I'd think he and his team do for every visitor. Peter and his gang run the place, and what a job they do for the Battle Harbour Historic Trust. So good that they've earned for this place a designation as a National Historic Site.

Our bags are whisked up the hill to one of the many charming wooden houses that the trust now uses as hotel suites, as Peter and his team give us a general orientation of the place. After a coffee, he encourages us to explore the island before supper, while it's still light. I ask him if we should start somewhere specific or just wander. He replies casually, like a fella who has no idea he is about to say something very profound, that he's about to give the definitive description of this well-off-the-beaten-track place. He opens his arms like Ricardo Montalbán on *Fantasy Island* and says: "The roads are wherever you want to go."

"That should be your slogan." I turn up the hill as Peter nods with a grin.

"Perhaps it should."

Over the next thirty-six hours we have an experience that defies expectation. Outdoors, we walk over rocky hills and through meadows to every corner of the island. We see sparse but well-used gardens for growing precious vegetables. We sit in small berry fields and spy more on neighbouring islands that provided some essential healthy sweets. We sit on rocks that seem to show you the inner foundation of the island itself. Peter reported one visiting student put it best when he said, "The geology of this place does not need to be uncovered. It's all just out there to see."

We fish off the wharves and catch full-size codfish. The same type Petty Harbour fishermen would head out to sea to catch. "I guess we are already out to sea," shouts Henry as he reels one in.

As eventful as it is outside, the real charm is indoors. Our room is like a captain's quarters in the best wooden ship ever. Painted wooden walls, floors, and ceilings, with warm rugs and homemade quilts. The main dining room is right on the wharf, and we feast on local fish, with desserts made from berries picked in the very fields we explored.

We take a walking tour that leads us into all the commercial buildings. Some still smell like salt, others like drying sawdust. I play a song on the old organ in the church. I play guitar in the pub above the general store.

It's as great an experience as I've had anywhere in our province or beyond. There is something so special about this place and about the people who work here. Most of the staff are locals who grew up here and in the area. Their knowledge and stories are not so much researched and book-learned, but real lived experience from their childhoods. Everything right down to the bun Daphne served me was extraordinary.

I am sad to leave so early in the morning. Sad to say goodbye not just to the incredible location, or the world-class treatment, but the very feeling of being somewhere separate from everywhere and everything. Separate from the clock itself. I shake Peter's hand and comment with my thanks: "Time travel is possible. Just come to Battle Harbour."

"Now, *that* should be our slogan." Peter recalls our first chat and I just nod with a grin as he did.

"Perhaps it should."

We jump down into an open speedboat and head back to the mainland.

As the boat brings us back to the present, I can't help but dwell on all we've seen and done since we rolled off the ferry in Quebec. I open my map on my iPhone and zoom in to the area of Labrador we have covered. I laugh out loud when I realize we have been in a pinch of this place. A teeny-tiny corner of it. Goose Bay is still around five hundred kilometres northeast of us. Lab West, the area we successfully fought for, is around a 960-kilometre drive due west of this minivan. You can't even drive to the tip. According to my quick and dirty calculation, a very cold crow would have to fly at least another thousand kilometres due north before it reached Cape Chidley.

"Jaysus, we haven't been hardly anywhere in Labrador."

After all that talk of the beautiful nothing, there sure is a lot.

The Big Land indeed.

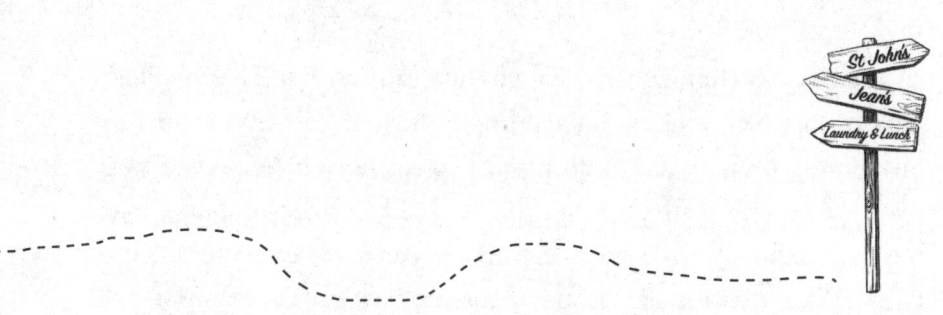

JEAN'S LAUNDRY AND LUNCH

"**D**ad, I am moving to St. John's."

It was late in the summer of 1987 when I finally summoned the courage to break the news to my dad. He was sitting in his most comfortable spot in the living room, on the end of the couch, with his thick eyeglasses lifted and resting on his forehead as he pressed the folded crossword section of the *Evening Telegram* to his ever-failing eyes.

He must have been stuck on a tricky word and didn't quite hear as he mumbled, "What's that?"

I repeated, "I'm moving to Town."

Dad folded the newspaper over just enough so I could see him tip his glasses down onto his eyes so he could visually confirm who was speaking with him.

"Oh, Alan . . . I thought you moved to Town long ago."

He quickly flipped the paper back up, and that's the last we discussed it.

Dad's cavalier confusion was not unfounded. By my last year of high school, I was spending a third to half of my time in St. John's. I suppose I didn't want to let myself believe it yet, owing to some guilty obligation to Petty Harbour, but I had already fallen in love with the city. I ran to it every chance I could. As I mentioned, in one of the luckiest breaks of my life, I had landed a job working Thursday nights and Saturdays and Sundays at the Museum of Newfoundland and Labrador in downtown St. John's. So, I would often leave school Thursday afternoons and hitch a ride to Town to be at work for 4:30.

I was to be a "museum interpreter," which I quickly came to learn was a Townie phrase for "tour guide." It was heaven sent. A Doyle getting paid to talk.

My older sister Kim and my brother, Bernie, were already living in St. John's as they attended university, and I often found a corner of their floor, or I crashed on a co-worker's couch till 7:30 a.m., then I'd hitch a ride back to St. Kevin's in The Goulds. Most of my Friday nights were spent playing with my uncle Ronnie's band or with our own band made up of my high school classmates. We were called First Attempt, a name I should regret, but really don't. In either case, I rarely made it back to Petty Harbour after school on Fridays, and I worked Saturdays and Sundays at the museum.

All this to say, in my last year of high school, I regularly left Petty Harbour around 7:30 on Thursday morning and didn't come back till around 7:30 Sunday night. So, we shouldn't judge Dad's nonchalance too harshly, as I had been spending over half my weeks in St. John's. Mom would always be ready for me on Thursday mornings.

"Take extra socks and underwear and some Cup-a-Soup packets." Mom would stuff freeze-dried soup and canned food into my backpack. "You can't be a dirtbag or be bummin' food."

I'd walk down over Skinners Hill on Thursday mornings like a roadie headed on tour. With my left hand, I'd sling a backpack loaded with schoolbooks, museum uniform, spare socks and drawers, and a toothbrush, along with several Cup-a-Soup envelopes and a can or two of Heinz beans. With my right hand, I'd swing my 1972 Fender Stratocaster.

I must have cut some figure hitching to school. Like a fella thumbing to Nashville to make it big. On a once-in-a-lifetime adventure. Every Thursday.

A note about all the hitchhiking. There was a school bus service to take us from Petty Harbour to the school some five kilometres away in the farming town of The Goulds. But if a kid wanted to participate in any preschool activities, the bus arrived at school too late. And if a kid wanted to do the same after school, the bus left too early. And this kid wanted to do everything. We did not own a car for much of my childhood, so if I wanted to go anywhere, I had to hitchhike. So I did. A lot.

I hitched to school and back every day for four years. I hitched back to The Goulds after supper regularly for band practice or social outings or sports, or anything else that might possibly be on the go. I hitchhiked to St. John's for shifts at the museum and for evening opportunities to sneak into clubs on George Street while I was underage. All of this hitching grew tiresome, and I moved to St. John's as early as I possibly could.

If I were to take you on a tourist walk through the famed jellybean houses in the heart of downtown, we would walk right past the first room I rented in the city. These houses almost always join directly onto each other and share a common wall, making them effectively all row houses. The "jellybean" part comes from the rainbow of unusually bright colours people choose to paint these dwellings. Bright reds, cartoon blues, flower yellows, deep greens—all make for a rainbow of a townscape that has made St. John's instantly recognizable.

The reason for this odd multicolour choice is a subject of great debate. Some say the limited paint choices that were available were surplus bright nautical colours from the boating world. But I prefer the argument that seems the most sensible to me. The houses are built onto the dark rocks of the St. John's hills. We live in a foggy place that is often overcast and grey. When fishermen made their way back into the harbour on a grey, foggy day, they needed, or at least wanted, to easily spot their home or neighbourhood. So, they painted the houses as opposite to grey and foggy as possible, and that tradition has been sustained to this day and I have always loved the look of it all. I was stoked to get a chance to live in one of them.

I actually sublet a room in a jellybean row house from a coworker at the museum who was headed to Europe on a trip for a few months. I couldn't believe it. I was going to Memorial University of Newfoundland and I did not have to hitchhike every morning. I lived within walking distance of everything downtown, and I'll tell you about the great things I discovered living there, as you might do on a visit yourself.

The first thing that struck me, and will likely strike you, too, is the waterfront. This long, continuous wharf runs parallel to Harbour Drive and to the harbour itself. I loved walking the full length of it and watching sailors running up and down gangways to busy ships from all over the globe. When the wharf wasn't that busy, you could see across the harbour and out The Narrows, the aptly named slender gateway between St. John's and the sea. I thought of it as the perfect place to start and get yourself oriented in a harbour town. Go down to the water, turn around, and look back up. None of the city is behind you, and all of it is in front of you. It's a simple, organic way to find your way around that has become part of my travelling DNA and has saved me many times when trying to find my way in Halifax or Vancouver, and perhaps is the reason why I still can't find my way around Calgary or Regina.

I became quite familiar with the harbourfront just from daily walks or special events, like the glory days when the St. John's City Council had the good sense to have New Year's Eve celebrations right on the harbour. It was, and remains, one of my favourite spots to walk in all of St. John's, and I could not imagine the city without it.

But one day at the museum, I sat at the desk across from the large black-and-white print of a photograph of old St. John's that had been there since I got my job weeks and weeks before. I must have sat in front of that picture a hundred hours, but on this day I saw something for the first time.

"Where's Harbour Drive?" I said to Bev, an older lady who'd worked at the museum for many years before I showed up. "And where is the waterfront?"

Bev looked over her reading glasses. "Alan, my boy, none of that existed till the mid-1960s."

As soon as she said it, so much made sense. All of Harbour Drive and the waterfront is wharf. All of it. The very roads that lead to it from Water Street are not called roads at all, but coves. "Because they were coves!" I pointed out the window to Beck's Cove, and Bev nodded. "Now you are getting it."

Beck's Cove. Baird's Cove. Job's Cove. All of them were little coves that led to the merchants' premises and were delineated by long finger piers that stuck out perpendicular to the modern waterfront that was built just before I was born. I could not believe this had never occurred to me. The very building I was working in, the Murray Premises, which currently sits inland from Harbour Drive, was once right on the water. I am happy to tell you that historical building is still standing and is used as retail, restaurants, and a hotel. One walk down the hall and you'll get a pretty good sense of what the harbourfront used to look like.

I loved walking on the waterfront and cursed when the city fenced part of it off, primarily to accommodate a few dozen cruise ships in the shoulder seasons. I loved the close proximity to the ships and all their activity and hearing conversations in foreign languages. And of course, if you are walking ever east, the whole waterfront is backed by the perfect view of one of my favourite sights in St. John's: Cabot Tower on Signal Hill looming over The Battery.

Cabot Tower might be the single most iconic image that the province has in its arsenal. It was built in 1897 to commemorate the four-hundredth anniversary of John Cabot's discovery of Newfoundland. The stone tower offers stunning panoramic views of the city, The Narrows, the ocean out to Cape Spear, and beyond. It is a delightful spot to whale-watch or gaze out over the cityscape, especially on the three afternoons a year when it isn't blowing a gale hard enough to take the braces off your teeth. Exhibitions on the lower levels explain the history of the tower's construction, its role in wartime, and, perhaps most significantly, its role in global communication.

Cabot Tower made history on December 12, 1901, when it received the first transatlantic wireless signal from Marconi's station in Poldhu, Cornwall, England. This groundbreaking event marked the beginning of long-distance wireless transmission, revolutionizing communication around the globe.

I confess that, for a very long time, I assumed this trans-atlantic signal was the very reason Signal Hill got its name. But, in one of my earliest days on the maritime history floor of the museum, I clocked an old poster with a variety of signal flags, each one above a well-known St. John's business. Bowring's had a flag, and so did Ayre's, and so did any company that required dockworkers when one of their ships was approaching and needed to be off-loaded quickly.

Long before telephones or text messages, a man in a lookout perch on Signal Hill had a telescope and a box of flags. When he spied a Bowring's ship approaching, for example, he would raise a Bowring's flag, and the dockworkers down in the city, with ever an eager eye on Signal Hill, would know they had to make their way to the dock for a shift.

I discovered in my earliest days living downtown that there are two ways to walk up Signal Hill and get to Cabot Tower. You could just take the conventional paved road up past what is now the wonderful Geo Centre, a geological interpretation centre, and the most excellent Signal Hill National Historic Site Visitor Centre. That walk is pretty much so straight up that you might want to employ a Sherpa, and in true St. John's form, it is also the easier and way less fun way to walk up Signal Hill.

By far the best way to get to the top of Signal Hill is to walk through the series of jellybean houses, known as The Battery, that cling to the rocks along The Narrows.

"The Battery is like they took a chunk of Petty Harbour and stuck it on Signal Hill just above the water on the way into St. John's" is how I regularly described the part of St. John's that looked most like home to me. As in Petty Harbour, the small, colourful houses seem to be randomly and desperately hanging on to the steepest part of the cliff, just above the cold ocean. It's like there were a few hundred of them up on the top, and a stiff wind blew the works over the side and all but a few fell into the ocean, never to be seen again. And those stubborn few are what we now call The Battery.

These days, I love taking first-time visitors in a car down the seemingly impossible road that snakes its way through the houses in The Battery. "Cars were definitely an afterthought." A pal tried to make light of it all while white-knuckling the dash and door, as I'm sure he was convinced I was about to either drive us into a living room or over the bank into the harbour.

But I had no car the first time I followed pals out from downtown to watch the sun come up on the oceanside foot of Signal Hill. I remember walking through the narrow footpaths between the houses, feeling like I was walking on someone's front step. You will feel this way as well. This is because you likely *are* walking on someone's front step, and you definitely are if you are headed for the North Head Trail.

This 1.7-kilometre trail leaves the Lower Battery and literally starts on someone's front step. Legend has it Parks Canada figured it should expropriate the few feet of land required to get to the trail, but the very agreeable owners of the house said they were glad to have the company, and they've let the park use it ever since.

This trail is not for the faint of heart. One website calls it "strenuous and challenging," as it heads directly out to sea over a beaten path between rocks and wooden boardwalks and steps. All of it hangs over the jagged rocks, where the cold, white water beats against the hill. There is one spot over a death-drop gulch, where the narrow path is just wider than a human foot. On one side a steep rockface, and on the other a steep plummet to the rocks and water. There is a chain attached to the rock in a very amateurish and not at all official-looking way, and you better hold on to it.

"Is this allowed?" I asked a pal the first time I walked it, and he spun round.

"Jesus, yes!"

I asked further, "Is it safe?"

"Jesus, no!" He spun around and continued.

About a kilometre out, the path to the ocean takes a sharp turn to the left, but there is an area big enough to sit and enjoy the view over to Fort Amherst, or out to Cape Spear, or down to the whales breaching below you. Yes, below you. If you pause for a bit, your heart rate just might settle enough to not pass out when you turn around and see what lies ahead of you if you want to get up to Cabot Tower.

Reaching up the steep back side of Signal Hill, you will need to climb a series of steep wooden stairs and boardwalks that total close to a thousand steps before you reach the stone castle. It looks like a background that a really talented CGI person would draw behind two characters in chain mail and on horseback in *Game of Thrones*. I always try to get a photo when first-timers turn around and realize what they've gotten themselves into. I love to take a video of them finally reaching the top, too. Legs and lungs burning, but with big, big smiles.

All this naysaying aside, hundreds of people do this walk every day, and I often argue that it is the best city-based nature walk in the world. That is to say, the best non-urban walk you can do without leaving the city. With all due respect to the sea-wall in Vancouver's Stanley Park and the Bondi to Bronte Coastal Walk in Sydney, Australia, the North Head Trail is the best.

The waterfront, Cabot Tower, Signal Hill, and The Battery were amongst my first discoveries when I moved to downtown

St. John's. Later, I'd fall in love with some of the older buildings, like the Court House and the Basilica and so many more in the heart of the old city.

It was such a wonderful way to ease into living on my own, as I was still very close to home. Once or twice a month, I'd head back out to Petty Harbour, where Mom would instantly try to look after me like she did when I was a kid. Washing machine and kitchen stove were immediately engaged.

Jean's Laundry and Lunch, me and my brother called it. We high-fived in our clean clothes as she would pack a box with food for us to take back with us.

Dad was not as enthused.

"Jesus! Where ye goin' with the bologna? I thought you moved to Town?!"

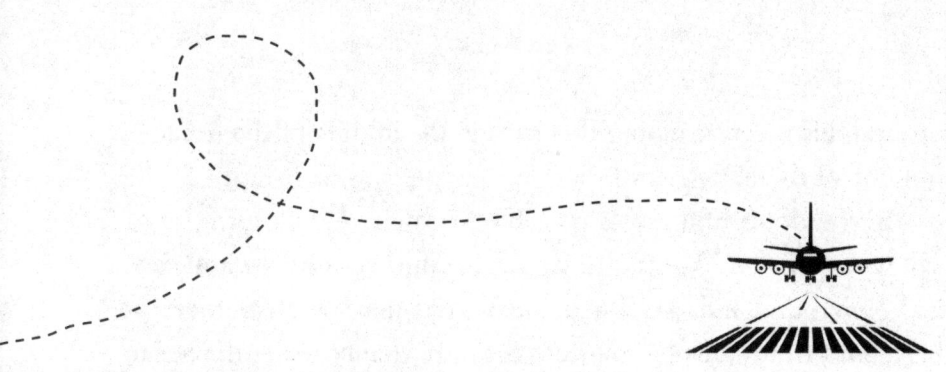

THE AIRPORT, NOT THE OUTPORT

"'Thank You for Visiting Scenic Green Bay'?!" shouts a confused Henry from the back of the van. I smile because this confusion is an age-old tradition for anyone travelling along the Trans-Canada Highway, crossing Newfoundland in either direction. He continues with the usual follow-up question from a first-timer:

"Did we miss the bay?"

I hate to break it to him, but he is correct.

"Yes, we did. We always do on this section of the highway, as we are currently nowhere near any bay."

I certainly don't want to dispel any romantic notions folks might have about driving across the Trans-Canada Highway in Newfoundland. I don't want to crush anyone's daydreams about a spectacular, ocean-lined highway drive across this huge island, but the hard truth is you are rarely in sight of the Atlantic on this road. While there are loads of eye-widening ocean-view drives around this place, crossing this rock in the middle of the ocean is not one of them.

If you don't blink, it is possible to catch a quick glimpse of salt water in a one-kilometre stretch around South Brook in central Newfoundland. My Bachelor of Arts math is elementary at best, but I figure this kilometre is the only chance to see the ocean in the four-hundred-plus kilometres between Corner Brook and Gambo. So, if you are driving the speed limit over this stretch, you'd have about thirty-six seconds to see the sea. Even then, it could be argued that you are just catching glimpses of the far-reaching arms of the ocean as you do in Terra Nova National Park and all the way to Clarenville in the lee of Random Island.

From the time you leave the Codroy Valley on the west coast till you hit the isthmus just outside the Avalon Peninsula, you are driving inland with many beautiful views of hills and meadows, with dozens of lovely ponds, lakes, and rivers, but only the odd saltwater arm or inlet to look for. It's over 650 kilometres from Stephenville to Chance Cove, where you can undeniably see open ocean. So, if it is ocean vistas you are after, take the side roads, because there is hardly a harbour to be seen for a whole day driving in Newfoundland on the TCH. Again, most tourists find this astonishing and surprising, and I might get in trouble with the provincial tourism department for admitting it here.

The "Welcome to" and "Thank You for Visiting" signs around this scenic place called Green Bay, which cannot be seen from the highway, are just to rub in the fact that if you were told that driving across this island was a blissful wander in and out of oceanside vistas, you were most seriously sold a bill of goods.

You could be forgiven for being as confused as Henry is today as we make our way through what most Newfoundlanders just call "Central." No other identifiers required. You don't need to say "somewhere between Terra Nova National Park and Deer Lake"; you can just say "Central" and everyone knows what you mean.

If we had time today, I'd be nudging the steering wheel north of the TCH, as there are quite a few places just off the highway that are worth a detour. South of the TCH, I have had amazing experiences in the Bay d'Espoir area, in towns like St. Alban's, and I was lucky enough to take a Zodiac ride from the mighty Conne River to the most impressive Miawpukek First Nation reserve. In Green Bay itself, I've spent time in Burlington and King's Point, and both are charming and beautiful. Further along the highway, I've had great hikes and river walks in this area and really wish we had time now for a slice of pizza at Lefty's in Grand Falls. The real shame of our haste today is that we don't get to dodge up to Lewisporte, which might be the visual gem of central Newfoundland.

A quick Wikipedia search will tell you Lewisporte is named after "an enterprising Scotsman, Lewis Miller." I was amused to read that Millertown, just down the highway, is also named for him.

"Must have been some fella!" I say to Jo and Henry. "Got towns named after each of his names."

There'd be a few reasons to head to Lewisporte, not least the stunning scenery and the fact that it offers more facilities for visitors than most rural Newfoundland towns of its size, but the marina is the big treasure. Believe it or not, traditional marinas are not that common in Newfoundland. Especially the ones that look designed to harbour any kind of non-commercial boat, like you would see everywhere in Prince Edward Island or Victoria, BC. There are a few around the outskirts of St. John's in Conception Bay, and an actual yacht club in the Corner Brook area, but that's about it. So, when you round the turn into Lewisporte and see a very organized and Charlottetown-looking lot of neatly-tied-up boats, it is a sight to behold. It'd make one think that what was just out beyond the breakwater might actually be a pleasant, hospitable ocean to play around in.

Let's put it top of the list for next trip, as today we can't detour into actual scenic Green Bay, or anywhere else off the highway, because we are headed for one of the most unlikely places to become globally essential in all of Newfoundland and Labrador. We are approaching a place where the population grew from what was effectively zero to over ten thousand people in a matter of months. A town that would cement its place in world history in the 1940s, and again in the '60s, and then once or twice more before really hitting it out of the park in September of 2001.

We are headed to Gander.

As the indicator clicks, we turn just off the TCH to what most folks from this province love to refer to as "The Airport, Not the Outport," which I learned a long time ago is fitting. This place does not look like any coastal community or any other type of community around here. You've heard me wax on about how beautiful and lovely many of the seaside places are in my home province, but Gander is not one of them and, in fairness, it was never meant to be one of them. I can tell you the people from this neck of the woods are fun and kind and generous and hard-working. I have played here many times and never had a bad night. They are truly the salt of the earth, and I feel bad confessing that I have never found the town itself to be breathtakingly beautiful. And, with the utmost respect, I think even the locals agree. When any of the numerous excellent Gander people I know boast about local-ish things, they almost always direct you just outside Gander.

"Oh, this is the best place in the world. Just head up the high-way fifteen minutes and you are at the head of Gander Bay" is a very common boast around here.

The reason to visit Gander is not to gaze upon its expansive ocean views or to go whale-watching. Rather, you should come visit Gander because it has one of the most fascinating histories—and very recent histories—on this side of the Atlantic.

A quick turn off the highway past a row of gas stations and what seems like a lot of hotels, and I am reminded that this place does not look like many or any other rural Newfoundland towns. Despite being surrounded by woods and lakes and rivers, this place looks solidly suburban. The very orderly streets are almost all lined with sidewalks, a rarity in rural Newfoundland. The houses on either side of those streets are of an eerily similar shape and layout, also a rarity around here. It's almost like this place was planned. And a quick look into Gander's very interesting history tells me that it was indeed planned, and recently. Actually, way more recently than I'd thought.

Gander was barely a town at all before the late 1930s and wasn't officially incorporated till 1958. After World War I, the world jumped into the flying age and needed an airport about halfway between western Europe and eastern North America. This flat middle part of a rock in the middle of the ocean was an excellent location, geographically but also politically, as Newfoundland was a dominion of the British Crown and firmly under Allied control.

The airport was built in a hurry, and built to accommodate anything that flew. At one point, Gander boasted what were con-sidered the biggest runways in the world. By the time World War II rolled around, this place quickly went from being an obscure island outpost to globally essential, earning it the moniker "The Crossroads of the World."

The airport opened in 1938. Before the end of the war in 1945, ten thousand British and American personnel lived in and around this shared air force base. It is estimated that over twenty thousand Canadian and American fighters and bombers and carriers came here en route to and from the great conflicts overseas. When the war was over, Gander International Airport, or CYQX, became a commercial airport, and beginning around 1950, a proper town was built a safer distance from the runways.

I blink twice as I assume I have misread that date on my iPhone. I've been to Gander many times, and the newness of the place has never struck me. Construction of the town we are driving through right now did not start till the '50s, which has to make it one of the newest, if not the newest, towns in Newfoundland. A town built near an airport, rather than the other way around.

"Why are we headed to the airport?" asks Henry. It's a fair question, as we are not flying anywhere today.

"We are headed to see the coolest airport lounge ever!" I try to make it as exciting as if we were headed to Universal Studios, but Henry still looks very doubtful.

Now, Dear Reader, I should say in advance of this next highlight that I don't blame you or Henry one bit for thinking me totally mad for even suggesting you might include an airport waiting lounge in your travels, unless you absolutely were flying in or out of that airport. But the International Lounge at Gander Airport is a delightful exception.

We park and quickly make our way into the small airport terminal and are immediately met with what looks like a movie set for a film set in the 1950s.

"This is like going back in time!" Henry picks up his pace and is quickly dwarfed under "Flight and Its Allegories," a twenty-two-metre mural painted by Ken Lochhead, a stunning collage of human and aircraft images. A few hurried steps later and he is surrounded by furniture and flooring that look somehow untouched since the Queen of England opened the place in 1959. I am not a student of design, but I've read numerous times that this is one of the most significant modernist rooms in the country. The flooring alone features extraordinary opposing and parallel rectangles tiled in what learned people call "geometric terrazzo" and I call "friggin' cool."

I was skimming through online comments and reviews of the place, and many, many expressed how they were flabbergasted that an airport waiting lounge could be anything but mundane. "This place is a perfectly preserved time capsule" summarizes many of the comments, but by far, my fave travel review made by one visitor was "Very surprisingly interesting."

I echo those sentiments here again, and repeat the fact that I wouldn't regularly send anyone to an airport on a sightseeing trip. But this is a special exception that is indeed very surprisingly interesting.

The global significance of this lounge can't be overstated. This airport was the crossroads of the world, and this lounge was where the world hung out for decades. During the 1960s and '70s, tens of thousands of airplanes landed here en route to and from Europe. I am excited to tell Henry more stuff I assume would be more exciting for him.

"Celebrities from every walk of life walked on this very geometric terrazzo. Frank Sinatra, Marilyn Monroe, Clark Gable, John Wayne, Elizabeth Taylor, even Winston Churchill!"

"I don't know who any of those people are," Henry shrugs. "Was Ed Sheeran ever here?"

"Ah . . . yes, definitely." I honestly have no idea, but I figure I should try to make this visit as satisfying as possible for my eighteen-year-old son.

Gander became a regular stopping point for aircraft from the Soviet Union, and this very lounge was a popular spot to defect and seek asylum. All a passenger had to do was walk up to a Canadian officer and say, "Save me," and they were immediately granted refugee status. Celebrated Soviet pianist and chess grandmaster Igor Vasilyevich Ivanov and Cuban Olympic swimmer Rafael Polinario both escaped communist regimes in the Cold War era by way of this lounge.

From the interpretation panels, we learn that Gander International Airport was the site of tragedy as well. In 1985, Arrow Air Flight 1285R crashed just after takeoff, killing all 256 people on board, making it the deadliest aviation incident to occur on Canadian soil. As most of those passengers were US Army officers, rumours and speculation of foul play ran rampant.

Media came from all over Canada, and especially the US. Reporters scoured the local area for weeks for any information possible. They interviewed hundreds of people from Gander who might have seen the crash, which led to the story of the "Big Tumpay."

I have to write some of this phonetically, as the story of the Big Tumpay is best told orally. Over three to six pints. I must also stress that this story is not intended to diminish or disrespect the tragedy that occurred or the losses suffered. Nor is it meant to poke fun at anyone with a local dialect, because I love local dialects. So, with respect, I'll proceed.

As noted above, in the aftermath of the crash, reporters from the mainland US and Canada and beyond descended on Gander. Most of those reporters would never have been anywhere near

Newfoundland before and would not have heard many or any of our awesome dialects. As reporters gathered at local hotels after a day or so of speaking with people on the ground here, many had the same question:

"What is a Tumpay? And in particular, what is a big one?"

Several visiting journalists had heard the same thing mentioned repeatedly and did not know what it meant. They'd canvassed the hotels and local media, but no one had ever heard of a Tumpay, big or otherwise.

Finally, one local media person at the gathering asked, "Where did you hear this term?"

A visitor spoke up and told of how almost everyone he interviewed had said, "There was a Big Tumpay." Still no one could figure it out.

"Wait!" one local jumped in. "Did anyone say they'd *heard* it?"

"Yes!" said an American journalist, raising his hand. The local grinned. He had finally figured out the mystery.

To explain the confusion, he spoke first in dialect—"Yes, my son, there was a Big Tumpay."

And then, slowly, with no dialect.

"Yes, sir, I heard a big thump, hey?"

Dialects are magical in Newfoundland and Labrador. Most of them have us speaking as quickly as possible and removing any syllables in a word that we deem unnecessary. Try to find a single Newfoundlander who pronounces "fishery" with three syllables instead of the far more efficient "fish-reee." In the Tumpay case, the speed of the speech combined with the effect of turning a *th* into a hard *t*, and dropping the *h* from *hey*, making it *eh*, almost sent international journalists into a spin. I couldn't love this place more.

And one of the main takeaways from that whole disaster was how friendly and generous and accommodating the Gander people were to the visiting folks who arrived under such awful circumstances. And generous and hospitable Gander folks put Newfoundland on the map. An act that would recur time and time again in good times and in tough times until the ultimate test on September 11, 2001, when Gander was a shining light on the darkest day the world has seen in a very, very long time.

With so much already written in the long and storied history of Gander, and the heyday of the airport presumed to be well in the past, I bet its residents believed the days of aviation excitement were long behind them as they entered the twenty-first century. Little did they, or any of us, know that the most famed chapter in this place was yet to come.

No one needs reminding about September 11 and how the horrible events in New York City shocked the globe and emptied the skies. Every plane had to land immediately. Well, try to imagine how many planes were flying around northeastern North America when that call was made. Planes halfway to Europe or back . . . all those flights that had left or were headed to massive airports in Boston, New York, Philadelphia, Washington, Montreal, Toronto . . .

Hundreds and hundreds of aircraft needing to land and park immediately. Where could they go? What airport has a runway long enough, along with the spare space to park dozens of jumbo jets on a moment's notice? The answer, of course, is Gander. The very place that thought for sure its days of global necessity were well behind it was about to become essential again.

So, the planes came. Big ones. One after the other after the other. This much instant, unscheduled activity would have flattened most places, but the people around here are very airplane savvy, and all aircraft landed safely and without incident.

All those planes, of course, were full of people. Three thousand people, all landing in a strange little town within minutes of each other. In the mostly pre-smartphone world, they were out of touch and confused. Waiting to be told why they'd been forced to land in what felt like the middle of nowhere and when they could get back on their intended routes. That was a lot of people for a city of a half a million to welcome, feed, and accommodate, as well as comfort and inform, during this time of tragedy and global uncertainty. Gander's population hovered just above ten thousand on September 11, and in one single morning, this place had to deal with a 30 to 40 percent jump in population.

Those people came from everywhere. From western Europe and North America. From India, Pakistan, Iran—everywhere. Some spoke English, others not. All of them needed food, bathrooms, and beds. As many of the baggage compartments of the planes were kept off-limits for security reasons, most of those people also needed clothes, toiletries, and medicine. There are a few hotels in the area, but with not even remotely enough spots to lay as many heads as needed laying.

The world was in shock. And the people of Gander saw a chance to do what so many around the globe wanted to do—to help. And so they did. And did they ever.

Just imagine the human effort needed for a town of only ten thousand—and that number includes the elderly and children, by the way—to welcome and look after three thousand unexpected guests. Try to imagine how disorienting that experience must have been for passengers born and raised in major cities in Europe, en route to major cities in North America, to find themselves sitting on a tarmac for twenty-four hours, and then bused around what must have looked like a tiny town in the middle of the woods, on some island in the ocean.

Imagine non-English speakers—or English speakers, for that matter—trying to decipher the dialect, where *th*'s are hardened and *h*'s are dropped. Try to imagine how much utterly heroic effort and organization these glorious Gander people demonstrated to house and feed and comfort all these disoriented people so quickly.

Well, lucky for you and me both, we don't have to imagine any of that, because Michael Rubinoff did it for us. And he enlisted the incredible talents of David Hein and Irene Sankoff to create an international theatre phenomenon and Tony Award–winning musical. And after a trip through Green Bay, through the brand-new town of Gander, through the coolest airport, we get to the biggest reason for our trip today. We have seats for opening night of the first-ever Newfoundland production of *Come From Away*.

In case you've been hiding in a bunker or living off the grid in the woods, you've no doubt heard of *Come From Away*. This Broadway and West End box-office record breaker tells how people from all over the world found something to smile about when the rest of the world was crying. And they found it in Gander. It is easily one of the greatest feats of performance storytelling I've ever seen. And I have seen it a couple of times on Broadway and a couple of times in Toronto. Each of these superb performances was of the same production, with the same sets and choreography seen in numerous touring productions all over the world. But now, myself and Joanne and Henry are three of the lucky folks attending opening night of a new and unique rendering of *Come From Away* made exclusively for the hometown theatre in Gander itself.

As we enter the best little arts and culture centre in the province, I am stoked to see how my magnificent friend, the genius theatre director Jillian Keiley, has reimagined the show. And I am not disappointed. The show is just sensational. Every bit as moving as the original production, if not more.

The most joyous scene in the show depicts a night when all hands made it to the Legion and here, in Gander, Newfoundland, in the midst of a global tragedy, a pub full of people took time out to have the time of their lives, in spite of it all.

This celebration, perhaps, requires some historical and traditional context. Newfoundlanders love to celebrate when times are good, and especially when times are bad. If you're ever invited to a wedding where I'm from, jump at the chance, as it's always a grand time. Jump even quicker if you get a chance to come for a wake. I'm dead serious. We've taken on the Irish tradition with a vengeance, and a send-off here for anyone who lived a full and happy life is a time of times.

We even go out of our way to adopt and invent reasons to celebrate. Guy Fawkes Night—Bonfire Night—around here is a grand time for drinks and songs around the biggest fire you can make. This despite the fact that all but the elderly around here were born in Canada and far, far removed from Fawkes' attempt to blow up the British Houses of Parliament. But there's a fire and a song, so why ask why? St. Patrick never led a snake out of Newfoundland or Labrador, but that doesn't stop us from celebrating on the 17th of March, or for the weekend before and after. "Paddy's Month" is a big deal for Celtic musicians like myself, as we get about twelve extra gigs.

I once tried to describe this phenomenon to a muso friend from Sweden.

"Every band in the world gets an extra payday on New Year's Eve. But if you play any kind of Irish music in St. John's, you get about eight extra paydays. One in December and another half dozen or so around mid-March."

If Bonfire Night and Paddy's Month are a bit of a stretch as Newfoundland celebrations, Tibb's Eve might just be complete and utter invention. Tibb's Eve is the night before Christmas Eve and the cause for great shenanigans in Newfoundland. You can look it up till your eyes go square and you can ask a couple of hundred locals about this "holiday," but you won't find any agreement as to its origins. I will go on record right now and say publicly that Tibb's Eve is nothing more than a completely made-up excuse to head out with your buds one last time before the real holiday season sets in. And the fact that I am from a place that invents a night out before a twelve-day stretch of nights out makes me love this place more than I can say.

But even Tibb's Eve is dwarfed by one of the most nonsensical and completely manufactured night or nights out that I have ever even heard of. I am delighted that I live in a city that annually practices Regatta Roulette.

Ed Roberston is the lead singer in the globally successful band Barenaked Ladies. He and the rest of the gang have been great supporters of me and lots of other ambitious Canadian musicians, and I'm so grateful for his friendship, which was quite likely cemented over Regatta Roulette. Ed called me one Monday night in August and explained he was filming segments in the province for his TV show *Ed's Up*. He and his crew were taking his Cessna around Canada in search of all kinds of whacky and interesting places.

"We just finished filming on the South Coast and have a day off tomorrow and thought about coming to St. John's, but I guess there's not much happening on a Tuesday?"

"Ed, Mardi Gras be damned, tomorrow in St. John's might be the greatest Tuesday night in the world." And the Tuesday I spoke of and am telling you about now is the first Tuesday in August, and its significance has everything to do with the Wednesday that follows it. And the events on the first Wednesday in August might make for the most fantastically impractical holiday ever ill-conceived, and that is exactly why I love it so much.

This requires some explaining. The Royal St. John's Regatta boasts that it is the oldest sporting event in North America, dating back at least as far as 1816. It has been held practically every year since, interrupted only by the Great Fire of 1892, the two world wars, and the COVID pandemic. This fixed-seat rowing regatta on Quidi Vidi Lake features amateur local teams in a daylong competition. All the while the teams are rowing, the lake is surrounded by a fair of sorts. Local charity organizations and sports teams set up booths and stalls for fundraising. Cheers ring out as someone successfully flops the frog onto a lily pad in one booth, while volunteer ticket vendors' shouts of "Two tickets left to sell . . . two tickets holding up the wheel" ring out across the crowd. There's dozens of food trucks and hot dog stands, and a beer tent to boot.

It's an excellent Wednesday. If it goes ahead.

As the heart and soul of the holiday is the race, it's weather-dependent. If the winds are too high at 6 a.m. and the forecast looks for no improvement, the committee makes a call and postpones the event till the next day. Think, for a moment, about what you just read.

There is a holiday on a rock in the middle of the ocean, and it's postponed if the weather's windy. So, the Wednesday event regularly gets punted to Thursday. Or Friday. Or Saturday.

How, then, does this affect the greatest Tuesday on earth? Well, that is how we arrived at the good-time-seeking Newfoundland tradition of Regatta Roulette. It totally makes sense to head out on a Tuesday night if you have Wednesday off work. But what if you might *not* have Wednesday off work? I'm not sure many around the world would want to risk a night on the town if there was a chance, and a good chance, that they would get the call at six o'clock the morning after, telling them that sleeping in is not an option. I am sure there are many communities who would never roll the dice on such a gamble. I am also sure that none of them are in Newfoundland, because as I said to Ed, "Tuesday is Regatta Roulette. The greatest Tuesday on Earth."

Downtown St. John's hops on this night and traditionally features the final hurrah for the George Street Festival, with an open-air concert blaring all over the city. No half measures here. It's like some sick and twisted masochistic partying endeavour. People enjoy it more knowing they may or may not be out on a school night. As if the possibility that this might all be a terrible idea makes it more delicious.

And it could all pay off and the wind might not blow tomorrow. On a rock. In the North Atlantic.

And when it does not pay off, a cityful of people stumble their way into work and open their shops with heads that have been shaken like paint cans at Home Depot. But then . . . but then . . . guess what happens at 5 p.m.? Well, you might have tomorrow off again . . . so . . . Regatta Roulette is on for the second night in a row. And it repeats till the wind subsides.

It makes me smile to think about the insanity of it. If I wasn't from here, I would consider moving to St. John's just so I could live with people party-hungry enough to go along with it all. For the record, I took Ed to the George Street Festival for Regatta

Roulette and he swears it is indeed the best Tuesday he's ever experienced. We've been buds ever since.

So, the folks singing in the Legion in *Come From Away* represent what went on in Gander that night, but also wave a flag that shouts to the world, "THESE PEOPLE CAN FIND A GOOD TIME IN A DENTIST'S OFFICE."

This show is a magnificent reimaging of the original. It has all the same songs and dialogue and story, but the presentation and trappings are distinctly more Newfoundland. As I leave the theatre, my eyes are red from tears, my sides are sore from laughing, and my hands are swollen from clapping. I hug Jill and tell her that she has once again done the impossible and made a great thing greater. Henry shouts, perhaps a little too loudly, "I have never been this proud to be a Newfoundlander!!"

The man who had this brilliant idea in the first place, and the driving force to get it onstage at its home in Gander, is here tonight. I extend my hand to Michael Rubinoff, but he hugs me instead and I hug him back while offering my congratulations. Michael is one of the cornerstones of the original musical sensation and the very architect of bringing it home to Gander. It's tough not to tear up as I explain to him what a service he has done to this area by staging this show about Gander *in* Gander. It allows us for one evening to look at ourselves in as flattering a light as can be shone. It is heartening to know that what we see up there onstage is a true depiction of our hospitality in good times and especially in bad. And it is incredibly humbling to know that something a little place like ours could offer was globally noticed and appreciated.

We share another hug and I head for the door to catch Joanne and Henry.

On the way out the door, I am stopped by a lady named Alice, who tells me she is from Boston and has seen many shows of mine over the years.

"I just had to come to Newfoundland to see what you've been talking about all these years." Alice hugs me and I hug her back and ask how she liked the show tonight.

"I've seen *Come From Away* in New York, but it was so much more special seeing it here, where it all happened."

She hugged me once more and we both joined our groups and headed off with smiles on our faces.

Come From Away is slated to run every summer at the Arts and Culture Centre in Gander, and you simply must come see it here. Even if you've seen the show on Broadway or in Toronto, or one of the many touring versions around the world, this local reinterpretation is worth the trip to experience it where you are surrounded by the people and places depicted onstage. It's like getting transported to nineteenth-century France for a performance of *Les Misérables*. You are literally in the story.

We head back to the hotel and crash after a long day travelling and a very satisfying visit to this very special place. I wake early and slip out of the room while my wife and son sleep in. I grab a coffee and walk around in the quiet. Walk through the downtown, and past the theatre towards a trail I remember from a previous visit.

It takes a while, but eventually I find Cobb's Pond Rotary Park. I played a festival here years ago and remember how lovely and serene it was to walk the trail around the pond. And my memory serves me correctly. The manicured trail is perfect for a casual stroll over boardwalks and through the woods.

"Hello again!"

My stride and solitude are broken by a quickly approaching smiling face I recognize immediately as Alice from Boston. We have another pleasant exchange and chat about my next planned trips to her area for gigs.

As she turns to go, she points to the trail and the surrounding woods as the perfect little pond glistens in the early-morning sun.

"Gander is beautiful, isn't it?"

I feel bad for thinking the exact opposite less than twenty-four hours ago, and quickly consider all the beauty I've discovered since we turned off the highway. I wave as I say, humbly, "Yes. It certainly is."

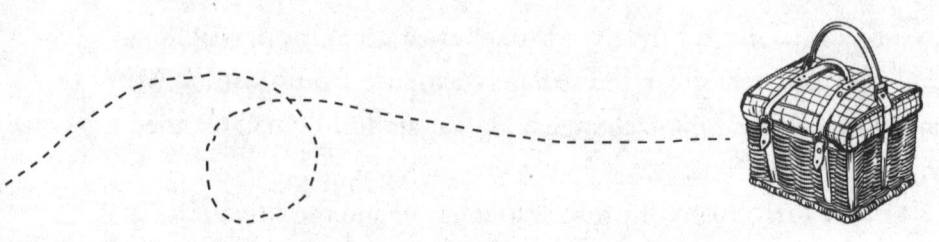

A Ferryland Picnic

"**T**oday we are headed up the Southern Shore!" I am trying to sell the day's activity to my somewhat reluctant son.

Henry's reluctance to get out of bed turns to skepticism as he ponders my choice of words. While unwrapping my bribe of a Tim Hortons plain bagel with butter, he asks, "What do you mean 'up the Southern Shore'? What is *up* about going south?" Henry could be smarter than me.

The Southern Shore is one of the best examples of Newfoundlanders' confused sense of direction. I'll explain. The Southern Shore is, well, south. It is, on practically every map, *down*. Yet all of us say "up the shore." Why, I have no idea. Likewise, I have no idea why for centuries, when fishermen sailed far north to catch fish, they would say they were going "down on the Labrador." Or, more famously, the line from the folk song "I'se the B'y" that sings "way down in Bonavista," when that town is decidedly north for way more than half of the island's population. In my hometown, I went down to Maddox Cove and back up to Petty Harbour, even though both are exactly at sea level. We are nothing if not wonderfully peculiar.

To make our way up the Southern Shore from St. John's, we first drive east to Cape Spear. And when I say east, I mean the far east. The eastest you can go. St. John's is the most easterly city on the continent, and a short drive brings you to the end of the road. You stand on the point at Cape Spear, look across the nothingness of endless ocean, and whisper, "Next stop is Ireland." If you step ahead of everyone else on the point, you can claim to be the most easterly person. Legendary local musician Sandy Morris often bills himself as the Most Easterly Guitar Player in North America. I've always loved him for that.

Making our way up the shore, Henry and I pass through my beloved hometown of Petty Harbour, then skip inland through the farming community of The Goulds, where I went to high school, then Bay Bulls, Witless Bay and on down—I mean *up*—to the south.

If the names of the towns seem colourful and odd to you, you are not alone. Often these odd names can be chalked up to some anglicized bastardization of the original name in French or Portuguese or Spanish, depending on which fishing country named it first. Petty Harbour was once Le Petit Havre, for example, and in Ferryland the name comes from what Portuguese fishermen called Farilham.

We are not good at everything in Newfoundland and Labrador, but we are excellent at shagging up place names in other languages, especially French. At least my hometown did the good service of changing the spelling to match. But in many cases, we didn't bother to even do that much. We just left the original French spelling but pronounced it whatever way we felt like. François is pronounced "France-way." Quirpon is pronounced "Car-poon." And don't get me started on Port au Choix, Grand Bruit, and Rencontre, none of which sound the way they're spelled.

In the most egregious cases, we have completely changed the intended identifying title of a place in a way that doesn't just make it sound different, but gives the wrong impression altogether. There is a place in Newfoundland we refer to as "Bay Despair," which makes this beautiful region sound far less inviting than its likely original name of Baie d'Espoir, which of course means "Bay of Hope." That's just poor marketing.

It could be argued that Witless Bay, here on the Southern Shore, originally named after a smart man called Captain Whittle, suffered the same fate.

But while the main town names may seem strange, at least a few of them are easily explained as lazy translation. The parts of these towns is another story. On the way up the shore, you will pass road and direction signs for Horse Chops, Hell Hill, Hare's Ears, and my personal favourite, Bread and Cheese. I'm serious. Bread and Cheese is a part of Bay Bulls. See my previous note about us being a wonderfully peculiar lot.

We are about halfway up the shore at the very southern edge of a town called Calvert when I see it. And it makes me pull off the road immediately.

"The Squid Jigger lives!" I thought Henry would be at least made curious by my bizarre exclamation.

It stands as a holy shrine. Well, for me, anyway.

"That is the very place I started this wonderful crazy ride in the music business." I glance over to Henry, who seems oblivious to the fact that we have stopped.

"What do you mean?" He looks up from his iPhone momentarily, which is a miracle, so I respond quickly.

"That is the first place I ever got paid to play music. It was the summer of 1985," I say proudly.

"Nineteen eighty-five?! God, how old are you?" Henry goes back to his phone.

The Squid Jigger is a legendary bar just on the Calvert side of the border with our ultimate destination of Ferryland, a town of around 350 people right in the middle of what Newfoundlanders indeed call the Southern Shore. For clarity, this refers to the shoreline of the Northeast Avalon Peninsula, running south of the capital city of St. John's. It really starts in my hometown of Petty Harbour and ends some two hundred kilometres south in Trepassey, and the Squid Jigger is smack dab in the middle of it in Calvert, even though it would be easy to stumble from its side door to find yourself in Ferryland. Don't ask me how I know this.

The Jigger looks quite homey, and dare I say wholesome these days, with signs advertising fresh seafood and home-cooked meals. But when I was a teen in the mid-1980s there was not a menu in sight at the Squid Jigger. This was a place for drinking and dancing. For about a decade between 1975 and 1985, the Southern Shore was dotted with Squid Jiggers, as a dozen or more towns boomed with the inshore fishery. What came with the boom was something these parts have not seen since: loads of young adults with pocketfuls of expendable cash.

When I was a teen in the early 1980s, Petty Harbour and practically all these towns along the Southern Shore never slept from May till November. At one point, there were three fish plants operating in Petty Harbour at the same time, a couple of them running two full shifts a day. Five-tonne trucks puffed their air brakes daylight and dark as the hum of forklifts and squeak of the offal-chute conveyor belts rang throughout the harbour at midnight as loudly as they did at noon.

People worked really hard, and when they got the chance to play, they played even harder. Long before the internet or even cable television came to this part of the world, hard-working, hard-playing people flocked to the local bar to socialize, drink, and dance to the music of the band.

And, lucky me, I was born into the band. Literally. The Doyles were, and still are, the band in Petty Harbour and one of a handful of acts that played in a dozen or more bars or Legions or halls up and down the Southern Shore. Folks from Petty Harbour and The Goulds went to the Crystal Palace or the Hayloft, while Bay Bulls and Witless Bay people danced at Darby's or the Hall, and Cape Broyle boasted Hayden's and the San Juan. Calvert had the holy Squid Jigger, and remember, we are only halfway up the Southern Shore yet.

There's a lot to do on this drive on the Southern Shore and around the Irish Loop, which extends some three hundred kilometres around the eastern Avalon. There's bird- and whale-watching in one town, kayaking excursions in the next, and fishing trips and kitchen music and ancient fossils and a caribou herd, and many great hikes and adventures. This drive is a must for anyone visiting the St. John's area.

The region is often referred to as the Irish Loop, and is one of the main reasons why Newfoundland has been called the most Irish place in the world outside of Ireland. The dialects along this shore basically echo the southeastern shore of Ireland, where the fishermen and families came from so many hundred years before. They left places like Cork and Waterford and remained so isolated where they settled that the dialects from the mother country never changed.

But it's not just the dialects that lingered. Luckily for me, the music did, too. Where I grew up, accordions were more popular than guitars and pianos. Irish folk music groups were more well known than the Beatles. The Clancy Brothers and the Chieftains were bigger than Bob Dylan. "Molly Malone" trumped "Sweet Caroline" every time. I was born into the beautiful noise of it. And it was that beautiful Irish noise, and how it mixed and brewed with other noises, that got this lucky fella down—I mean up—this shore all those years ago.

I make Henry take a photo of me outside the Squid Jigger. I have no idea how he could possibly take it while rolling his eyes so hard.

"You started here in 1985? How many concerts have you played, anyway?"

Henry asks a valid question. I have to think about it, as it has never really occurred to me to add them up. How many professional gigs *have* I played since my first one at the Squid Jigger around four decades ago? In three years of high school, I played at least once a weekend, so I estimate that to be around 150 gigs before I started university and moved to St. John's in the late 1980s. I quickly started playing the pubs of downtown, and by the time we started Great Big Sea in 1993, I played at least three times a week. So that would be about 150 per year for five years, and if we add that total to the approximately 150 in the high school years, I get to around a thousand gigs before Great Big Sea even started.

And when we *did* start, we hit George Street running. This was long before a Google calendar was available, so I'll have to estimate. I know from looking over my handwritten calendars, the one from 1993 shows over 250 gigs. The next year, 1994, shows about the same. So, by 1995, around thirty years ago, I had already done 1,500 gigs. Most of these would have been in pubs and bars. We were about to become a concert act, which meant fewer but bigger gigs. But still, the pace has been steady.

From 1995 till the present day, I have maintained a schedule of between 90 and 110 concerts per year, so let's just say a hundred for easy math. I estimate that by the time you are reading this, I will have luckily, oh so luckily, played somewhere in the ballpark of 3,500 professional gigs.

If I stay healthy and folks will put up with me, I'll happily make it to five thousand by the time I am seventy years old.

It is considered a marathon of a hockey career to play in a thousand pro games. I have already had the good fortune to play around twice as many professional gigs as Gordie Howe played professional hockey games.

I figure that none of this estimating will mean much to Henry, so I just say, "I dunno, bud. Thousands and thousands."

"And you did one here? It looks small." Henry looks like he doesn't believe me.

Henry can be forgiven for thinking that this place does not look like where he sees me working. He was born in 2006 and started coming to my shows in 2009. He's seen dozens of outdoor festivals with thousands of people. He's seen me play in glorious theatres like Massey Hall, and huge amphitheatres like the Budweiser Stage in Toronto. Come to think of it, I don't think he's ever seen me in a venue that held fewer than a thousand people.

"Yeah, bud. And lots of small places like it." I watch Henry quickly and deftly take a couple of pics on an iPhone the way only young people can, and I giggle at how I foolishly thought my son would be super impressed that his dad was a popular musician.

He has never thought of it as anything more than Dad's job. And that is exactly how it should be. If I wasn't so enamoured with the stage and all that comes with it, I might have realized that having a dad as a touring musician isn't necessarily the be-all and end-all for a little boy.

There were early signs. When Henry was about five years old, he came running into the house, cute as a kindergarten button. I was just about to hug him by the kitchen counter when he heard hammering in the pantry.

"What's that?" Henry looked more excited than puzzled.

"There's a carpenter in there, bud. He is building new shelves for our pantry and—" I think I expected Henry to immediately ask me about my day writing songs, but instead he bolted enthusiastically to the pantry before I could even finish my sentence. I snuck over to the door to eavesdrop.

"Are you a real carpenter?" Henry looked up at Paddy, an expert cabinetmaker in the St. John's area, and Paddy quickly responded, delighted to have a cute visitor.

"Yes, sir, I am."

"So you can actually build stuff?" Henry loved *Bob the Builder*, as most little fellas do, and I guess Paddy wanted to respond in a way that made me look good to my son.

"Yes, and what about your dad? I bet he can build stuff too."

Then Henry said something that made me realize long stretches in front of a notepad and a recording console are not quite as impressive as a reciprocating saw and a nail gun.

"Dad? Nah. He don't build nothing. He's just a rock star."

I giggle at the memory of it, and we jump back in the minivan.

One of the first few houses you'll see in Ferryland is the Hynes House. I don't think it is marked as such, but it does not need to be. We all know it is where legendary songwriter Ron Hynes lived.

"I wrote a song with Ron Hynes there." I point to the very modest dwelling.

"The 'Sonny's Dream' guy? He had a small house." Henry is right again.

But it would be difficult to overstate how big an impact Ron Hynes had on the artistic community of our province, or the general population just as well.

They say the moment Ron died, the lights went out in downtown St. John's. Sounds like a fairy tale, doesn't it?

Ron was born in 1950 and was raised right here in Ferryland. He became a leader in the performing arts scene of downtown St. John's when local music, theatre, and visual arts boomed in the early 1970s. This renaissance brought us painters like Gerry Squires, comic geniuses like Mary Walsh, and, most significantly for me, a TV show called *The Wonderful Grand Band*.

When I was a kid, the biggest show in the world was not from Los Angeles or New York, it was from St. John's, Newfoundland. It didn't feature songs from California or Nashville. It featured Newfoundland traditional songs and the original songs of Ron Hynes. The entire province stopped for thirty minutes during the season to watch the sketch comedy and hear Ron's and the Wonderful Grand Band's music.

Later, Ron had a modest recording career, but somehow his brilliant songs never propelled him to national or international success the way he and his catalogue deserved. But his legacy here in Newfoundland is unprecedented. It is tough to imagine this place without him. His songs are about us. About a lonely mom who doesn't want her son to leave her alone, even though she knows he should. About a knock on a door that would haunt the widow of a victim of a tragedy at sea. About Newfoundlanders leaving and coming home. About the perils of trying to make a career in the music business when you live on a rock in the middle of the ocean.

We loved him. And he loved that we did.

They say the lights went out in downtown St. John's the moment Ron died because the lights *did* go out. Word had not yet fully made its way around town that the Man of a Thousand Songs had passed, when, *boom*. Darkness.

Days later, the province came to a halt as what I can only describe to you as a state funeral took place at the largest church in St. John's. The event was one of the only multi-denominational services ever held at the Roman Catholic basilica and was broadcast live on radio and television.

I suppose I was lost in reflection and uncharacteristically quiet as we passed the Hynes House. Henry doesn't fully understand what's up, but he quietly asks, "Was it a good song? The one you wrote with him?"

"Oh, yeah, buddy." I snap back to the here and now. "I think it was a good song, and it was a thrill to get to work with a hero."

"Did he play at the Squid Jigger, too?" Henry's question is one that had never occurred to me.

"Yes, now that you mention it, I bet he did." And it made me feel good to realize me and a great like Ron might have actually started out in the same place.

Just round the turn, the wide and beautiful harbour of Ferryland comes into full view.

The bay is immediately differentiated from others on the shore by some unique islands, but what really stands out— actually sticks out a couple of kilometres into the ocean—is a narrow strip of land.

"What's that?" asks Henry, noticing through the mist a house and a tower of sorts at the end of the peninsula.

I'm so glad he's noticed it. "That is the famous Ferryland Lighthouse. That's where we're going." I pause for a second to turn off the main road and then finish with "But not yet. First we are going for a walk on the railway track."

Henry looks confused. "There's a railway here?"

"Not anymore." I've pulled into a gravel parking lot next to a kids' playground. I turn to Henry. "But there used to be."

"We can't walk on a track that used to be here." Henry is exactly right.

"The railway track is gone, but the railway bed is still here, and it makes for an excellent trail."

Newfoundland is defined by its failures as much as its triumphs. Most places are, I suppose, but the history of our place is dotted with missteps that seem to reverberate for generations. The Newfoundland Railway is one of them. I once asked a learned acquaintance why Newfoundland became so impoverished in the 1940s that we voted away our independence and joined Canada. He quickly pointed to two reasons.

"The losses in World War I were devastating, but easily the main cause of the economic failure was the disaster of the Newfoundland Railway."

The main line ran east to west from St. John's to the ferry in Port aux Basques, with smaller lines branching off. Henry and I are walking on the remains of one of those branch lines right now.

Local people call this trail The Track, and because of the unusual location, it affords expansive views. Most of the trails I've explored around Newfoundland and Labrador are as close to the water as possible. One of the most magnificent things to do in this part of the world is walk on the mighty East Coast

Trail, which boasts around 350 kilometres of hikes through and between dozens of coastal communities.

Unlike most of that trail, this one does not run along the ocean. Rather, it runs high up on the hill, behind the town of Ferryland. We are looking down over the backs of the houses and church and out over the long, narrow peninsula to the lighthouse. If we were making a film about the place, this would be the perfect establishing shot.

I close my eyes and let my other senses take over for a moment. A lonely but somehow reassuring moan of a foghorn drifts out to sea. Funny how a sound meant as a warning could bring comfort. But it does. Almost as much comfort as the smell of baking bread wafting up from one of the houses below. The long, narrow, rocky beaches that line both sides of The Downs leading to the lighthouse are covered in beach rocks smoothed and rounded by the sea's constancy. The loud wash of the waves across them fills the air. It's a unique geographical feature that gives us a sound like no other place, up or down the shore.

"Look at all the large gardens right down by the water," says Henry as another peculiarity of the landscape strikes him. His comment opens my eyes to see what he does. These are, by east coast of Newfoundland standards, larger-than-normal flat family plots. They're delineated by fences and rock walls and look very fertile. And they are right down by the ocean. Surprising for a Petty Harbour fella who assumed all the Southern Shore's harbour towns to be like his. And I can tell you, there is not twenty square feet of usable farm or garden land down by the water in rocky Petty Harbour.

"What is the square pond? Did they have a swimming pool?" Henry is looking at a perfect right-angled, clearly man-made—or at least man-aided—rectangular pool.

I so badly want to answer and look informed to my young son. I really, really don't want to say, "I don't know." So I say, "Oh, it was likely an irrigation pond carved out to give fresh water to each house in the lower part of the harbour." I must have stammered or something, because Henry does not look convinced.

"You don't know, do you?"

I am gonna be caught, so I do what any parent trying to look smart would do. I shout, "Hey, look—a stone church!"

Henry does not look fooled but drops the point as we head off to explore the church hung on the rocks over the town.

Stone churches are not at all common in rural Newfoundland. These towns were filled with boat builders who knew their way around a sawmill, and wood was ever-plentiful. So, wooden churches are scattered all over the place, while stone ones are scarce as hen's teeth. And the one towering over the main road as Henry and I stroll towards it casts an impressive shadow.

Charlie Dunne lets us in the building and explains that the first rocks were laid in the construction of Holy Trinity Roman Catholic Church in 1863. Fishermen lugged stones from the aptly named Stone Island in nearby Calvert Bay. Charlie and a group of people have most nobly looked after this gem for years, and you immediately feel their love and affection for it.

This Catholic church occupies a special place in the history of this town, and this town occupies a special place in the history of the Catholic Church. The very fact that it was allowed to exist here at all, as early as it did, is significant. Over a century before the official establishment of the Catholic Church in Newfoundland, the governor, Cecil Calvert—also known as Lord Baltimore—followed the policies of religious tolerance of his father, George, and allowed and encouraged people to have Church of England and Catholic services as they saw fit.

The province is rich in whacky names. Where else can you direct a visitor to go past Widow's Walk, just above Deadman's Pond, and through Cuckhold's Cove to get to The Gut?

Fogo's memorial to the great auk. Sadly, they were too slow—and tasty—to escape extinction.

The former St. John the Evangelist in Fogo, where I performed a song inspired by one of Fogo's most tragic, deeply personal stories.

Rush hour on Fogo Island.

On the ride south to Rocky Harbour, Henry concentrates hard on his father's fascinating commentary.

One of my favourite road snacks. Follow me for more recipes.

There are twenty branches of the department store chain, a provincial institution. This one happens to be on Fogo.

Fishing—and what feels like time travelling—off a wharf in Battle Harbour.

Magic hour in the heart of Gros Morne National Park.

Family time:
Joanne with ADHD
in Point Amour.

I have never seen anything like it. Battle Harbour, an impossibly perfect act of preservation.

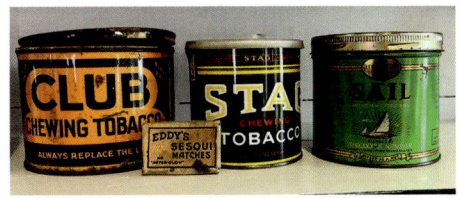

Who's with me?

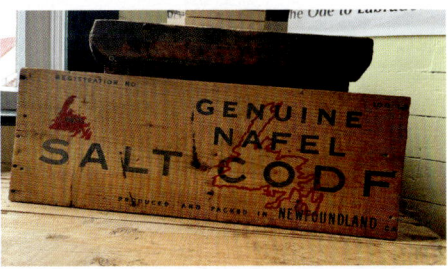

St. Anthony is the biggest town in these parts, accommodating about 25 to 30 percent of the Northern Peninsula's population (not pictured).

Newfoundland delicacies, past and present.

Ferryland: a pretty good lighthouse offering spectacular sandwiches. Henry went for custom grilled cheese on white.

Harbour Grace's monument to the legendary Ron Hynes, by artist Jud Haynes. "His songs must be way better than yours," said photographer Henry.

Back to my roots—or do I mean tentacles? —in Ferryland. I played my first paid gig in this bar.

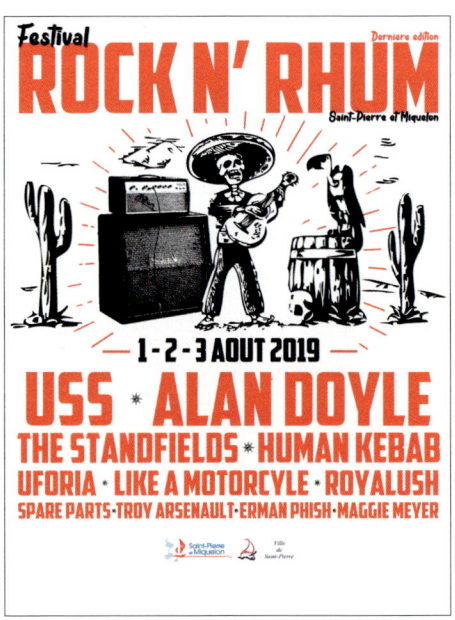

A couple of the other musicians on the bill got too heavily into the rhum . . .

We have branches everywhere, including the southwest coast.

The icebergs of Harbour Grace come in all shapes and sizes. Here's one that's suitable for a family audience.

Highways and byways of Harbour Grace.

Channel-Port aux Basques. Make a crazy U-turn in the middle of a nearby four-lane highway to see the sign saying "Welcome to Newfoundland and Labrador."

Hello and goodbye. My pilgrimage is complete. For now, anyway.

This was unheard of at the time. One historian called Ferryland "the birthplace of religious freedom," as it was the first place in British North America where an English-speaking priest said a Catholic mass.

Ferryland was ahead of its time. But more about that in a moment. Charlie is too entertaining to miss. He beams with pride for this building and the central role it has played in the town he loves. He has a story for every stone in the place. I hope you get to meet him.

My chat with Charlie starts with how the churches in our towns were often the centre of the social life. I tell him that many notable church services in Petty Harbour did not go as planned. Midnight masses where everyone, including the priest, drank too much. Baptisms where someone shouted, "That's not even his youngster!" Funerals where there was almost inevitably gonna be a fight if Jerry got the gall to show up. "Jerry" always showed up in Petty Harbour, and he did in Ferryland, too.

I told him about my years as an altar boy, and about myself and my cousin serving on the altar for our grandfather's mass. How he and I, at the reflective, deeply spiritual conclusion of the service, could not get the large baptismal candle out of its stand. As the very serious and very bald archbishop scowled at us and impatiently gestured for us to get on with it, my cousin and I yanked up hard on the thick, tall candle, which had been burning for over an hour. We should all have been more aware of the hot, molten liquid wax that had pooled around the wick. We all should have known that said hot, molten liquid wax would fly out when we yanked at the candle and jerked it out of the stand. And I suppose we all should have known that said hot, molten liquid wax would fly through the air directly at the arch-bishop's bald head.

"What's an altar boy?"

Henry's question, clearly indicating the lack of organized religion in our house, is still bouncing off the beautiful stone walls, I'd say.

I figure it's a good time to say thanks and scurry out of the holy place. We thank Charlie and head out to continue the Ferryland Adventure.

As we make our way towards the Colony of Avalon site, we pass the Interpretation Centre. There, next to a large public building, we see a monument that was recently erected to the very fella we spoke of earlier.

"That's a monument to Ron Hynes, bud."

"A statue?! His songs must be way better than yours." Henry doesn't blink, and I giggle as I say, "They are, bud. They are so." I ask Henry to take a photo of me leaning on the beautiful metal art piece of Ron's guitar-playing silhouette. I give him a quiet wink and we move on.

As we look around the area, Henry says, "I can picture how this could be a bigger, busier town."

I am chuffed and cannot hold back my enthusiasm. "It was!" I say. "And they are still discovering just how busy it was."

I turn my son's head to the point of land where the peninsula meets the mainland. You can see unearthed rock walls and uncovered building foundations, all surrounded by archaeological tape and grids and flags.

"The Colony of Avalon is one of the most significant archaeological finds in Canada." I am about to blather on, but Henry asks, "What is the Colony of Avalon?"

"That is." I point to Ferryland. He looks confused. I can't blame him, because what I am pointing to is not a town or colony now, of course, but an expansive archaeological dig that is slowly but surely unearthing a bustling village founded about four hundred years ago.

The Colony of Avalon archaeological project in Ferryland, Newfoundland, began in the 1980s with the discovery of a seventeenth-century English colony established by Sir George Calvert, the first Lord Baltimore, and was continued by his son Cecil, mentioned earlier. Gradual excavation revealed more and more about what early colonization actually looked like. The project has uncovered artifacts, structures, and evidence of the daily lives of the colonists and their families.

The site and the Interpretation Centre make for a great visit and a very interesting window into a time that served to kick-start the Newfoundland we know today. Highly recommended.

Though it started before the cod moratorium, this archaeo-logical curiosity quickly grew and became an ongoing project when the inshore cod fishery fuelling this place was shut down in the early 1990s. Government-funded programs to retrain displaced workers in the fishing industry came to all parts of rural Newfoundland. Local people who'd become instantly unemployed went to work with the archaeologists. Makes me wonder how many other post-moratorium projects were this successful. Some? A lot? No doubt Battle Harbour, and this proj-ect, would be big wins in that category. It will be interesting for history to judge just how many actually worked and replaced the inshore fishery in rural Newfoundland.

Leaving the dig site, Henry and I take one of my favourite walks in the whole province. I've done it before and I speak of it often. And not just because it has the world's best ham sandwich at the end of it. Henry pauses mid-stride.

"Wait. Dad, did we come all this way so you could have that ham sandwich you keep talking about?"

"No, no, buddy, we are here for the book I'm writing." I quicken my pace in hopes he doesn't continue this line of questioning. But he does.

"Are you getting the ham sandwich?"

"Yes, Henry." There is some shame in my answer. "Yes, I am." Henry definitely might be smarter than me.

The walk leads us over The Downs, the long, raised narrow peninsula that juts unusually out into the bay. It leads to Ferryland Head and the lighthouse, with a few meadows and a small, wooded area at the end, but is mostly treeless and open to what must be ferocious winds at times. Ferryland Head is connected to the mainland by this isthmus just wide enough for a narrow off-road vehicle to drive on, with steep banks leading down to the rocky beaches we saw and heard so clearly from The Track. From this close, the loud washing of the waves sounds like a beautiful orchestral cymbal swell.

It is remarkable to stop and just listen. It occurs to me that while we think of travel as being about what to see and do, our memories of it are very often triggered by what we hear and smell.

"Come on, Dad, I'm hungry." Henry remembers I got them to do a grilled cheese for him, and we don't want to let it get cold. After a short walk down a winding road through Ferryland Head, the Ferryland Lighthouse rises up into view.

The lighthouse was built in 1871, and after a gent named Kearney got it rolling was continuously operated by one family, the Costellos, for about a hundred years. A fourteen-metre-tall bright-red cylinder reaching to the blue sky from its perch on the cliff's edge, it cuts a fine figure, but it is not its appearance that makes it stand out. Not to me, anyway. What makes it stand out for me is the one and only Jill Curran and the most awesome Lighthouse Picnics she has been running for over two decades.

Jill has many connections with this place, including the fact that her grandmother was one of those Costellos who were born right here in the lighthouse itself.

The picnics always make for one of my favourite days in Newfoundland and Labrador. I recommend them to everyone who is visiting this part of the province.

A trip to Ferryland followed by the walk out to the lighthouse is rewarded with a picnic basket that Jill and her gang prepare. They also provide you with a blanket to spread over the grass and sit upon with your woven basket filled with sandwiches on warm bread baked right there in the lighthouse. Ham and brie on warm oatmeal molasses bread is my go-to, among a selection of others that I've no doubt are just as good. But to be honest, I've never tried any other ones because the ham and cheese is so spectacular. Henry goes for a custom grilled cheese on white. There's also homemade salads and desserts and lemonade. You can sit on the blanket and watch the whales dancing below you while you munch on superb freshly made food. Come on. It's just awesome. Henry and I get into it.

I devour my sandwich, as Henry does his. We agree we definitely could eat another one, but in truth we are well satisfied. Henry runs around to look for whales as I see Jill rounding the lighthouse. We hug and I tell her what a wonderful day we've had so far, coming up south like we do around here. We laugh together about our common oddities, and she asks if I had a good look around the church and the Colony of Avalon. I tell her I have, and that I've explained to my son all about Lord Baltimore. Henry has made it back from his run and is standing with us. I introduce him to Jill, and he thanks her for the sandwich. He is no doubt thinking at this point that his father is a wicked-smart man who clearly knows loads about everything.

"You mentioned Lady Sara Kirke, of course," says Jill. I respond with a blank face.

"He didn't," says Henry. He is correct. I've never heard of this lady, who Jill now explains was considered the most successful woman entrepreneur on this side of the pond in the seventeenth century.

Lady Sara came to Ferryland with her husband, David, and they ran the colony together for a few years, till he got recalled to England by an unsupportive Oliver Cromwell and later died in prison. She not only kept the ball rolling, but went on to become a force to be reckoned with. Census figures from the 1660s and '70s show that Lady Sara Kirke owned more stages, boats, and cod liver oil vats, and employed more fishermen and processors, than almost all other English shore planters at that time.

"So, you are not the first smart lady to run this place?" Jill and I share a laugh and I ask her to remind me when she started this whole deal.

"The love of the place came before the business idea. We started Ferryland Lighthouse Picnics in 2003. Had no idea if the picnics would be popular, but we really wanted to save the building."

Before Jill came along, few might have predicted such a happy fate for a building that had been left empty and neglected for some twenty years, but she and her gang succeeded wildly. Hundreds of picnics are served every week to the thousands who make the walk every year. Which means the future of this building is now secure, and I couldn't be happier.

"It was decommissioned as a manned lighthouse in the late 1960s or early 1970s and they automated the light. Then, of course, the last person to live here was Gerry Squires."

I break stride as I realize what Jill has just said.

For me, Gerald Squires is one of the most, if not *the* most, inspired and inspiring visual artists in Canadian history. I know many of his works, including several of the Ferryland Lighthouse, but it's never occurred to me that he lived here.

Jill explains that, not long after the decommissioning, the house portion was meant to be torn down, but the Ferryland Historical Society saved it and rented it to Gerald, who lived in the attached house for a decade or more. I comment on how inspiring this lighthouse and surroundings must have been for someone as gifted as Mr. Squires. Jill nods as we walk around the grassy hills that drift down to the ocean, where more than one pod of whales are entertaining the picnickers.

"Gerry freely admits that he came into his own as an artist here. He was inspired by the bleak days, and he did three whole series out here."

"The Boatman" and "The Ferryland Downs" are two of his early series that propelled him and his art around the globe, making him one of the province's and the country's most celebrated artists.

The stroll with Jill is constantly interrupted by her phone buzzing and beeping. She's clearly the central figure in a busy, busy operation.

Jill asks if my son and I have already stopped by the Ron Hynes monument. Henry answers for us.

"Yeah, and the house, too. Dad says he wrote a song there."

I can tell he doubts my claims. Perhaps he is on to my attempts to look smart.

"Ron was the last person to ever sleep at the lighthouse. He stayed there after doing a small concert there. I'll never forget it."

Again, I break stride, and have to ask: "Jill, are you telling me two of the last people to stay at the lighthouse were Ron Hynes and Gerald Squires? This place is holy ground!"

As we make our way back to the car park, I hear Henry catching up from behind. He quickly asks Jill, "So, you know lots about this place . . . what is the square pond for?"

Henry's clearly trying to fact-check my bluff about the pond being part of some kind of irrigation system. But there's no time for me to intervene before Jill comes back with:

"Oh, that's just for ice hockey and skating."

Henry mutters "*Dad*" as Jill wonders what's up.

I just say, "Henry is smarter than me."

He shakes his head while sliding into the minivan for the drive up to—I mean down to—home in St. John's.

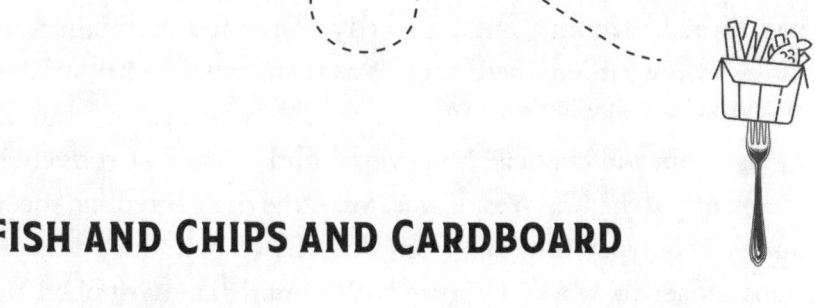

FISH AND CHIPS AND CARDBOARD

"Jesus! Ye got it made. Ye can't afford not to drink!"

Freddie's dad, Jim, was scratching his head as Freddie and I sat in the cab of his truck, counting out dozens of five- and ten-dollar bills we'd just gotten at Brewers' Retail, the best place to recycle beer bottles in St. John's. He and I and a revolving cast of two to four others were renting a de facto frat house in a part of St. John's about halfway between downtown and the university, known as Rabbittown.

I have found two possible explanations for how this mainly residential area got its name. The first is obvious: that it comes from when St. John's was quite small, and this was a place on the outskirts of town where men would set snares to hunt wild rabbits. The second is scandalous and argues that the area was settled primarily by poorer Irish Catholics who were morally obligated to not use sinful birth control and hence bred like rabbits.

Freddie, my brother, and I found this three- or four-bedroom house for rent on Suez Street and jumped on it for the simple reason that the asking price suited our budget at a paltry $650 per month. I say three- *or* four-bedroom place because it really had three bedrooms, but I covertly converted the main floor dining room into my bedroom. Was it an actual bedroom? No. Did it have a closet? No. Was it completely separated from the living room and kitchen? Not even slightly. Was it effectively in the front porch? Yes. Yes, it was. Sure, the draft lifted the sheets on my bed every time the front door flew open, but I was ten steps closer to work, I figured. We immediately dubbed the house "Le Château du Suez." We thought it funny to give such unregal digs the name of a palace.

The three of us and a pal moved in there in the fall of 1988 and paid a whopping $162.50 each for rent. My brother and other housemate were engineering students, and prone to binge-drinking parties on their one night out a week. And we had the perfect house to host the madness. Then, once a month, we'd gather the empty beer bottles. A lot of beer bottles. It was not uncommon for us to have over 150 dozen, requiring a favour from Jim and his pickup truck. We'd load his truck to the limit and he'd drive us to Brewers' Retail.

There was not a month that passed when we didn't make at least $150, which we would quickly use to pay our phone and light bills—prompting Jim once to utter in disbelief:

"Jesus! Ye got it made. Ye can't afford not to drink!"

I hadn't really wanted to move away from downtown, but this house made total sense as it was a fifteen-minute walk both to school at Memorial University and work at the Newfoundland Museum. I can't count how many times I did that walk and back in the six-plus years that I lived at Le Château du Suez.

The museum that played such an important role in my life has moved locations and grown to become one of the most compelling cultural destinations in the country. My first job was at the Newfoundland Museum in the Murray Premises, a branch off from the main museum, located in a perfectly preserved historical building on Beck's Cove, between Water Street and the harbour. I later moved up to the main museum, located on Duckworth Street in a beautiful old building that previously housed the Gosling Library. Both buildings still exist to this day, but the museum isn't in either of them. For it's now one of the three reasons why a magnificent cultural and educational facility known as The Rooms should be high on any visitor's agenda.

Designed by the PHB Group with Philip Pratt, Charles Henley, and Paul Blackwood, The Room's structure is inspired by Newfoundland's traditional tall and narrow fishing rooms used for storing dried salt cod and fishing gear. This spectacular facility officially opened in 2005, welcoming visitors to explore its exhibits and artifacts. Each of the Provincial Museum, Provincial Archives, and Art Gallery of Newfoundland and Labrador occupies one of the three towers that dominate the skyline of St. John's, and each contains treasure you don't want to miss. The museum, in particular, is world-class. Take a walk through, for example, the exhibition *Beaumont Hamel and the Trail of the Caribou*, which explains and honours the heroic efforts the tiny but plucky Dominion of Newfoundland made in World War I. It is more of an experience than a visitation. You are *in* something, not looking at something.

Oddly enough, the excellent content in the towers of the museum, archives, and art gallery is upstaged for me by my favourite part of The Rooms, the glass atriums connecting all the towers. The stairways and landings encased within the floor-to-ceiling glass walls afford views of The Narrows and the harbour and Signal Hill that are just glorious. As you ascend, each landing looks over a different section of downtown, giving you a more and more impressive vantage point, till you reach the restaurant at the top, which might be the best place to sit and have lunch in all of Canada. It even has an outdoor patio, where you can lord over the harbour and feel the sun or the rain or the wind or the fog, or most likely all four if you stay there for an hour.

The views are breathtaking on a clear day, and even more astounding when the wind blows the fog off the ocean in through The Narrows. Like an ocean giant took a long drag on his pipe and exhaled it directly into the tight opening into town.

I always suggest that visiting pals "save The Rooms for a rainy-day activity, and if you are the only person in history to not have a rainy day on your visit to St. John's, just go on your last fine day." It is a national treasure.

The Rooms being effectively right next door to the Roman Catholic Basilica of St. John the Baptist is an embarrassment of riches. There are several amazing Old-World churches in the neighbourhood. The Anglican cathedral, Gower Street United, and my personal favourite, Cochrane Street United Church, are all worth a look if cool old churches are your thing. But undeniably, the basilica is literally at the top of the hill.

The basilica was completed in 1855, and is not only a place of worship but also a cherished symbol of the city's heritage and spiritual identity. Until The Rooms came along, it was this grand structure that completely dominated the skyline of the city.

The basilica's architecture is a stunning blend of Romanesque revival and neo-Gothic styles, characterized by its towering spires, intricate stonework, and awe-inspiring stained-glass windows. One step inside and the scale of the place is as imposing as it is impressive. It is enormous for a city the size of St. John's. The cavernous interior is adorned with ornate altars, intricate woodwork, and magnificent frescoes, all bathed in the warm glow of candlelight.

Beyond its architectural splendour, the basilica holds deep cultural significance for the people of St. John's. It has witnessed countless weddings, baptisms, and funerals, serving as a cornerstone of community life for generations. The acoustics are legendary. I have sung there on dozens of occasions, and it's been a joy every time. Most notably, at legendary songwriter Ron Hynes's funeral, hundreds of couples filled the aisles behind him and waltzed him out as I sang his iconic "St. John's Waltz."

I walked by the basilica each time I left the Château to walk downtown. And that, let me tell you, was a lot of times. My schedule for four years of university quickly became a weekly dance of trying to serve three masters: school, work, gigs. By the time my fourth year rolled around, I was working full time, nine to five, Monday to Friday, at the museum on Duckworth Street. I was also doing a full courseload towards my degree at MUN. I took one correspondence course, which was all done by snail mail at the time. I did four night classes that ran from 7 to 10 p.m. on Mondays, Tuesdays, Wednesdays, and Thursdays.

Monday, Tuesday, and Wednesday were as follows: work, nine to five; walk to Château; eat a can of beans or a frying pan full of Hamburger Helper; walk to MUN for night class.

Thursday would have looked the same, but I had a regular gig at the Rose and Thistle on Thursday nights that started at 10 p.m. I had to somehow bail twenty minutes early on English 4000 so I could get to my gig downtown. I nervously approached my professor before the first class of the fall semester.

"Hey there, Professor Roberts . . ."

"Yes. Alan Doyle is your name and I know exactly what you are about to ask me." He barely looked up from his leather-bound notebooks. "You want to pip off my class every week so you can make a racket at the dirty old Rose on Water Street."

I thought I was done for, until he looked up and smiled and said, "You certainly can leave at 9:40 if you like. I'll be done here by around 9:50, so you'll only miss ten minutes, and I can fill you in on your first break at the pub."

I was confused till he smiled broader and confessed:

"I've been there every Thursday the summer. You got a great voice. You can go to be there for ten. And I'll be there before 10:15. Save a few Stan Rogers songs for me. Deal?"

We shook on it, and my Thursday night gigs were saved.

On Fridays, I worked nine to five at the museum and then raced to one of a few pubs that booked me for happy hour. Then I'd walk up George or Water Street and start my night gig. Saturdays, I usually played at least two gigs, and every Sunday night I was back at the Rose till midnight.

It was busy, but I loved it. I played so much downtown that I just left my gear down there. A guitar in the closet at Humphrey's. Speakers and stands under the bench at the Rose. Microphones and cables left downstairs at Trapper John's.

I'd usually make between fifty and a hundred dollars a gig, and there were a few free drinks here and there and I'd get fed sometimes, especially at the happy hour or brunch gigs. At the Sunday night Rose gig, the owners basically told me to clean out the fridge.

"Whatever's cooked in there, you can have, Al," Ron would say, wiping down the bar after last call. I would go through the leftover tubs from Sunday brunch, where the Rose featured a mixed grill breakfast. I'd scrounge and plate up whatever I could get. I would regularly sit at the bar with Ron and drink a beer while chowing down on a plate with two sausages, a pork chop, blood pudding, and baked beans. On rare occasions there would be something deluxe left over, like a piece of steak, or my fave, a Scotch egg. I'd never even heard of this sausage-wrapped Scottish delicacy before I started playing the pub circuit in downtown St. John's, but it quickly became my second-favourite new food. My number-one favourite discovery was fish and chips.

Now, I expect many of you will be surprised to hear that Alan Doyle from Petty Harbour did not really discover fish and chips till his very late teens or early twenties. But this is the case, and it was actually a very common thing for fellas like me from small fishing towns to start our love affair with fish and chips later than you might expect, and not just because Freddie and I needed an affordable late-night ride from Power's to Petty Harbour.

When I was a kid growing up in Petty Harbour, it felt like fresh codfish was everywhere, all the time, and free. We ate it constantly at home. Mom pan-fried it. She made stews of it. She salted it and made fish cakes of it. She even stuffed it like a Thanksgiving turkey and somehow made cod gravy of it. We ate cod tongues and cheeks and heads. Mom was one of those high-level cod connoisseurs who ate the "britches," roe sacks that adorably look like a pair of wee purple pants, and the "sounds," a thin elastic piece of flesh along the sound bone that inflates and deflates when the fish wants to rise or dive. All this to say, when we got a chance to eat at a restaurant or even at a takeout, fish was the last thing we would think to order.

These days the magnificent Chafe's Landing offers amazing meals in Petty Harbour, but when I was young, we rarely had a takeout of any kind. When we could find one in a neighbouring community, we usually went for burgers, or sub sandwiches, or deep-fried chicken and chips. Fish just wasn't our go-to when we wanted a treat. Moreover, our parents, and certainly our grand-parents, would think it wasteful and even immoral to order fish in a restaurant or takeout when it was readily available for free at home.

But as my time in St. John's became permanent, and certainly after a few decades of travelling the world, I feel confident making a statement that would cause folks to rage with offence in places like England, Scotland, Australia, and New Zealand. Likewise, folks closer to home in Nova Scotia, PEI, eastern Quebec, and all along the coast of British Columbia. And that most controversial statement is:

We have the best fish and chips in the world.

Yes, we do.

Yes, we do.

Yes, we do.

And any visit to this province should include eating as many fish and chips as your heart can suffer, simply because once you leave, you will not find anything close to it. It only makes sense that this meal is top-shelf around here. The island is surrounded by fish, and one of the only food groups that grows reliably is root vegetables like potatoes.

So, the fish is almost always fresh. I was showing mainland friends around Petty Harbour once, and as we entered Chafe's Landing, I said, "Around here, when you ask when the fish was caught, you don't mean *what day*, you mean *what time today*." The best places lightly batter fresh cod and deep-fry it to a golden crust ever so quickly, so the outside is crunchy and inside is flaky and snow-white.

The chips—or fries, as most North Americans call them—are always fresh cut and never frozen. I know this sounds obvious, but I am constantly astonished how many places, even chest-pumping fish-and-chip places, will serve you frozen fries. I spent a delightful summer in Prince Edward Island, globally known to be one of the potato capitals of the world, and I was astonished how few restaurants and takeouts served fresh-cut fries.

We cannot discuss fish and chips in Newfoundland and Labrador without addressing the dressing. And gravy. Any come-from-away could be forgiven for looking lost at a St. John's fish-and-chips counter when they are inevitably asked if they would like dressing and gravy on their meal. I'll make it simple for you. Yes, you do.

The dressing is akin to what most North Americans would call stuffing, like the bread and spices you might stuff in a Thanksgiving turkey. Around here, the dressing is almost always bread crumbs mixed with a little onion and a tonne of dried savory, one of the only herbs you'll regularly find in traditional local cooking. The gravy is almost always brown turkey gravy. The Quebec crowd will tell you that poutine, with its cheese curds and gravy, is the best fries-and-toppings combo in the world.

The Quebec crowd are wrong.

Yes, they are.

Yes, they are.

Yes, they are.

Chips, dressing, and gravy is the best. Full stop. Thank me later.

How this combo came to be is not agreed upon. Some say it came from fried hash—or "bubble and squeak," as the Brits love to call it. You know, leftover cooked meat and vegetables from the Sunday roast, refried in the cast-iron pan. Some argue that, at some point, someone had the good sense to splash leftover gravy on it, which eventually led to putting gravy on other fried food. I think it developed from restaurants serving hot turkey sandwiches, where it is easy to see how the dressing got on the plate and on the fries and under the gravy. As soon as the lucky first person had tasted dressing and gravy on fries with their hot turkey, they also wanted it with their deep-fried fish or burger or anything else.

As far as fish-and-chip purveyor options go, I've mentioned Chafe's in Petty Harbour, and there are a few more not in the downtown core of St. John's but in the greater city area that are worth a trip. Keith's in The Goulds, where the fish likely came from Petty Harbour, is consistently excellent. Dick's (wonderfully pronounced "Dickses") on the ferry dock in Bell Island is astounding. There are others all over the province, but as we are chatting about downtown St. John's, here are three options to consider.

The Duke of Duckworth might sound familiar to anyone who read my previous book or watched the many seasons of the CBC-TV series *Republic of Doyle*, as the Duke is a prominent setting in both. If you want a traditional English Newfoundland pub experience, this is the spot for you, as the pints and the sports and constant chatter are as good as the food.

Ches's Fish and Chips might be the most famous place with tourists and out-of-towners. It is a hike up Long's Hill to Fish and Chips Row, where this place is the heart of the zone. And despite the climb, the place was often jammed as the bars closed late at night, though I confess I'm not sure they still serve the post-pub-hours gang like they once did.

Leo's is just up the street from Ches's, and many Townies swear it to be the better of the two. "Ches's is for the tourists, but Leo's is for the local diehards," a museum pal once told me as we bolted up Long's Hill at lunchtime.

I would happily eat in either of these places, and I encourage you to eat in as many of them as your doctor advises. Okay, two more than your doctor advises. Though, sadly, I can tell you first-hand that the caloric intake of irresistible St. John's fish and chips is not the only potential danger to your health. It is so tasty that if you are not careful, you could hurt yourself eating it.

I'll explain.

I was at the end of a normal week of studying and working and playing. I recall it was late in spring, as the NHL playoffs were on when I finished a gig at the Rose at around midnight. It was a West Coast game, and the first period had just got rolling when I left to walk up the hill back to the Château. As I passed through the fish-and-chips zone, I was surprised to find that Scampers, a place that had consistently great food but inconsistent hours of operation, was still open. I ran in and convinced the fella to make me one more before he closed, and he obliged with a monster three-piece smothered in dressing and swamped in gravy as per my instructions.

The weight of it was something. I walked the remaining kilometre or so up to the Château and had to continuously switch hands, it was so heavy. I could feel the heat of it all through the large cardboard boat of a container. The hot gravy was making its way down through the dressing and fish and chips to the cardboard, so I picked up my pace.

I ran into our frat-like house at about 1:30 a.m. to find no one around on the main floor. I sped to the kitchen and took the cardboard boat out of the paper bag, and as it was starting to get wet on the bottom, I laid the whole works of it, boat and all, on a porcelain plate, grabbed a metal fork, and went quickly to the living-room TV to see if I could catch the end of the hockey game.

"We are into extra time here and next goal takes it!" The unmistakable voice of Newfoundland-born sportscaster Bob Cole rang through the living room as I sat with the porcelain plate under the cardboard boat filled with fish and chips and dressing and gravy. I bit open two white vinegar packets and drowned the works of it before becoming entranced with the game under Bob's mesmerizing call.

I pushed the metal fork into the fish. I brought it to my mouth, and it was perfect. I ate it without blinking, for fear I'd miss the winning goal. A few forkfuls later, I was through the fish and dressing and into the gravy-kissed chips soaked in vinegar. I pushed the fork in time and time again. I did it without looking down as the seconds in the nail-biter of a playoff game ticked away. One more push with the fork, and I felt it scrape the white porcelain. I moved it left and right and front and back, but it found nothing but the porcelain. I still didn't look down as the play was deep in one zone.

Wait. Did I just hear the fork on the porcelain plate? I thought to myself and wondered why I would wonder such a thing.

Then I remembered why this sound was noteworthy and even alarming.

I looked down to see the sides of the cardboard boat intact and effectively licked clean. My eyes followed the sides down to where they should intersect with the bottom of the container.

But they didn't.

It was gone.

There was nothing but shiny white porcelain where the cardboard bottom used to be.

Bob Cole shouted, "He scores!"

I shouted, "Jesus, I ate the cardboard!"

We both said, "Game over" at the same time.

HARBOUR GRACE EXCURSION

"Dickie Berg is trending!" I grin like a fifty-five year-old teenager. Harbour Grace has made international news. Not because of its rich history in global marine shipping, or its esteemed place in the settling of the New World, or its notoriety as a haven for pirates. No. On this day in 2023, Harbour Grace is closing every news broadcast on Earth because of an iceberg that bobs and floats just offshore. An iceberg that looks a lot like, well, like a dickie berg.

I'm struggling to keep it wholesome here. I'll do my best.

Icebergs are common sightings on the east coast of Newfoundland, and my young life in Petty Harbour was decorated with them every spring.

One of our icebergs is famous for having sunk the *Titanic* in 1912, something that's provided me with an easy way to familiarize people with where I'm from. In the States, for example, I usually say to confused concertgoers, "I'm from Petty Harbour, Newfoundland."

Crickets.

"I'm from northeast of Maine."

Confusion.

"It's where the *Titanic* sank."

Subtle nodding.

If that doesn't work, I continue with: "I'm from the newest island province, like you have the newest island state.

"Yes, that's right. Newfoundland is Canada's version of Hawaii. Come see us in February."

I know I'm eventually going to get punched on Duckworth Street on a snowy Valentine's Day by a very upset Texan, but it'll be worth it.

Luckily, I usually don't need to go past mentioning the *Titanic*.

The iceberg that downed the *Titanic* is just one of thousands and thousands that have floated past me and most of Newfoundland and Labrador for as long as I can imagine. These prehistoric mountains of frozen fresh water break away from glaciers up north and make their way past Newfoundland in a spectacular annual runway show on the ocean. Some big and square, some tall and pointy. One summer, an iceberg got jammed onto the rocks of the narrow ocean entrance to Petty Harbour, and every time the high water came or went, it spun on the rocks and made horrific crashing and scraping sounds. It was like a nightly plane crash at the turning of the tide. It changed shape and size every day as it twisted and melted and cracked. Most icebergs do.

Inevitably, these ever-changing icebergs will sometimes present themselves in strangely reminiscent shapes. "That one looks like Granda's Datsun," I remember saying about a growler—a small iceberg, in this case shaped like an automobile—while peering over the breakwater when I was very young. In 1905, photographer Thomas B. Hayward snapped a pic of a berg off St. John's with a tall pillar on one end that he and Archbishop Michael Francis Howley swore was a perfect representation of the Virgin Mary. Devout Christians ran to it with rosary beads flying and binoculars brandished and searched for any sign of stigmata from Mary's icy hands.

All this to say, icebergs have been trending in Newfoundland for a long time. In 1905, Madonna Berg; in 1912, *Titanic* Berg; and in 2023, Dickie Berg—which, if you haven't figured it out by now, was shaped much like a penis. A—ahem—tall, proud penis. I guess it had drifted past Dildo on its way to Harbour Grace. You can't make this stuff up. Just google Dickie Berg— no, wait. Maybe don't google it at the office. Just trust me.

My search for this infamous iceberg is taking me to Harbour Grace, and the drive down this peninsula that juts north out into Conception Bay is lined with great little towns like Avondale, Brigus, Bay Roberts, Spaniard's Bay, and the hub town of Carbonear on the eastern shore. Most notably, you pass through Cupids, which rightly claims to be the oldest official town on the island, and the oldest continuously settled place in the entire British colony of Canada. Established in 1610, Cupids is as old as colonial Canada gets. I remember the celebration of Cupids' four-hundredth anniversary and discovering just how old that is compared with some other Canadian towns.

On the western side you'll find a Dildo, followed by Heart's Desire, Delight, and Content. Please read the previous sentence one more time. Thank you. Further along that western side you'll find Old Perlican, which has a couple large fish plants and often appears as busy as most of rural Newfoundland did in the 1980s. My favourite spot on the western side might be Winterton, where a fantastic wooden boat museum, and the incredible music venue Trinity Hall, makes for a great stop.

I'd love to linger more along this wonderful shore, but I have a famous iceberg to find.

Harbour Grace was almost the capital of Newfoundland. It probably should have been. It sits a hundred kilometres north and west of St. John's, and the road between the two has been commonly travelled for the past seventy-five years or so, but the seaway between the two harbours was quite possibly the busiest travel route in Newfoundland history. For centuries, boats and ships and schooners and every other kind of nautical vessel went back and forth between these two hubs, carrying everything from fish to seals to people to workboots.

The route was so heavily frequented that it has inspired more than a few shanties and songs, the most famous being "The Harbour Grace Excursion," or as we in Great Big Sea called it, "Excursion Around the Bay." It remains one of my favourite traditional Newfoundland songs, as it falls perfectly into the category of happy ditties about dire tragedies. In this case, a fella's wife gets pulled on board a St. John's boat bound for Harbour Grace and gets so seasick that "the screeches from her truly, you could hear in Carbonear." In true Newfoundland traditional-song form, the poor lady dies on board and her body is buried in the ocean, "wrapped up in a Union Jack," while the not-so-bereaved fella sings about how he'll get another lover shortly and "we're off for Harbour Grace" again. A jaunty singalong chorus of "Oh Me, Oh My" wraps up this joyous, joyous tune about a death in the family.

I turn off the Trans-Canada Highway and eventually reach the Harbour Grace exit, where signs direct you to take Back Track Road. It occurs to me for the first time that driving into the backs of towns is a recurring situation in Newfoundland. So many of our settlements were meant to be accessed by water, and driving cars and trucks on paved roads into Harbour Grace was not at all part of town planning when it was settled in 1517. So, if you are in a vehicle, you are almost always arriving through the back door. And inevitably, the first things you see are not the best features a harbour town has to offer. In many cases, there's a town dump and a rock quarry, but here today there is at least a sawmill and what appears to be a former dance hall. But let's not judge a house by what's been discarded on the back step.

As I crest the last hill of the highway and catch my first sight of the water, I am struck by the incredible size of the harbour.

"More of a bay than a harbour," I say into my voice-recorder app, feeling kind of lonely as I do. I am on a rare solo mission today, as Joanne and Henry are at work and school, respectively.

Whereas the entrance to the actual capital city of St. John's is called The Narrows, the entrance to Harbour Grace is anything but. The opening into St. John's has been dredged and widened several times, and if you ever want to give yourself a sick thrill, try watching a massive cruise ship navigate the skinny entrance between Signal Hill and Fort Amherst. The mouth of Harbour Grace must be well over two kilometres across, and judging from the massive ships over at a shipyard that occupies much of the landscape of the north side, water depth does not seem a significant issue.

I almost get lost in the ocean view, but two peculiar sightings break the spell. Two things so strange and out of place that not even the glorious Atlantic can compete for attention.

The first is rather disorienting. After having spent a few days researching the extensive nautical history of Harbour Grace, the first thing to greet me is not a ship, but an airplane. The *Spirit of*

Harbour Grace is a Douglas C-47 built in the US in 1943, and after a long working life it was brought to Harbour Grace in July of 1993. It sits by the water without a runway in sight. Like I said, I find it disorienting and odd at first, as I am predisposed to assume all of Harbour Grace's charms to be nautical ones. I confess I snicker a bit and scoff at the notion of this trophy airplane in such a ridiculous location—but please stand by for more about *that* whole deal.

The second sighting is indeed a nautical feature, but not one you'd expect to see in a place rich in successful maritime history. There, right behind the seemingly out-of-place airplane, is a ship-wreck, run hard aground and listing slightly to one side. Most odd is that the ship seems to have run aground there an hour or so ago, yet no one around is alarmed. It is not rusted out like a wreck of years past. Rather, it shines in the morning sun with what appears to be a recent coat of paint. It takes me a few moments to see that this ship is firmly nested on a sandbar.

Then I spot the name close to the front and realize, of course, I am looking at the *Kyle*, a legendary steamship that in its fifty-plus years of service carried supplies from Nova Scotia to Newfoundland and up to Labrador, served as a sealing vessel, and even had a stint carrying infantry in World War II. This vessel was made famous for me and many others by legendary Newfoundland storyteller Ted Russell, who penned, amongst other great stories, "The Smokeroom on the *Kyle*," a tale as tall as you've ever heard about a string of squid of biblical proportions. (Look up Ted Russell's *Tales from Pigeon Inlet* and thank me later.)

The *Kyle* was into its sixth decade of dutifully serving the people of Newfoundland and Labrador when, in 1967, it broke loose from its moorings in Harbour Grace and ran aground on a mussel bed here on the Riverhead side of the harbour. Much debate ensued about how to best honour the ship. Some were shocked to see it left there to rust and felt it should be towed off to a proper ship's burial in deep water, while others thought it fine to prop it up here on its final resting place and slap a fresh coat of paint on it every now and again.

A corpse of a ship with fresh makeup for the never-ending wake.

Turning towards the heart of Harbour Grace, I instantly understand how this place competed for Newfoundland supremacy with St. John's. Driving towards the historic Water Street, I'm struck by how Harbour Grace looks like it was supposed to be bigger. A quick look at the population density tells the story, really. The most recent census shows about 2,700 people in Harbour Grace, down a few hundred from the previous counting in 2016. In 1857, there were well over five thousand, plus who knows how many temporary residents living on dozens of ships that came and went regularly. In short, this used to be a boomtown.

The ghosts of a previously thriving place are everywhere. Storefronts along Water Street with display windows, an incredible courthouse, and other public buildings all point to the undeniable relic of a once-thriving place that was expected to keep growing. I pass the store and warehouse that housed a boot factory and a window of a shop that appears to have once sold ladies' clothing and shoes.

There is so much to show what Harbour Grace hoped to be, and it might easily feel like a place of the past, if there were not some very significant landmarks that look to pave a future for this place that is very promising.

The Harbour Grace Ocean Enterprises shipyard holds significant importance to the past, present, and future as one of the oldest and most productive shipbuilding facilities in the region. Established in the early 1800s, the shipyard quickly became a hub of activity, crafting sturdy vessels for fishing, trade, and exploration. The skilled workers and craftsmen at the shipyard were renowned for their attention to detail and dedication to producing high-quality ships. Throughout the years, the shipyard played a crucial role in the economic development of the town and contributed to the marine and offshore oil industry.

But as prominent as the shipyard is, another landmark literally towers over everything else in sight. The Cathedral of Immaculate Conception dwarfs Harbour Grace. Its stone walls and bell towers are nothing short of awesome.

"This church is so impressive. It could easily be one of the main tourist attractions in any European city. If this sat next to St. Paul's in London, you would definitely go see both." I am still trying to focus my eyes to the scale of the place as I speak into my notes app. "There are cathedrals in dozens of German cities I just visited on tour smaller than this one. This cathedral would not look out of place in Cologne or Munich—cities of millions of people, not a few thousand."

I continue: "Putting a stone cathedral of this size in Harbour Grace would be like putting the SkyDome in Petty Harbour."

I get bored talking into my phone and step out of the car to stand beneath the spires. And standing beneath them, it is hard not to wonder what in the world could be done with this monolith in such a beautiful but sparsely populated place. How could a massive cathedral have any future in Harbour Grace? As if they heard me ask the question, around the corner come Brenda O'Reilly and Craig Flynn.

I've known these two for a few decades and have eaten and drunk and sung in a few of their great places in St. John's, all of which are located in wonderfully restored or reimagined histor-ical buildings in the heart of the old city. Their dedication to preserving the architectural culture of the province is super-human. I can't imagine downtown St. John's without a few of their spots. My favourite is in the basement of their craft brewery, Yellowbelly, right on the corner of the famous—or infamous—George Street. The UnderBelly is so old, it literally runs under what is now our Bourbon Street. It contains burnt beams from the great fire of 1892. A storey or two underground, where the world disappears. It might be the best hidden speakeasy in North America, or the best bomb shelter in the world.

So, I was excited and curious to hear they had taken on ven-tures outside the capital city in what very well should have been the capital city. I am impressed and astonished by their out-standing vision. Where I see a massive, aging, empty cathedral, they see a bright and prosperous future for the cathedral and the town itself. They have taken on the monumental project of restoring the cathedral and converting it into a modern restau-rant and performance space.

I should probably regret starting the conversation with "Are you both crazy?!" but I stand by the question.

The three of us exchange greetings while the smacks of hammers and the buzz of saws fill the air around us. I can tell instantly that these two are not just starting this restoration, they are well into it. Men and women in steel-toe boots, hard hats, and work vests rush around us with a nod as we walk through the stone entryway.

I don't want you to think, Dear Reader, that I'm being a lazy author when I say this cathedral is very much like the great cathedrals of Europe. I say this because of the surreal feeling I got upon entering the grand nave and realizing how out of scale it is with the local population. This cathedral is not a small version of the ones found in major cities in the UK or Germany. It is a match for them. The high arches, the long parallel pews, the magnificent altar, the choir loft and pipe organ. This church would be impressive in Dublin or Munich or Lisbon. It is nothing short of amazing in Harbour Grace.

Construction started in the 1890s on this Gothic revival church, which boasts two towering spires, lancet windows, stone buttresses, and so many other classic features that make it a must-see when visiting the area.

"You could fit everyone in town in this place twice! The Stones could play here! Are you building a restaurant or a Vatican?" I probably should be more reserved.

Chatting with them is nothing short of invigorating. Brenda and Craig are exactly the type of people we need in Newfoundland and Labrador if we are to pave a way forward, especially in our smaller rural places. Their energy is infectious.

"You'll have to walk through the confessional to get to the brewery," Brenda grins as she describes their plans for a restaurant in the cathedral and a craft brewery and "beer spa" in the basement. I confide that I don't know what a "beer spa" is. I also offer to purchase the first membership.

"As well as craft beer, we are also doing clear spirits, and we are also putting whisky on, and"—Brenda leans in—"we are calling it 'Holy Spirits.'"

After I tell her I love her even more now, Brenda explains that the greater plans for the site include a full-scale export brewery and packaging site, a hotel with more than fifty rooms, and a spa, as well as a garden events facility.

I ask, "What is your blue-sky hope for Harbour Grace?"

Brenda does not skip a beat. "We are building an international destination resort. It's also going to be a catering facility for events and weddings and conferences and live performance events. We will be marketing this outside of Newfoundland and Canada as an experience that is truly singular."

If you are getting the picture that these people are ambitious and forward-thinking, I am doing my job properly here.

"And of course, we already restored the courthouse across the street." Brenda mentions this as casually as if she had fixed up a hooked rug. As if the cathedral down the road wasn't enough of an accomplishment.

The stone courthouse and jail was erected in 1830 and survives as the longest-standing public building in all of Newfoundland and Labrador. Brenda and Craig have impeccably restored the main courtroom to its original splendour, and it now serves as a function and performance space. The lower judge's chambers are a speakeasy with an iron door that leads to the original jail cells and a prisoners courtyard. If I hadn't just walked through the cathedral, this place would have blown my mind even more.

The original building was paid for by a tax on the folks in the area. Public records tell me that for every thousand quintals of fish, a buck was sent to the courthouse fund. The presence of this extremely rare grand public building in rural Newfoundland surely confirms that Harbour Grace was not only suited to be the capital, it was preparing to be the capital.

"This town is just incredible," I say. Brenda is quick to not only agree but supply me with a list of additional stuff I may not already know.

"There's two other churches as well."

I am quick to look informed. "Yes, I walked around St. Paul's this morning."

"And the walking trail." Brenda wants to make sure I don't miss anything, but I am on it.

"Yes, the Pirate's Path. I am headed there shortly."

"You know it's named for—"

"Pirate history like Peter Easton!"

Brenda looks assured now but adds, "And don't forget the airstrip."

Brenda's comment turns me around and provides me with the perfect opportunity to make a snarky Townie comment about the absurdity of mounting a plane on the side of the road in a fishing town. I am just about to say, "Yeah, that plane is kind of out of place," when Brenda reminds me of a fact I had known at some point but must have stored in a brain cell that went missing in a bar somewhere in Iowa in the 1990s.

"The airstrip is worth seeing." Brenda gestures to the hill behind the town, and I nod in a way I think clearly shows I know exactly what she is talking about. But, of course, Brenda has worked in pubs for years and she can tell when someone is full of shite from a mile away. She continues like she is talking to a forgetful fella, because she most definitely is. "Amelia Earhart flew a plane across the ocean? First solo woman to do it. Big part of Newfoundland's aviation history!"

"Oh yeah." I'm not sure why I'd try to indicate I've been planning to go to find the airstrip, but foolishly I do. Finally, I fess up. "Holy frig. I forgot about Amelia Earhart. One of the most famous people in the history of flying and exploration and human achievement! What a tour guide I am."

As I follow the "Historic Airstrip" signs ever higher up the slopes behind Harbour Grace, I repeat aloud almost involuntarily,

"Harbour Grace was almost the capital of Newfoundland. It probably should have been." Even for someone like me, with a limited visual imagination, it is very easy to picture how this slope would make for a spectacular San Francisco urban hillside town. And as the slope gives way to the plateau, a pond that would be called a lake anywhere else commands an area that would surely be a city planner's dream.

I can see how the streets would wind gently up from the lake like they do in Zurich, Switzerland, or Queenstown, New Zealand. Again, I cannot help but think how much easier it would have been to develop a large urban centre here, compared to the craggy rocks of St. John's.

The icing on the cake for my urban daydreaming would be just a few hundred metres from my imagined lakeside city: an airport. And Harbour Grace effectively had one.

The landing strip is a kilometre of grass so tidy and level and flat that it is almost shocking to the eyes of a fella from Petty Harbour. I don't need to look it up or confirm the fact that there is ten times more flat lawn at the airstrip in Harbour Grace than in the entire town of Petty Harbour.

I hate to sound simplistic, but the whole thing is very impressive. It is over a kilometre long and over sixty metres wide, cut neatly out of the trees and brush. It is uncanny to stand on a patch of grass that is groomed and manicured, straight as, well, as a runway. Readers from PEI, Ontario, or Nebraska will think me ridiculous here, but I just need to express how incredibly odd this sight is in Newfoundland and Labrador.

The sign reads "Harbour Grace Airfield," but if it read "Alien Landing Site" I could not have been more surprised. Constructed in 1927, the airfield was an essential first or final stop in the daydreams of those eager to encourage and develop international long-distance air travel. We need to remember that in the 1920s, airplanes had a range of about the length of your living room, so finding the shortest route from North America to Europe inevitably meant a runway was needed somewhere on the island of Newfoundland. In a few short years, the resulting airfield would cement its place in the history books.

From this beauty of a meadow, in May of 1932, a lady just thirty-two years of age named Amelia Earhart took off in a plane about as big as my minivan and flew it across the Atlantic Ocean by herself. I repeat, by herself. She has a grocery list of other accomplishments to her name, but of course she is now globally famous for being the first woman to complete a solo transatlantic flight. A flight that started right here in Harbour Grace.

I lift my head from the info panel like a kid who's just realized he missed 50 percent of the test by forgetting to turn the exam page over (yes, I did this in Grade 12). The fact that I had giggled at the airplane by the water now fills me with Townie shame. Despite my know-it-all snickering, Harbour Grace, as it turns out, has a perfect right to put an aviation monument in your face.

What a place this is. And what a jerk I am. I whisper an apology to no one.

On the way back down from the plateau, I see a large, newer building I can't identify. Upon investigation, it turns out to be the Danny Cleary Recreation Centre, named for the man responsible for bringing Newfoundland its first Stanley Cup.

Home to the first solo flight by a woman and the province's first Stanley Cup. Jaysus. "How," I wonder aloud into my notes app, "is this place not the capital of the province?" I am a massive hockey fan, and we even featured Danny's accomplishment in one of our band's music videos. And yet, just like that solo flight across the Atlantic, the Stanley Cup slipped my mind.

I take my shame to the edge of town—to the Pirate's Path. The walking trail, like other equally memorable ones in rural Newfoundland towns, starts where the harbour ends and follows the oceanside ever out to sea. It rises and falls gently on this beautiful day and makes its way through thick woods into open, sloping meadows that would have been cleared for gardens or firewood or even dwellings if they were closer to the fishing grounds.

An interpretation panel or two remind me who this trail is named for, and of the grim history in which he played a prominent part. It's the reverse side of *Come From Away*'s story about wholesome, hospitable Newfoundland. Pirates roamed these coves for centuries, waiting for a shipwreck to raid, and if a wreck wasn't occurring naturally, well, there were lots of ways to encourage one. Strap a lantern around a cow's neck and have her wander one of these meadows on a foggy night. You'll be collecting booty by dawn, guaranteed. That kind of story does not fit with the one about the lovely, friendly gang who welcomed the stranded air-travelling world during 9/11, but both stories are equally true.

Peter Easton was one of the more famous fellas who pillaged the North Atlantic. And his home base for several years was right here in Harbour Grace. After a tenure as a legit sailor starting around 1602, Peter said, "Shag the high road," and turned to piracy. And what better spot to build a pirate's fort and headquarters than here—the town they most likely assumed to be the inevitable future capital of the bustling British colony. He established a fort on these hills in 1610 and went on to become one of the most feared people in North Atlantic sailing history. At a high point, he had enlisted as many as 1,500 Newfoundlanders in his fleets of marauding pirate ships.

I cannot help but think what a spectacular place this must have been at that time. Who among us wouldn't want to be in Peter Easton's home pub when a thousand or so of the lads rolled back into town with a load of God knows what. I'd be the first fella on the stage with a song. I'd have loved this place on a Friday happy hour. I'm not sure I should be particularly proud of that. But I know it is true.

The walk on Pirate's Path is just oceanside glorious, and as I round a bend in the trail I see it. Bobbing in the tide. The source of all those news broadcasts around the globe.

Dickie Berg is not as—ahem—not as proud as he was yesterday, or the day before. He . . . ah . . . appears to have lost his enthusiasm for whatever had him . . . ah . . . so enthused.

"Dickie Berg is melting," I announce into my voice recording app. I put my phone in my hoodie pocket and, without planning to, I raise my right hand to my forehead and offer a respectful salute.

DOWN IN BONAVISTA

I hates camping.

There. I've written it exactly as I've said thousands of times. I've noted it publicly and for the record. Finally. I have never really proclaimed myself a camping lover, but I've often been aware that people assume I am one, and I have never corrected anybody, so this confession might surprise some.

I love the outdoors. I love everything about it. I love the walks in the city, the hikes in the woods, the views, the boat rides, the bridges, the birds, and even the bees. Anyone who knows me is keenly aware that one of my more annoying traits is that I positively adore walking in the rain. I love cooking and eating in the outdoors. I love an open fire. A propane stove and a wiener on a stick. A screaming kettle on a bow hung over the flames. A sandwich in a meadow. A pot of fish stew on the gangboards of a boat on the bay.

I love everything about the outdoors.

I just don't want to sleep there. I like to go indoors to sleep.

My wife loves camping. Daydreams about lying in a hammock with a warm breeze rustling the pages of a book. She loves a tent. Loves a sleeping bag. I'm convinced the sound of a zipper connecting canvas flaps is like a lullaby for her. If there's one thing she likes more than actual camping, it is the idea of camping. She loves to search the buy-and-sell mags and websites to see if there's a vintage hardtop or jack-up camper for sale.

"A 1981 Trillium for six grand in Bay Roberts!" is a typical exclamation in our kitchen as Joanne scrolls through Facebook Marketplace.

I wanted to get her something special for a recent birthday and found a fully preserved 1976 thirteen-foot Boler trailer. I was charmed immediately by its classic two-tone exterior: white on top and dark brown below. A cupcake of a camper. I thought she would love it, and she did. I thought it would look cute in our backyard, and it did. I never thought she would actually make me go camping in it, but she did.

So, here we are, piled into the minivan in the early-morning hours, headed west on the Trans-Canada Highway. Me, my wife, and son, and Spencer, our Cavalier King Charles spaniel, towing the Boler trailer behind us down the highway about two hundred kilometres west of St. John's. Quite unusually for our family, I am driving.

I hates driving.

There. I've written it exactly as I've said thousands of times. I've noted it publicly and for the record. Finally. I have never really proclaimed myself a lover of driving, but I've often been aware that people assume I am one, and I have never corrected anybody, so this confession might surprise some.

I love travelling and being in new places, but I really don't like manning the vehicle that gets me there. I am happy to look around, daydream, write notes and song ideas, and generally take in the experience of being in motion. That's if I can stay awake. And quite often, I cannot.

If you're looking for one superpower to help you survive three-plus decades of touring, I suggest you train yourself to fall asleep the second you are in the passenger seat of any car, truck, bus, boat, or airplane. With any luck at all in your career, you will spend a lot of time going from one place to the next, and not a lot of time sleeping in a proper bed. In a country as big as Canada, and especially for someone like me who lives in, arguably, a remote part of it, it will serve you well to learn to use the time in motion for sleeping. Easier said than done, but if you can master that skill, it will prove more helpful to you than singing a high C, I promise. I won't brag about much. But I am a superhuman sleeper. The second a vehicle starts moving, I start dozing off. In five minutes, I can be as completely asleep as if I were in a king suite at the Ritz.

Joanne swears I fall asleep in mid-sentence when she is driving us to and from our cabin, and she regularly curses me on airplanes as we arrive at our destination after I've slept for six hours straight while she's white-knuckled through turbulence next to me. I once flew from Sydney, Australia, to Honolulu, Hawaii, and did not stir for practically the whole eleven-hour flight.

"Are you okay, sir?" the attendant asked me as she lifted my seat into the upright position for landing.

"Me? Yes, grand. Why?" I was honestly puzzled by the question.

"Sir, we've flown for over ten hours and served three meals around you. I've been your flight attendant for basically half a day, and I have not given you so much as a glass of water!"

I felt bad for her and replied, "Oh . . . I'd love a glass of water."

My friend Bob Hallett, who started Great Big Sea along with me, Séan McCann, and Darrell Power back in the early 1990s, is not a good sleeper. He once offered in envious frustration, "Alan can get twelve minutes' sleep in a fifteen-minute cab ride."

I roomed with Bob for the first three or four years of touring and would somewhat proudly proclaim, "I have never seen Bob asleep." I regularly stumbled into our hotel room to find him awake, reading his third book of the week, and before he could lay it down to ask me how the pub was, I'd be asleep. When I awoke in the a.m., he was always up and often gone.

All this to say, when it comes to our family, I am rarely in the driver's seat.

Wow. That sentence says way more than I meant it to.

Joanne usually drives, but for some reason I can't quite comprehend, she wants me to drive when we tow the Boler . . . which has happened exactly twice before this trip.

Like it or not, I am helming this van and trailer as we turn off the TCH at Clarenville, a thriving rural Newfoundland town that serves as the government services hub for the area, but also has industry success of its own. Along with elements from the fishing industry, Clarenville hosts a marine repair facility, a hardwood manufacturing mill, and dozens of small businesses. At any given time, this place is hopping with activity. It is wonderful to see a rural Newfoundland place so commercially active.

Clarenville is also in very lucky proximity of a national park, a ski hill, and two major industrial sites that have, at different times, hosted hundreds of workers on massive projects.

Terra Nova was the first Canadian national park in the newly assumed province of Newfoundland. You could be forgiven for thinking it an odd choice as it feels rather, well, random. The area within the park does not look radically different from the area around it. It has lovely deep inlets and wooded areas, but so do Clarenville and Shoal Bay and dozens of other places. A quick bit of research shows several sources agreeing that the park was established to protect the boreal forest, but then they also point out that boreal forest exists basically everywhere on the island east of Deer Lake. It makes you wonder why Joey Smallwood, the first premier of Newfoundland, insisted this place would be the first national park in the late 1950s. At one particular supper with some folks far more learned than me, I wondered this aloud.

"Why was Terra Nova chosen as the first national park? It is lovely, but how was it selected before Gros Morne, with the fjord and mountain? What was particularly remarkable about Terra Nova?"

"One remarkable thing about it," said an extremely well-read friend of mine, "is that it is really, really close to Joey's hometown and his elected district."

Whatever the reason for its selection, the park is quite lovely, and boasts over eighty kilometres of hiking trails and, most confusingly, an excellent golf course. The Newman Sound area is a wonderful spot to camp or get out on the water. The resources of the park, and the tourism it brings to the area, have been a tremendous benefit to the growth of Clarenville, especially in the summer months. A nearby downhill and cross-country ski facility, the White Hills, gives this place the same boost in the winter.

Clarenville is within a short drive from two massive industrial sites: the Bull Arm Fabrication Site, and an oil refinery in Come By Chance, my favourite of our whacky place names. Both of these facilities have seen their ups and downs over the decades, but their massive industrial areas right next to deep, deep ocean makes Bull Arm ideal for the manufacturing and dry-docking of massive offshore oil rigs and vessels, while Come By Chance is a perfect spot to refine, store, and ship industrial oil products. When one or both of these facilities are in full swing, it makes for a bit of a boom in Clarenville.

And Clarenville is indeed one of the few Newfoundland places outside the greater St. John's area that has consistently grown in my lifetime.

"This place is one of the only rural Newfoundland towns—if not *the* only town—that has seen a massive population growth in my lifetime," I say to Joanne as the Boler bobbles around behind us. "In fact, the population has basically quadrupled, from around two thousand to over seven thousand in the past fifty years."

"Dad, that's just above tripled. Your math is not good." Henry makes his mom giggle, because they are both way, way better at math than me.

With all the attractions in the area, you might wonder why we are not stopping, other than to let Spencer out by the Irving gas station to do his business. Truth be told, we own a family cabin (a cottage, for many ye mainlanders) close to Clarenville, so we are here quite often. It has become the downtown for our home away from home.

We have some favourite spots, especially Rod's for fish and chips and, of course, Mercer's Marine, which could be the greatest retail store on the globe. One-stop general stores are widespread in rural Newfoundland. You know the type: where you can find food and hardware and clothes all in the same shop. Well, Mercer's Marine could be the Canadian Tire of general stores. You can get a sharp steak knife, a sharper pair of dress shoes, a home-crocheted dishcloth, a bilge pump, a handle for your gaff, a kettle, a galvanized bolt, a raincoat, an AC/DC T-shirt, a coil of rope, and a high-tech fish-finding sonar, all in the same aisle at Mercer's Marine. I insist you go there when rolling through Clarenville. It is just delightful.

A more recently established attraction is the high-end Bare Mountain Coffee House. I remember hearing a few years back about a new spot where you could actually get an espresso-based coffee in rural Newfoundland. Thankfully, there are now quite a few, but a few years back, you'd be hard pressed to find anything but drip or even freeze-dried instant outside of Town.

The first time we went in search of the newly opened coffee house spawned one of our favourite family games, where Henry and I trade voiceover intros to a fictional TV show that we both swear should get made. Henry started it with his best announcer voice as we and our friends searched Clarenville for an americano.

"This week on *Townies Around the Bay*, a dentist tries to find espresso in Clarenville . . ."

The game has grown to always have three entries, one for each segment in the TV show in our heads, which usually mocks the misadventures of urban folk in rural places. A typical one for Henry to announce might be: "This week on *Townies Around the Bay*, a St. John's doctor finds 'moose tracks' while cows graze all around him, a city councillor gets lost in Whitbourne, and Alan Doyle gets shamed for walking a purebred dog on a leash in Bunyan's Cove."

There are many entries.

Spencer is done, so off we roll. I've strategically parked the Boler with lots of space around us so that an easy forward-rolling exit is possible. So, the latest episode might be: "This week on

Townies Around the Bay, Henry hunts for rare Doritos at the Clarenville Irving, Spencer pees in front of a tourist bus, while Alan is terrified to back up the camper in public."

Clarenville is a service hub for the immediate, ever-growing area, and also for the Bonavista Peninsula, which juts out into the ocean on the northeast side of the town for about a hundred kilometres. I'd guess its widest point to be around twenty kilometres, so it is a long, narrow peninsula lined on each side with smaller fishing towns, all leading to the town of Bonavista, one of the most historically significant places in the New World.

The Boler bounces behind us as we make our way out the peninsula past another of my favourite Newfoundland place names, Morleys Siding. I've always loved that unusual word for a place name: not *harbour* or *cove*, but *siding*. There are a few sidings around here, including Blundons Siding and New Country Siding.

"What's with all the sidings?" The battery must have died in Henry's iPad for him to have noticed the repetition.

I instantly have another moment of desperately wanting to look smart in front of my son. I really want to answer his very reasonable question. A question that has never occurred to me. Not one time. I panic.

"Oh, *siding* is just probably how they pronounce *sighting*, and I guess they regularly saw this Morley fella around here, and that's how the town got its name."

I can't see Henry, as he is in the back seat, but I hear a sigh and know his eyes are rolling.

"Mom, Dad doesn't know, does he?"

The question hangs in the air as I hear Henry tapping his iPhone. He quickly reports his research.

"*Siding* refers to a short piece of parallel track where engines and equipment are parked when they are not in use."

My son now double-checks every fact I offer. I hope that's a good thing.

We drive in silence for a while as we approach a split in the road offering a choice of a northern or southern route to Bonavista. As we'll be looping around and camping later near Trinity on the southern side, we opt for the northern route through beautiful places like Long Beach and Summerville and the delightfully named Birchy Cove. These coves and harbours are idyllic little villages lined with woods on one side and ocean on the other.

But as we drive further and further out into the ocean, the woods around us start to thin. By the time we crest a hill and look down on the sprawling town of Bonavista, the trees have all but vanished.

Bonavista is as much in the ocean as next to it. It sticks out as far as the island will let it, and unlike many of the tight woodland-protected harbours that led us here, this place is wide open to the North Atlantic and all its gifts and gales. It is so far out there that it makes it very easy to imagine how and why it might be one of the first places you would lay eyes on if you were sailing in this direction from Europe.

And this is exactly what happened when John Cabot clapped eyes on the place and made Bonavista a place name known around the world.

John Cabot sounds like he was cool fella, I figure. To start, he has multiple names, depending on the language being used to talk about him. Jean Caboto, Giovanni Caboto, and Giovanni Chabotto are all handles of his. But my favourite is Zuan Chabotto, which apparently is Venetian, which I confess I didn't even know was a language. He was one of those guys who went around Europe in the mid-1400s with extensive sailing experience as a resumé, convincing rich people to sponsor their explorations out into the vast unknown ocean.

As we drive through Bonavista, with not a tree around to cast a shadow as big as a milk carton, I look out into the cold North Atlantic and try to imagine what that proposal must have looked like over five hundred years ago. The ocean looks daunting and dangerous to me, and I live in the age of the internet—I know how far it is to the next piece of dry land. Neither John C. nor any of the people he courted for sponsorship had the slightest clue what they were getting into. As we head out towards our first stop at Cape Bonavista Lighthouse, I envisage how one of Gio's sales pitches must have gone.

"Hello, good king," says Zuan, his CV of seafaring experience at the ready. "I would like a mountain of money to sail out that way and see what's up."

The king would no doubt ask, "How far are you going?"

And Zuan would reply, "Don't know."

And this pattern of varied question followed by same answer would continue.

"How long will you be gone?"

"Don't know."

"What do you hope to find?"

"Don't know."

"What are you even looking for?"

"Don't know."

"Will I get anything in return for my sponsorship?"

"Don't know."

"Are you and all your men going to die a horribly cold and wet and salty death?"

"Most likely."

Cabot, like the famed Columbus and other counterparts, must have put on quite a show, because King Henry VII commissioned him to head out onto the open Atlantic in 1497.

As we turn out towards the lighthouse, and the full breadth of the North Atlantic is as much around us as before us, I wonder if we, in the present day, have any equivalent to the expeditions these men took on. Outer space is more well known to us than North America was to them. The far reaches of the universe currently have more maps than fifteenth-century explorers had for what lay beyond the horizon. Yet, off they went.

"Mad as hatters," I mutter.

"Who, us?" Henry sounds concerned. "For towing the Boler out here?"

I really want to say, "Yes, yes, we are mad as hatters to be sleeping in a six-by-thirteen-foot fibreglass tank," but I don't want to be a downer, so I just say, "No, buddy, I was thinking about how hard it must have been to sail across the ocean five hundred years ago."

"I finds it hard to fly across it now." Joanne loves camping in fibreglass tanks but hates flying in airplanes.

No wonder John Cabot uttered, "*O buono vista*" when he finally laid eyes on land, securing Bonavista's place in history as one of the earliest bits of North America to ever have had a European walk upon it.

One account of his landing reports that Zuan walked ashore and raised a crucifix with banners to the king and Christ on it, no doubt believing he was the first living soul to ever stand upon these rocks. Imagine how weird he must have felt when he and a party of his men followed a well-worn path into the woods and came across a firepit and a spear.

Though the exact landing spot is unknown, many assume it to be somewhere along the shore between Bonavista and Cape Bonavista Lighthouse, which has just come into full sight.

The lighthouse has a rich history dating back to 1843. It was built to guide mariners through the treacherous waters of Trinity Bay and to mark the eastern entrance to Bonavista Bay. The original wooden tower was replaced in 1855 with one of stone. Over the years, the twenty-two-metre lighthouse has undergone several renovations and restorations. We pull into the parking lot, and I am delighted there is a wide spot with space in front and behind it so I can just slide in and out of there with the Boler in tow.

We have a look at the tower and light, and I am struck by the simplicity of it all. After centuries of radar and satellite technology, a simple light on a tower still helps guide ships around the globe. A candle in the window still lights the way.

As with most of these lighthouse properties, I find the sparse living quarters the most interesting. I am forever fascinated with how these lighthouse families lived in such remote places. It's a long, long walk to borrow a cup of sugar. I am a people person. A self-confessed social-holic.

"I would go bonkers if I lived out here," I say, perhaps a little too loudly.

"Yes, you would." Joanne and Henry speak simultaneously.

We exit and I immediately clock that disaster has struck. Someone has parked in the space in front of the minivan. The time has come for me to do something I've really never done before.

I have to back up the trailer in public.

Dear Reader, I feel I need to be clear about one thing here, so there is no confusion as to my feelings about being regularly recognized in this part of the world.

I likes being famous.

There. I've written it exactly as I've said thousands of times. I've noted it publicly and for the record. This fact will surprise no one. I'll happily and gratefully stand in front of ten or ten thousand people and sing a song and be very happy to be the centre of attention.

But there are times, when I'm about to do something I am no good at, when I wish no one was looking at me. At all. And just now, just as I sheepishly get behind the wheel and put the van in reverse, a forty-five-foot tourist bus pulls up to the lot, consuming almost all the available space, and all fifty or so passengers aboard instantly recognize me.

We have backed this Boler up before. We did it in our own side parking spot on our quiet street. We did it on a massive empty lot, early one Sunday morning while the city slept and no one was watching. Yes, we've done it before, but it was not pretty. Here in the now-quite-busy parking lot of the Cape Bonavista Lighthouse, we have no such solitude and the pressure is on. We take our places and I turn the wheel hard to the left and take my foot off the brake.

Jo and Henry stand behind the Boler and shout instructions into the side-view mirrors. Every time they shout, Spencer barks from the back seat. It is utter chaos.

"Turn the wheel the opposite way!"

"Woof."

"Put your hand on the bottom of the wheel!"

"Bark."

"Why are you going that way!"

"Bark. Bark."

"You are gonna hit the fire hydrant!!"

"Woof. Bark. Bark."

And my least favourite: "STOP!"

"Whimper."

"Wrong way!" Henry shouts. The tourists giggle.

I spin the wheel completely in the opposite direction and I hear a loud clang.

"You jackknifed it. Pull ahead a bit!" Joanne shouts as the tourists are in full laugh now.

I pull ahead and a man's voice shouts, "Stop! Don't look behind when you are moving forward!"

I recognize the bus driver by his uniform as he's just stepped down from the tourist bus. I am a hair away from hitting the car that parked in front of us. I can see two tourists actually slapping their knees, they are laughing so hard.

I look up over the dash with more than a little bit of Townie shame and meet the surprisingly sympathetic eyes of the professional bus driver.

"You want me to back that up for you?" I can hear people giggle further as he speaks, which stings a little, and I want to refuse his kind offer. I go to open my mouth, but it is Jo's voice I hear, not my own.

"Yes, please."

I am about to object again, but when I open my mouth it is Henry's voice I hear, not my own.

"Thank you. Dad hates driving." I assume for a second he's finished, but he continues: "And he's not very good at it."

I get red-faced pics taken with tourists while the professional driver moves the van and Boler. In two flicks of the wheel it is pointed back towards Bonavista. I thank him and hear faint applause as we pull away.

Henry starts immediately.

"This week on *Townies*—"

"That's enough, please." Joanne knows I'm not in the mood.

We three do not speak till Bonavista is all around us. I can see why there has been so much optimism about this area in the past couple of years.

"This place is on wheels" is not a statement you hear a lot in rural Newfoundland, but I say it happily as we make our way past the fish processing plant that is, well, processing fish. I can't tell you how the sight of it warms my heart. When I was a kid in Petty Harbour, the wharf around the fish plant—both fish plants, actually—was buzzing with forklifts and trucks and offal chutes, and that is exactly what I see here today.

I am whimsical as I steer the van and Boler into a very, very wide-open parking lot.

"I had no idea how much I've missed these sights and sounds," I say as we all start a stroll up the main drag of Bonavista, which is quite pleasantly lined with shops in old, refurbished buildings and coffee shops and cafés in beautifully restored houses. Not many rural towns have bounced back from the cod moratorium as well as Bonavista, and it is delightful to be one of many people walking the street and taking in the sights.

While Joanne and Henry walk with Spencer to an awesome-looking food truck, I nip into one of the gems of this place.

The Garrick Theatre, a bright clapboarded flatiron building on the corner of the main road, has been entertaining folks around here since the 1940s. Like much of the bustling town of Bonavista, it was quite a busy movie cinema and hosted live music and theatre successfully till the dreaded cod moratorium of the early 1990s. When that industry died, the fate of the theatre seemed to be sealed. Luckily, the Bonavista Historic Townscape Foundation took over the building in 2003, and their efforts to preserve this place are a treat to behold. The Garrick is one of the most charming little theatres in all of Canada. And I've been lucky enough to see a lot of them.

The lobby and bar area are welcoming and warm, and the theatre itself is a wonderful portal into old-time entertainment. The old footlights and the painted wood immediately transport me to the days of vaudeville and big bands. I recommend this place to anyone who's visiting the area. It is delightful in so many ways.

After a quick bite, I suggest we leave the van-and-Boler combo parked and walk to the other stops in Bonavista. There is so much history here, and much of it still stands in the public buildings that have been preserved and are open for visitors. The Ryan Premises—a series of domestic and commercial buildings that were used by merchant James Ryan as far back as 1869, when the first structures were built—is a National Historic Site of Canada. It's like strolling into another century. Similarly, the Provincial Historic Site of the Mockbeggar Plantation dates back to 1839, when the main house was built. This plantation was a key player in the development of Bonavista as a hub in the global cod fishery.

But we have got to get this camper parked before dark and can only visit one more Bonavista site today, so we opt for the home of John Cabot's boat, the *Matthew*. Okay, fine, it's not the actual boat, but rather a really cool replica built for the five-hundredth anniversary of Newfoundland. Not only did they build a full-scale, ninety-two-foot replica of the ship that carried Cabot from Bristol, they dropped it in the water and sailed it across the sea!

It was quite a big deal in June of 1997 when the *Matthew* once again sailed to the shores of Bonavista, five hundred years to the day since the first arrival. Queen Elizabeth was here to greet it. And so was I, as Great Big Sea played a few of the ceremonies and concerts, including one in the hockey rink in Bonavista itself.

It was an even more than typically windy day, which made for a less than ideal visit for Her Majesty. There were formal hats flying off heads left, right, and centre. One local politician was scolded for breaking protocol and putting his arm around the Queen. I would say it's a good thing he did, or she would have been blown halfway home before the *Matthew* got ashore. That faux pas was not the first time we've gaffed with visiting regal types. Perhaps we are not a good fit for the formalities of royalty. I love the story of one local serving lady approaching the Queen's supper table after the main course and, as she lifted the place setting away, putting the used fork back on Her Majesty's side plate and saying quite loudly and proudly, "Oh, keep your fork, my dear. There's pie."

But my favourite story comes from a previous royal visit to Purity Factories in St. John's, where fantastic local candies and cookies are the stars among their many excellent products. The story goes that Queen Elizabeth was visiting, and the workers were lined up at their stations to show off their wares. As Her Majesty approached one station, she asked a local worker, "And what do you make here?"

The man stepped up, politely removed his hat, lowered his head respectfully, and said, "Only $7.25 an hour, Your Highness."

The Matthew Legacy is a small museum that wraps entirely around the replica of the ship itself. Myself and Henry have a good walk amongst the information panels and exhibitions, but the best part is getting on and in the ship itself. At only ninety-two feet, it is hard to believe this boat could make the trip from Bristol, England, to here in current times, with its modern technology, much less than under wind and oar power in 1497.

"They sailed across the ocean in *this*?!" Henry is right to be astounded.

We have a lot yet to do on this Bonavista Peninsula day, so we jump back in the van. Thankfully, I don't have to reverse. We head out of town towards Elliston, but I make an unexpected turn off the paved road onto dirt. Henry looks up and I let him know: "We cannot depart on our quest just yet. No visit to Bonavista is complete without seeing the Dungeon."

I intentionally make it sound like something from *Game of Thrones*. Dungeon Provincial Park really should have been a set for that TV show. The park is situated on the bluffs just outside the edges of Bonavista proper. The grassy meadows roll right to the steep cliffs and to jaw-dropping views of the ocean and rocks below. The park's name refers to a natural, cave-like rock formation. We jump out of the van and have a quick look at this impressive and rather daunting piece of landscape. It is somehow peaceful and imposing. Lovely and discomforting. Dreamy, but dangerous.

We stand on the edge and peer down at the dungeon.

"I wouldn't want to fall down there." I nod in agreement with Henry and we run back to the van.

We are bound for a campsite near Trinity, but we have a pit stop before we can unhitch the trailer for the evening.

Elliston is not a big place, with only three hundred or so people. It really should not have three excellent reasons for stopping there. But it surely has that many. At least.

"Are those hobbit houses?" Henry has immediately spotted one of the local attractions: the road into and around this town is regularly lined with wooden doorways that seem to lead not to a house, but to the inside of a hill or a mound.

"Those are root cellars, bud," answers Joanne before I do, as she wants me to keep my eyes on the road and not take out someone's perfect picket fence with the camper. "They are rooms dug into the hill and ground to make a space away from the heat of summer and cold of winter to store vegetables and things all throughout the year."

"We used to use them before we had fridges and electricity, bud. They worked very well and didn't cost a cent to run." I'd wanted to join in, but with one quick and obvious question, Henry makes me feel like I should have stayed out of it.

"If they work so well and don't cost anything, why don't we still use them?" Henry looks back and forth between me and Jo. Neither of us knows the answer. I still don't.

There are dozens of these root cellars around the town, and it is a very cool (no pun intended) thing to step inside one. When we explore one that's open to the public, the change in the air around us is shocking. We have gone from hot and humid to cool and dry in three steps. It's kind of amazing.

We step back out into the sunny afternoon and stroll down the hill to what gets my vote for the best small museum in all of Newfoundland and Labrador. The John C. Crosbie Sealers

Interpretation Centre was named for the man who championed the sealing industry and defended the honour of the sealers when it was very, very unpopular to do so.

This building might be small, but it is packed with information and insights into an incredibly dangerous and labour-intensive industry that both fed the people of this area and provided employment during the dead of winter when folks really needed it. This place provides some much-deserved respect and dignity to sealers who were demonized by the anti-sealing movement, which effectively ruined them by ending what for centuries had been a way to sustain a year-round life in places like Elliston.

The perfect ending to any visit to the museum is to walk down to the shore and spend a moment in quiet reflection near the Sealers Memorial statue.

Created by renowned artist Morgan MacDonald, the bronze sculpture depicts locals Reuben Crewe and his son Albert, who perished in the sealing disaster of 1914, a horrific tale of tumbling circumstances and weather changes that left 138 sealers stranded on the ice in a vicious storm. Seventy-eight of the men and boys perished. Many of their bodies were found frozen in embraces like the ones depicted by MacDonald. This tragedy is well known to our people, and to many beyond who learned about it from Cassie Brown's famous book, *Death on the Ice*.

We have what is an unusually silent moment for the Doyle family.

"Let's see the puffins," I say, to break the weight of the moment. For me as much as anyone else.

Now, you might wonder why I would make a special trip to this place in order to see puffins. In truth, they live and thrive closer to my home. There is even a sanctuary and long-established boat tour there on the Southern Shore. But this place is different.

I park the van on the side of the road and we walk to what is effectively an unmarked area just outside Elliston. Very little fanfare is made of this place, and as we pass through one gate that might have had *Puffins* written on a wooden sign, I wonder if I have led us to the wrong spot.

About fifty strides later, I stop worrying. Spencer sees them first, but they are not bothered by his Townie Dog woofing.

On the surrounding cliffs and islands around us, one, then two puffins jump from their burrows down to the ocean below. Then ten or twenty more. Then a hundred. Then more than I can count.

There are a few places in Newfoundland where you can go to watch puffins. This is the only place I've ever been where you can practically park your car amongst them. It is an incredible experience to be among this many wild birds who are puttering around and sunbathing and dropping down for a swim or to chase a school of capelin.

They are very funny little birds, and I mean that sincerely. Like, they are funny to watch as they really don't look like they could possibly fly. Their fat little bellies seem too big for their fin-like wings to lift them. But they do manage it. They fall off the cliffs like divers and plunge into the water. The funniest thing is watching them take off from the surface of the ocean. Especially if their colourful beaks are lugging a fish. It's almost like they run along the top of the water and flap their wet, tiny wings as hard as possible in a dance that looks destined to fail. But somehow, they get air and make their way back up to their cliffside apartments. It looks like a major victory every single time.

They are delightful company and I wish we had more time to stick with them, but, "We've got a hike to do!"

I try to sound enthusiastic as I know how much Henry hates hiking.

He does a mini stand-up comedy set about it:

"Hiking is basically walking to nowhere. And all the while you are exposed to flies and bees and moose and bears, only to find yourself right back exactly where you started. Walking makes sense. I walk to the grocery store and come back with a pizza. Hiking is stupid. I hike in the woods and come back with nothing . . . except fly bites."

We park at the start of the Skerwink Trail in Port Rexton. I have to come here every time I am in the area. I love hiking and this—get ready for an argument—is the best trail in Canada.

This five-and-a-half-kilometre trail is challenging and takes us along the rugged coastline, and with every turn and switchback offers views of the ocean and rock formations. The trail's name comes from the local dialect, *skerwink* meaning "corner" or "turning point." Along the way, we spot whales, icebergs, and seabirds. It is so good that Henry only complains 6,347 times. Oh, and Spencer stopped walking for the last eight hundred metres, so I carried him.

"This week on *Townies Around the Bay* . . ." Henry gets his dig in as I lug an eight-year-old spaniel who is snoring in my arms before we get back to the van and Boler.

You should hike a bunch of trails in Newfoundland and Labrador. But you simply *must* hike Skerwink. It is spectacular.

As we finish the trail and walk out of the woods, I see the beautifully appointed Fishers' Loft on the hill. They have charming guest rooms there. With hot showers and real beds. The voice in my head speaks sarcastically, "I am *so* glad we are not staying there in a suite. Delighted we are all jamming into a thirteen-foot fibreglass tank instead." I think about saying this aloud, but decide not to as I don't want to get divorced.

I do protest aloud that we have not had a beer all day, and I successfully turn us to the Port Rexton Brewery, where Henry and Spencer drink cold water and share a grilled cheese sandwich while Joanne and I neck a pint of beer each like two sailors on leave.

We load up for one more stop, and many would argue we saved the very best for last. We are rolling a few kilometres up the road to Trinity.

Trinity might be the most photographed and painted town in all of Newfoundland and Labrador. For good reason. It is just the most impossibly postcard-perfect, quaint little rural Newfoundland fishing town. If you've seen a Newfoundland tourism commercial with a little red-haired person skipping along the water as homemade quilts hang on clotheslines attached to colourful clapboard saltbox houses, then I bet you've seen Trinity. It has been painted and photographed and filmed by everyone from me to Hollywood's best. It has served as the backdrop for numerous TV shows and movies. If you watched the 2001 film *The Shipping News*, you have seen Trinity.

The landscape is like many other spots around this coast. Almost an island, Trinity is barely attached to the rest of Newfoundland. It is effectively surrounded by water, with sturdy, rocky hills and beaches, but also long-flowing meadows that crawl up the hills on the back side. It is easy to climb up and get an amazing view of the ocean and town, but as good as it is, the landscape is not at all the main draw here in Trinity.

There are two big reasons to come to Trinity versus many other rural Newfoundland towns. The first is undeniably the perfectly preserved and restored wooden houses and churches and public buildings. Again, there are many places in the province that have quaint clapboard houses with old wooden windows, but in this town practically *every* house does. Likewise, an impressive, enormous wooden Anglican church and a charming and quaint little Catholic one are two of the many public buildings in this town that look exactly as they would have in the early 1900s and before.

This town, famously, was one of the first to buy into the notion of the value of historical preservation. Many hands and heads lead this glorious act of preserving the built heritage, including the Trinity Historical Society, which started in 1964 to "preserve, present, and promote the built and cultural heritage of the area."

When plastic siding and mass-produced vinyl windows were replacing the old rough-side-out clapboard and handmade wooden windows in the 1970s and '80s, Trinity effectively made it illegal to do so. The introduction of building material controls as far back as the 1950s must have caused quite an uproar, but this place bought into it, and that decision has made this area one of the most lucrative tourism destinations in all of Atlantic Canada.

As we walk to Dock Marina, one of a few excellent restaurants in town, we are just engulfed in the physical history of this place. It lives in every picket of every fence. In every stained-glass wood-clad window. In every chimney and woodpile. As we take a seat on the wharf in front of the restaurant, Spencer lies in the shade underneath. The pooch is pooped.

While trying unsuccessfully to eat my fish and chips slowly, I spy a couple of people in old-timey clothes headed around the wharf, and I instantly recognize them as characters in the second big reason to visit Trinity.

The *Trinity Pageant* is the anchor show in a summer theatre festival created and administered by Rising Tide Theatre. The Summer in the Bight season features the pageant, along with a few other shows. Rising Tide made a name for itself back as far as the late 1970s doing many kinds of shows, but their annual political sketch comedy, *Revue*, spoofing the politicians and headlines of the year, made them a household name in the province.

In the post–cod moratorium world, Rising Tide set up in Trinity and established this summer festival, along with the buildings and infrastructure that host the shows. They set about retraining people who had just been ousted from the cod fishery to be actors and comedians and stage technicians. I would not have bet on its success, to be honest, but I and so many others have been proven so wrong. It worked. Really well. And it still does. This could be the most successful use of cod moratorium money in all of the province.

I have been lucky enough to see a few of Rising Tide's shows over the years, from hilarious dinner theatre in the hall to more dramatic shows in their purpose-built theatre, and I have enjoyed them all, but the jewel is the pageant.

The *Trinity Pageant* is a piece of musical theatre like nothing else I've ever seen. Characters in costumes of various periods take you through the history of the town and area on a sometimes amusing, other times tragic, but always fascinating journey. But this is more than theatre. Rather, this is a real journey around the town—and in and out of the church and over the beaches and all over the place. They don't re-enact the pulling up of boats onstage under lights with a prop punt. In the *Trinity Pageant*, the characters walk you down to the landwash and pull up the boats on the very beach from the very story that's being told. It is just delightful.

I wish we had time to join the pageant today, but the evening sun is falling and we have a frigging campsite to assemble. We drive past a dozen or more excellent B&Bs on the way out of town. I dream of a hot shower and a restful night under handmade quilts while we cross the highway and head into the woods on a muddy dirt road.

We roll into Lockston Path Provincial Park just as the last of the summer sun is peeking over the hills near Trinity. There is a series of these parks around the province. All planned and administered by the provincial government for the public's easy access to and appreciation for our great outdoors. Most of them have hikes and ponds or lakes or harbours, and varying levels of services like powered lots or washroom and shower facilities. Unlike my young self, who spent his summers on the wharf cutting out cod tongues, my wife spent hers camping and swimming and generally having a great time in provincial parks just like this one.

From the time the rubber hits the dirt road, I can see the smile rise on her face.

I'm not sure if it was the tiredness or just good luck, but I back the camper onto the campsite on the first attempt.

"Too bad no one was looking." Joanne says exactly what I was thinking.

We unhitch the camper, and while Jo sets it up, me and Henry and Spencer go to the pond. I flick both of them in. Henry shouts. Spencer barks. But we are all better for it.

We walk back clean and tired from such an awesome day. The sun is long gone by the time we get back to the camper. By lamp and firelight, we assemble the sleeping quarters. Henry and Jo take the comfortable beds in the back. I am about to get on the small bunk in the front, which would be tight for a full-grown fella like me, but there is a whimper as I settle in.

I look down and Spencer wants up. I had made him a bed on the floor with his own decent-sized doggie mattress, but he is having none of that. He jumps up on the front bunk and slowly but surely sinks down behind me and the inside of the bunk. In five minutes, I can hear him snoring, jammed down behind my legs, and as he settles, my knees fall off the bunk and I am not too far behind them.

I lie on the camper floor. There is not a sound. That is, except for the sleeping breaths of my wife and son. And the loud, contented snore of the dog who took my spot. I fall asleep with my head on his doggie mattress and my jean jacket for a blanket. I mutter one thing before I fall asleep:

"I hates camping."

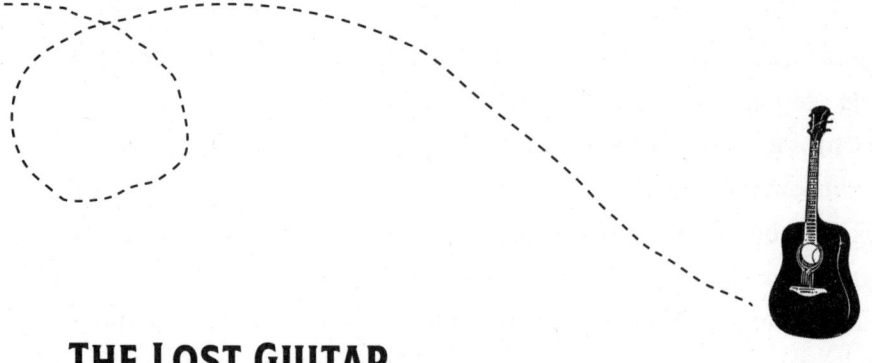

THE LOST GUITAR

"When is the last time you cleaned under your bed?"
Joanne was asking me an honest question, and I wanted to answer her honestly, but I really worried that if I did, she would come to her senses and reconsider her dating options.

When me and the various frat-ish fellas finally shut down the Château, in the fall of 1993, about a dozen people had come and gone over a half a decade. I had been its only start-to-finish resident and had lived in that dining room-turned-bedroom for over five years. Lots of people moved in, and when they left for the semester, they asked if they could leave some stuff there till they got back. Of course, many of them never returned and never bothered to collect anything, so on the final days of moving out, the sidewalk was piled with assorted gear awaiting sale, donation to the needy, or garbage collection. In that pile you could find twelve bicycles, or parts of bicycles, six full sets of old hockey equipment, fifteen assorted sports balls, three televisions, two full stereo systems, and a dozen Walkman-type cassette or CD players. I didn't even try to count the textbooks and novels and magazines, but I did count the six mattresses, because it looked kind of ridiculous seeing them all piled up on top of each other on the sidewalk, and we were about to add one more to it. Mine.

Joanne had helped me move out my stuff, which took about seven minutes. I had some clothes in a hockey bag, an amplifier, and three guitars. I should have had four, but I just couldn't find my black Ibanez Roadstar. I had not played it a lot in a year or so, as it was really a hard-rock electric guitar, and I had been mostly playing acoustic music downtown. I had misplaced it somewhere in the mix. I figured it must be out at Mom and Dad's in Petty Harbour.

I grunted a bit as I lifted the mattress off the metal frame and up on its side. I was about to ask Jo to help me slide it out to the pile when we both paused at the sight of what was below the mattress on the floor below.

We stood in silence, giving our brains a moment to try and decipher what our eyes were looking at. Was it a second mattress? No. There, on the floor, sat a black and grey and brown rectangle of dust, exactly the same shape as the mattress itself, only a little deeper, at around a foot thick, I guess. It was so dense that you could not see through it at all.

I wonder if my face showed shame or embarrassment or if I still just looked confused when Joanne asked:

"When is the last time you cleaned under your bed?"

We had not been going out that long. I had two choices. I could lie to her and tell her I cleaned it regularly and this must have accumulated quickly in the move. Or I could tell her the truth and confess that never once in over five years had it even occurred to me that cleaning under your bed was a thing that people did.

"That's where I sweeps the dirt?"

I raised my voice like I was asking a question, and in a way I most certainly was asking a question, which was: "Are you gonna break up with me now that you've discovered this horrible truth about me?"

I got into action with the broom and vacuum. Slowly but surely from the bed of dust emerged stuff of mine that I'd assumed had been missing for years. A pair of dress shoes I used to wear at the museum. A goalie stick and mask. An unopened twelve-pack of Molson Canadian that I must have stashed there during a party and forgot about.

"What's that?" asked Joanne from under the T-shirt she was holding up over her mouth and nose as she pointed to a long, black, rectangular case that was gradually being unearthed with every suck of the old vacuum.

"Hey! My guitar!" I was delighted to find my Ibanez Roadstar in fine shape. Joanne shook her head and went to wait in her Honda Civic.

We had met a few months before in one of the famous jellybean row houses that line the hills of downtown St. John's. Great Big Sea had just started, and I was helping one of the fellas in the band with his move into the second floor of a three-apartment house on Victoria Street in the heart of downtown. As I lifted the last of his stuff up the stairs, a beautiful young woman met me at the door, and I assumed I had gone to the wrong unit.

"Oh, hi." I was about to apologize when she smiled and said, "Hi—"

"That's Joanne. She lives on the main floor." My bandmate was behind me on the stairs and interrupted her, and I could have shoved him back down the steps as I just wanted to hear her. He continued: "She's here to collect the rent, I'd say." Jo nodded in agreement.

I figured I should turn on the charm and try to impress her with my quick smooth-talking.

"Oh, that's cool. You collect the rent for the owner in exchange for a break on the rent or whatever. I got you figured out."

I did not have her figured out. She took the box from me and laid it in the corner as she spoke.

"No. I own this house. I used the grant portion of my student loan for the down payment. Then I quickly returned the loan portion without interest or penalty. The rent from the other two units covers the mortgage, so I basically live for free while building some equity here as I finish my naval architecture program."

I guess I just stood there with my mouth open, because after a while, she spoke again.

"And yes. I am Joanne."

A few weeks later, I asked her if she'd join me for a night out listening to music in a downtown pub. We've been together ever since.

We lived in a couple of jellybean houses, and then we built one of our own—the one where we now live with Henry and a couple of dogs.

It sits quietly in the jellybean mix. Bright yellow. In downtown St. John's.

We met because of the St. John's music scene, and that is a wonderful place to meet.

St. John's and music are synonymous. It's hard to imagine this city without it. I was once asked to speak to the provincial government about the importance of funding for the local music industry. "St. John's without music would be like Paris without the Eiffel Tower," I told them. "The downtown live music scene might be the leading factor that makes this good city a great one. It is one of the things we have that so few others do. We are the envy of Atlantic Canada and beyond for not just live music, but excellent super-high-level live music, in almost every nook and cranny."

Sure, there might be someone in the Irish bar in Etobicoke singing "Wild Rover" while reading the lyrics from an iPad, but O'Reilly's on George Street has award-winning Irish/Newfoundland singer Fergus O'Byrne singing from his Irish heart. At happy hour. No cover charge! (Look him up. Thank me later.) Mick Davis is probably singing an incredibly cool song at the Black Sheep, before he walks down to the Bull and Barrel to sing another one. (Look him up. Thank me later.) Meanwhile, Spirit of Newfoundland are in their fourth decade of leading singalongs and laughter just down the hill. You'll have to walk past a couple of dozen live music venues to get from one end of downtown to the other, and you might not ever make it because the accordion player at Bridie Molloy's is just too good to pass. There's singers and sessions. Bodhrans and ballads. Whistles and whistlers.

It's an embarrassment of riches. And that's just to speak of the music around the various venues in town. Festival season is another matter altogether. The first breaths of summer kick-start a season found in no other city in the country. The Iceberg Alley Tent Festival on the banks of Quidi Vidi Lake (more about that name in a bit) begins mid-June and leads very quickly to the Newfoundland and Labrador Folk Festival, cozily tucked into historic Bannerman Park. Harbour Voices, a globally renowned choral festival in the middle of summer, has singers from all over the world. The George Street Festival comes right after that one and leads to the Regatta Day celebrations. You might have time for a quick nap before the Churchill Park Music Festival begins, because you won't want to miss a second.

I always argue that music is one of the biggest, if not the biggest, reasons people get on airplanes to visit St. John's. It may sound self-serving, but I honestly believe it. This is a music city. It is not the only one in the world, but it is the only one in Canada. If you were to list the world's best music destinations in North America, you'd likely have New Orleans, Nashville, and New York pretty high up, and for very good reason. They are huge, well-populated cities with lots of good music. But St. John's would be on that list, too. And with a population of around 250,000 it punches way, way above its weight.

We not only have lots of music, but perhaps more importantly, we have our own music. Our own instrument combinations and singing styles. And songs. Dear God, do we have songs.

We surely inherited a mountain of traditional songs and international sea shanties that we love to claim as our own, but we also have a huge canon that is uniquely and undeniably ours alone. And . . . And! (As you can probably tell, I get excited talking about this stuff.) And, not only do we have a huge canon of our own songs, but everybody knows them. By heart.

Walk up to any Newfoundlander and shout, "Fogo, Twillingate, Moreton's Harbour." If they don't shout back, "All around the circle," I'll eat my hat. Ask a hundred people around here, "What colour is Lukey's boat painted?" and exactly one hundred people will tell you it is most certainly green. We take it for granted here, but it is worth noting.

Most people in the English-speaking world will tell you they have no memory of learning the lyrics to "Happy Birthday" and "Jingle Bells." Every other song in their heads, they had to actively learn over the years. I'd be willing to bet that the average Newfoundlander has a dozen or maybe even twenty songs that they have no memory of actively learning. Like most people from around the English-speaking world, they automatically know "Happy Birthday" and "Jingle Bells," but they also automatically know "I'se the B'y," "Lukey's Boat," "Rant and Roar," and a dozen more songs as well.

Every touring band I know rates St. John's high on, if not at the top of, their list of favourite touring stops in the country. The audiences here are just top-shelf. Quick to sing and dance and give back to the folks onstage.

All this to say, when you visit St. John's, you'll be coming to a place where music lives in the air. Where the singer onstage isn't the only one who knows the song. Where live music isn't something you just watch and hear, but something you partici-pate in. I could offer countless reasons to come to this beautiful place I call home, but one might suffice.

Come sing a song in downtown St. John's. You won't be the only one singing. There's nothing like it, anywhere.

Even after Great Big Sea started really growing and we finally started making some money, I never had any interest in cars and still walked all over St. John's. I still do. I loved finding the hidden little alley streets among the jellybeans. Paths that I thought were driveways that led to a hidden little street with four houses on it.

Perhaps my favourite walking discovery was a part of St. John's that looked like Petty Harbour to me. We've spoken about The Battery, but there is another gem that is even more a slice of outport in the city. A chunk of Bay in Town.

Quidi Vidi (pronounced "kitty vitty," and sometimes, mysteriously, "kwida vida") is also known as The Gut, a term we use to describe a small harbour cut sharply in the jagged, rocky oceanside cliffs. This self-contained traditional fishing-harbour hamlet is about a twenty-minute walk from downtown St. John's, if you take the road. A far cooler way to walk there from downtown is to take the previously discussed North Head Trail, but when you finally reach the top of the stairs, don't head straight down the road, but turn north and follow the cliffs . . . carefully!

The trail to Quidi Vidi is marked and safe, but don't venture too far off it on the water side or we'll all be sorry. You'll see signs that will send you down through Cuckhold's Cove and on to Quidi Vidi. You heard me correctly. Cuckhold's Cove. I got in trouble once at the museum when a rather conservative-looking British visitor asked me how Cuckhold's Cove got its name. I shouldn't have said, "I'm pretty sure you know how Cuckhold's Cove got its name." But I did. I apologized when she turned red.

As you'll know by now, I love the fact that we have so many bizarre place names and titles. I cherished every time someone asked me how to walk from Cabot Tower down to Quidi Vidi, and I could utter this sentence with a straight face:

"So, you walk north—not up, but down—from Signal Hill, past Widow's Walk, just above Deadmans Pond, through Cuckhold's Cove, and you'll find yourself in The Gut."

Imagine saying that sentence anywhere in the English-speaking world and expecting anyone to understand it. There's not a Townie around who wouldn't nod and say, "Yes, that's a lovely walk there."

God, I love St. John's.

The origin of the name Quidi Vidi is the source of much debate. It's quite funny to research it, as so many arguments are made with complete confidence when, in reality, no one seems to know for sure where the name comes from. Some argue with great certainty that it is from Irish Gaelic and means "beautiful village," while others swear it is from a Latin phrase meaning "divided land." My favourite one is the staunch belief that the name derives from a popular neighbourhood cat named Kitty, and the kitty village became "kitty vitty."

Whatever the origin, or whatever the route you take to get there, don't miss a chance to walk around Quidi Vidi Village. The steep rocks on one side are decorated by iconic little fishing sheds that are literally hanging off the cliff face. The entrance to the little harbour is so narrow and shallow that boats of any size have to wait for a high tide or the seventh wave to pass from harbour to ocean or back again. A long wooden slipway is still a fairly active small-boat launch, and the wharves are often busy with fishermen cutting and cleaning fresh cod, all of which makes for wonderful sights and sounds.

You can hike in through Cuckhold's Cove and out the other side on yet another walk along the East Coast Trail. But the walks are just part of the reason to visit this delightful little St. John's zone. The hospitality industry has taken off here in Quidi Vidi in recent years, and there are several destinations for your day in The Gut.

Linda's Bar has been here for as long as many can remember, and you really should pop in for a drink and a chat with the lady of the house. You'll be surrounded by hundreds of pieces of local memorabilia. You might find a flag from a military group or a jersey from a hockey team. It is as charming and quirky as I've ever seen. The Plantation is a city-run arts and crafts space where you might just stumble upon an artisan making the very thing you hoped to find. Two breweries occupy space on the waterfront at Quidi Vidi. Landwash operates a beer garden and food truck park that is just delightful, especially on a sunny afternoon. Quidi Vidi Brewery actually brews beer in their building right on the wharf, and the tasting room upstairs offers the coolest views of the water and cliffs. You can sit on the deck outside and watch a fishing boat make its way back in through the narrow entrance to the harbour while sipping on a local brew. They also have a performance space where they regularly feature sessions and full performances.

But with apologies to all the awesome stuff around, the gem of The Gut is Mallard Cottage.

Mallard Cottage could very well be the oldest wooden structure in the province, its construction said to date back as far as 1820. It has been used as a residence and, for many decades, an antique shop, but around 2014 chef Todd Perrin and restaurateur Steve Lee took a leap and purchased the building and meticulously converted it into a restaurant. A few years later, Mallard Cottage was deemed one of the best new restaurants in the country and a destination for culinary tourists from around the world. Happy to say, this award-winning restaurants is still in operation.

I've loved Quidi Vidi since I first discovered it so many years ago, and I bet you will, too.

I love to tell everyone about it, and I love to tell them like this:

When in St. John's, don't miss The Gut.

SAINT-PIERRE SWEARS

"F—K ALAN DOYLE! F—K ALAN DOYLE!!"

It's not what I usually hear when I am about to play a gig. Walking towards a stage, I am more accustomed to hearing "Are you ready for Alan Doyle?" and then a few cheers or whatever. But here on the sidewalk wharf that wraps the harbour in Saint-Pierre, "F—K ALAN DOYLE!!!" is not just aimed at me, but shouted to, well, everyone in town through an impressive PA system that sends the words across the festival crowd of about 2,500 and bouncing off the walls of the houses and churches to the remaining 2,500 or so inhabitants of this most unlikely French town on a most unlikely French Island.

And when I say French, I don't mean Québécois, or Acadian, or any other subset of the French-speaking population of Canada. For I am not in French Canada. I am not in Canada at all. Nope. Today, I am being sworn at in *France*.

You are probably asking, Dear Reader, "Why is Alan now taking us not only outside the province, but to a foreign country?" To this very fair question, I would offer the same response I give any time I'm asked about why anyone would leave Newfoundland and travel to this ocean speck of France:

You barely have to leave Newfoundland. Saint-Pierre is right there.

Most Canadians, and just about everyone else, tend to be very surprised to learn that an actual part of actual France is less than twenty kilometres off the shore of Newfoundland. But this patch of islands is indeed a part of France, and every trip here reminds me just how French it is, and how Newfoundland and Canadian it isn't. You could be forgiven for expecting that this place might have assimilated somewhat to a North American way of life. It hasn't. At all. Quite the opposite. This place has clung to all things France. The language, the cars, the food, the works of it.

So, with an authentic chunk of a European country a hop, skip, and short ferry ride from Newfoundland, a better question might be "Why wouldn't I take you here?" In truth, it is significantly easier to get to than most parts of the province. It is also one of the living examples of how closely Newfoundland and Labrador was—and in fact, still is—connected to the European countries that fought for and settled the place.

I am here to play the wonderfully titled Rock and Rhum Festival. I can scarcely recall being as eager to get a festival T-shirt, as this one features two of my favourite things—one of them with the coolest French spelling. A few hours ago, I flew into the tiny airport across the expansive harbour from the town itself. If you fly in on one of the six days a year it is not socked in fog, you will appreciate just how remote and, again, unlikely, this place is.

I have been here a few times over the years, and it has always struck me the same way. It is a dozen or so streets of France. Not streets *like* in France, but a dozen or so streets of actual France. These streets have Citroën cars zooming around past bistros and baguetteries. Not a Ford or a Tim's in sight. It is truly bizarre that this place has existed a few kilometres from North America for this long and has so actively and passionately refused to integrate in the slightest.

"*F—k Alan Doyle!*" rings out once more, and a few more people seemed to have joined the chant, so instead of turning into the festival site, I figure I should head in the opposite direction and let whatever is happening in there run its course before I come in to play or run for my life.

I double back past the legendary Hotel Robert, which for the longest while was the only real hotel in Saint-Pierre. I giggle as I recall the first time Joanne and I came here. We were in our early twenties and had been only seeing each other a few months. We booked the last room in the Hotel Robert, and when we checked in, we discovered it had two small single beds. When I went back down to remind the lady that I had booked a bed big enough for two, she winked and said in her best broken Franglais, which I will try to write phonetically as I heard it:

"Ah *oui, oui*. Zis iz fine, fine. Deez two small bunks, you know? D'ey h'ar separate now. But you can *pousser* d'em togedder to make ze love."

"I see. *Merci*," is all I thought to say.

I keep my head down as I walk further from the F—k Alan Doyle Festival past the tourism office. I giggle again as I recall when Jo and I visited this place and found the folks inside somewhat confused that we had come in, and they had more to say about the lady at Hotel Robert than anything else.

"Ah! You are at ze Hotel Robert?! Did ze lady ask you to *pousser* ze bed togedder?" I guess the lady at Hotel Robert was well known for her advice for wannabe lovers with single beds.

A few steps later and I am upon what I would call the main square in Saint-Pierre. Place du Général de Gaulle is a small but welcome patch of well-groomed grass and mini botanical garden in a town that feels like it has very, very little of those things elsewhere. It is difficult to avoid words like *rocky*, *barren*, *foggy*, *windswept*, and *sea-beaten* when describing this place. It's funny how a fountain and a few flowers jump out in a bleak spot. You would walk past this little park in almost every other town in North America, but here amongst the pavement and concrete and stone, it is a bit of an oasis.

It overlooks the port's main terminal, where the ferry ties up and French customs officers regularly surprise Canadians who didn't think they needed a passport to come here. And as I turn seaward, I nod and say, "Oh yeah!" aloud at the sight of the most prominent Saint-Pierre building, standing French tall and French proud, dominating the waterfront and square.

The post office building was constructed in 1932–33, in a style reminiscent of eastern France, and has been used for postal and customs purposes, amongst other official processes, over the years. At the time, only the central part of today's building existed. The wings on either side were added later. I recall reading one travel site that referred to locals saying the building resembles a praying monk, but for the life of me, I cannot see it. Maybe I need a drink.

I stroll by the Musée Heritage. It is closed this evening, but I can say from previous visits that this is a quaint little stop where you can quickly learn a lot about the history of this place. And the history of this place is tumultuous, to say the least. It has been fought for and won and lost and abandoned and established and re-established since 1536, when Jacques Cartier, who seemed to get everywhere in these parts, claimed the islands for France.

The result of all this claiming and taking and settling and ousting by the French, British, and Americans didn't really come to a halt until the end of the Second World War, when Saint-Pierre and Miquelon became a French overseas territory; later, in the mid-1970s, it switched its designation to a "territorial collectivity." I confess I find it tricky to spot the difference between these two titles, but it seems the latter affords the place slightly more autonomy and ability to self-govern.

I hear some loud and poorly played rock music being blasted over the PA, so I am hopeful the anti–Alan Doyle rally might be winding down. But just to be safe, I figure I should wander some more before heading over.

As I round the corner heading back into the streets of the town away from the water, I pass the beautiful stone front of Saint-Pierre Cathedral, the most impressive church on the island.

This church has gone through a lot since it was first built back in 1690, facing winters and gales over the centuries. A fire in 1902 saw it all but destroyed, but the local parishioners would not let her go and refurbished and rebuilt to make the grand structure that I see here today, which was officially reopened in 1907. The rugged stone bell tower stands out from the smooth painted exterior walls of the main church, drawing my eye in a most pleasant way. It almost appears as though the church exterior was done industrially, while the bell tower was done by the hands of the locals bringing one stone after another by hand.

I grin as, once again, the stained-glass windows are the most impressive—one of them donated by Charles de Gaulle himself.

It's always the way. Say what you like about organized religion, but man, they make cool windows.

A few streets deep into the heart of the domestic area of Saint-Pierre and I am once again astonished by how France, and how not Canada or Newfoundland, it is. The streets are not like ours. The houses are not similar. The fishing stages aren't really stages at all, and though they fish the same stocks as fishermen from just across the bay, the fishing boats here are not the same either. They're not even hauled up out of the water in the same way.

At home, the flakes and stages reach out into the water to meet the boats. Here, they lash them to round winches, which are hand-cranked by walking them in circles to drag the boats in over the beach rocks. It is a head-scratcher to me that so few, if any, signs of assimilation can be found anywhere.

I record a voice memo to remind myself of this moment: "I wonder if they even know Canada is right there?"

I turn and walk up towards the cemetery. From this height I can look out over the entirety of this tiny little fascinating place. Houses built on solid rock in the middle of the ocean. It is a calm evening, so I and all the festivalgoers enduring someone swearing at me are above the water line. I bet there's lots of windy days when we would not be.

It is not hard to see why France was so eager to hang on to what could be the only remaining vestige of their hopes and dreams for a massive New France in North America.

Over a few hundred years, Saint-Pierre ran in the race for North Atlantic cod and had great success establishing a flourishing local economy trading and selling salt cod back to Europe and to the West Indies. The strategic location, coupled with the sometimes-booming fishery, made it worth keeping. This was the ideal location for restocking of vessels—and later, refuelling of planes. Come to think of it, this place has made for a lifetime of stories about very unlikely events brought about by its most unique geopolitical location.

I am reminded of a crazy interview I had with an American journalist a few years back.

It was a "phoner day"—a day when I did a run of phone interviews one right after the other in fifteen-minute intervals to promote a Great Big Sea album and tour. Four an hour for eight to ten hours. I called a US journalist based in the New York area, explained that I was speaking from my home in St. John's, and asked him if he had ever been to Newfoundland.

His response puzzled me. "Almost." His ensuing long pause told me he wanted to be asked what he meant, and since I'd had a dozen or more identical conversations that day, I was happy to oblige him for the chance of an unusual one.

"Almost?"

"I've been to Saint-Pierre." Again, nothing but a lingering buzz on the line till he added, "For four hours."

I had to bite. "Why Saint-Pierre, and why only four hours?"

He went on to describe an unlikely circumstance. One that is very oddly indicative of this most unlikely place.

"A few dozen entertainment journalists and I were loaded onto a charter jet and flown directly into Saint-Pierre. We went directly to a screening of a film, and then the director, Roman Polanski, took questions at a press event."

I figured it was my time to let silence indicate I wanted more info, and he bit as fast as I had.

"You see, Roman Polanski has charges laid against him in the United States, and if he steps foot here or in any of the countries where America has extradition treaties, he would most likely be immediately arrested. I guess France isn't one of those places. So, in order to promote his movie in the US press, the most efficient thing for the film company to do was to fly Roman to a part of France that is as close as possible to the US, and then jet in the American journalists for a few hours and then jet them home again.

"When I got word of this assignment, it was exactly the first time in my life I'd ever heard of Saint-Pierre and Miquelon. And I was shocked that I could travel from New Jersey to France in about six hours, round trip."

As big as the fishery was, and as politically strategic as it may have been for France to keep Saint-Pierre, there is one piece of history that literally put it on the map. Sure, you'd still have to zoom in, way in, on that map, but if this place is locally and globally known for one thing, it is smuggling.

Smuggling booze (and a few other heavily taxed items like cigarettes and perfume) from Saint-Pierre is a huge part of southern Newfoundland's history. It is especially a big part of my childhood, as I am partly from the area where most of the contraband landed. You see, the Saint-Pierre ferry lands in Fortune on the Burin Peninsula, which is about sixty kilometres from the hub town of the area, Marystown. I was born a Doyle from Petty Harbour, but my mom was born a Pittman from Marystown, and every Newfoundlander knows that running rum from Saint-Pierre to Fortune and Marystown and St. Lawrence and Spanish Room and all the other Burin Peninsula towns was big, big business.

The stories are legendary. The fishing boats from Newfoundland meeting French fishermen on the fishing grounds between the two countries. The tales of boats with false bottoms with a few hundred pounds of fish on the top of a hold built to take a thousand pounds. The bulk of the hidden compartment beneath loaded with dozens or hundreds of bottles of contraband rum and vodka.

The French *gendarmes* turned a blind eye to it all, mostly, as it was such big local business, which left the Newfoundland authorities to do their best to catch the smugglers on the open water. But the vast, often foggy fishing grounds were practically impossible to police, especially as everyone on the Burin Peninsula and beyond was rooting for the smugglers to outrun The Man.

The savings and cash grab were no doubt the biggest reasons for the efforts. But let me offer one more reason, even though I know I might get some flak for saying this out loud and for speaking for any Newfoundlanders on the southern half of the island.

We liked it.

Yes, we did. We thought it was fun. Running booze from the Frenchmen. Dashing across international borders in speedboats under the cloak of night. Outrunning the local cops gave great delight, but nothing—nothing!—compared to getting one over on Canadian Customs Officers, duping the government out of tax from our hard-earned dollars. It was great sport. People enjoyed devising ingenious ways to dodge the authorities and get their illegal haul ashore.

I have heard of cod traps sewn into huge bags big enough to hold hundreds of bottles of booze. They were towed behind the boat and affixed, loaded with heavy chunks of salt in the bags with the bottles. The smugglers would drag the contraband in the net across the bay, and if a customs boat came speeding around the point, they cut the line and took a mark of where they were. The heavy salt chunks would sink the net like a stone, dragging all the booze down with it.

"Nothing to see here, officer."

Of course, in an hour or so, after the authorities had left, the salt chunks would start to melt and eventually disappear. As soon as they did, the buoyancy of the rum bottles would lift the load back to the surface, where the lads could easily recover it.

And once they landed the booze on the Burin Peninsula or beyond, there was no end of the shenanigans to hide and sell it.

I had a friend, Sam, who was from Salt Pond, a little town halfway between Marystown and Burin. I was delighted to be invited to his house for a supper and a night of family fun. The backyard of his parents' house was a well-kept family garden with a firepit, raised beds of vegetables and flowers, and a rusty old tractor.

"What's with the tractor?" I knocked at the rust on the bucket.

My pal quickly responded, "Oh, that's been broke down for years." But then he winked and grinned, which I found curious.

Once after-supper drinks were in, about eight of us set out to the backyard fire. As darkness fell, and songs flew almost as quick as the drinks, we found that we had drunk the bottle dry.

Upon discovering this, my pal and his entire family shouted, unprompted and in unison, "FIRE UP THE TRACTOR!"

They all jumped into duty like a fire department at the sound of the alarm. One sister ran to the main road to take watch, while the other ran to a shed and lifted a large rock right next to it and retrieved a key. She flicked it to the dad like a quarterback executing a well-run drill as he climbed up on the broken-down tractor as quick and easy as the Lone Ranger mounted Trigger.

Sam just stood there and grinned like a drill sergeant proud of his platoon. "Come with me," he called out as he strode confidently towards the back of the tractor as his dad turned the key. That thing started like a Formula 1 race car.

"Fadder put an extra baffle on the exhaust so it hardly makes a sound," said Sam, beaming with pride.

Sam Sr. rolled the tractor ahead about six feet without barely making a sound. Sam Jr. kicked off about six inches of dirt, revealing a hatch. After an "all clear" from the sister on watch, Sam lifted the hatch and escorted me down to what I can only call a rum bunker.

Below ground—or I guess I should say, below tractor—was a wood-floored, rock-walled cellar. There must have been three dozen bottles of rum in there, along with half as many of vodka, and enough cigarettes to last a fella a lifetime.

"This will all be sold by Tuesday," Sam smiled. "But not this bottle!"

He picked a forty-ouncer, and the makeshift militia reversed the process as quick as a flash. The whole operation took less than five minutes, and we were back at the fire singing songs like it never happened.

In the strangest twist of fate, my own uncle Ted ran the government liquor store in Marystown. My dad used to torment him. "Jesus, Ted, who in their right mind is buying legal liquor in Marystown? It must get lonely in there, does it?" And then he would finish with the banger line: "Ted, you are like the Marystown Maytag repairman."

Dad wasn't wrong. And neither was the logic of those avoiding the taxable liquor and smokes. Sure, you could go to the government liquor store and pay full price for a bottle of Screech, but why would you, when you could also buy a smuggled bottle of Saint-Pierre rum for a fraction of the cost? Financially, it just made total sense. People bought it for their own use, while every single club and pub and Legion and bar was pouring smuggled rum into empty legal booze bottles for decades.

And again, the sport of it was half the jolly. As one skipper in Petty Harbour used to say all the time, when asked about shopping at the legit liquor store, "Sure, where's the fun in that?!"

As I walk up the narrow Euro street past some houses and a few warehouses, I note that many of these buildings played a role in Saint-Pierre smuggling and bootlegging, but not just on a local and Newfoundland level. For Saint-Pierre and Miquelon played a globally significant role in the smuggling world for several decades. You could even argue that during Prohibition in the US, this was the centre of the smuggling universe.

The Prohibition era in the States ran from 1920 until 1933, and during that period, this little archipelago was not subject to the alcohol ban. So, the importing of illegal alcohol to America became the biggest industry in Saint-Pierre and Miquelon. One publication called the islands "The Warehouse of America," and Al Capone is well understood to have set up operations here. American bootleggers frequently made the short voyage to Saint-Pierre and Miquelon to procure alcohol. The local economy benefited from this influx of revenue, and bars and establishments catering to American tourists flourished. French authorities, while officially respecting prohibitionist policies, often turned a blind eye to the lucrative trade. For a decade, many historians agree, illegal alcohol was the biggest industry in Saint-Pierre and Miquelon.

The presence of organized crime in the region was significant, and the islands gained a reputation as a haven for those engaged in the illegal alcohol trade. This situation persisted until the US repealed Prohibition in 1933. Afterwards, Saint-Pierre and Miquelon's role in smuggling diminished, but the period left an indelible mark on the islands' history, highlighting their strategic significance during a unique chapter of American history.

Show business knows all about it. As I type, my pal Allan Hawco is filming a new crime drama titled *Saint-Pierre*. Fans of the most awesome Netflix show *Peaky Blinders* know that the opening episode of season six sees the hero gangster, played by Oscar winner Cillian Murphy, strolling menacingly along the wharves of Saint-Pierre and Miquelon in 1933. He finally enters a building at the start of what is an amazing scene about the end of Prohibition, where Capone and others are mentioned. And what building does he enter? The Hotel Robert, of course. And I'm sure he "*poussé*-ed the beds togedder to make ze love."

From the direction of the festival, I hear another poorly played rock song end to very little applause and maybe even a boo or two, so I keep walking up towards the cemetery. I pass a bakery that, like most everything else this evening, is closed so that everyone who works there can be at a festival booing some fella called F—king Alan Doyle. But I do recall going into that bakery on a previous visit and eating what I can 100 percent surely say was the best apple turnover I ever had anywhere, including Paris.

The apple turnover—and all the food scene here—might be reason enough to jump on the ferry and come for a visit, but the road to the ferry is well worth the ride as well.

As noted, I came here this afternoon via airplane, but an equally popular route is to take the short one-hour ferry from Fortune on the bottom of the Burin Peninsula, or what most

Newfoundlanders refer to as "The Boot," as it is shaped like a man's lower leg, bent at the knee with a well-worn workboot on.

I am potentially biased with romanticism about the Burin Peninsula as my beautiful mom is from Marystown, and I spent quite a few summer days there chasing cousins up and down the meadows right around the heel of the workboot. I've also mentioned that me and Joanne and Henry have a cabin right where the man's lower leg attaches to the main island. So, with those confessions over, let me give you at least a few notes about driving down The Boot to get to Saint-Pierre and Miquelon.

Once you turn off the TCH in Goobies—yes, Goobies—and travel about twenty kilometres, you'll find yourself in Swift Current, which crowns the head of Placentia Bay and I think is in the discussion for the prettiest little town in all of Newfoundland and Labrador. The main road snakes right exactly at the edge of the water, and you might feel like you were driving your car across the bay, not next to it. There's a most unusual grove of birch trees that line the road out of town, and along the way they engulf the wonderful Kilmory Resort, a fantastic place to stay or camp and pop a kayak in where the salt water meets the fresh water plunging down from Pipers Hole River.

It makes for a stunning drive to start the journey down the peninsula. You couldn't be blamed one bit for expecting the next hundred kilometres to be postcard-picturesque.

And they are not.

At all.

The drive down the middle of the Burin Peninsula is the best (or worst) example of how this island of Newfoundland was 100 percent meant to be travelled by boat. There are all kinds of beautiful bays and harbours and towns on both sides of this narrow leg of land, and you can't see a single one of them once you leave Swift Current.

Instead, there's a unique barren landscape to look upon and a few million moose to dodge, and that's about as exciting as the bulk of the Burin Peninsula highway gets. But don't be discouraged. There's beauty in The Boot. You just got to turn off the highway to see it.

Grand Le Pierre, Bay L'Argent, and the wonderfully named Jacques Fontaine are all visually incredible places. A little further down the road, Spanish Room and Jean de Baie are just as impressive. The larger towns of Burin, St. Lawrence, and Fortune are all worth a visit, but my fave is my mom's home of Marystown.

"Marystown is Newfoundland's Glasgow," a well-travelled British engineer pal of my brother once said. I didn't know what he meant until I went to Glasgow, where people work hard and play harder. "Nowhere better than Glasgow when the whistle blows on Friday," he'd say, always with a glimmer in his eye.

In the best of times, Marystown has a bustling fish plant and shipyard as well as playing host dock to a fleet of fishing boats and draggers and offshore oil supply boats of all shapes and sizes. Add all this to the booming smuggling economy mentioned earlier, and you got a hell of a Saturday night.

Around here, we use the word *tear* to describe a great night out, as in "What a tear we had!" The main motel in Marystown was always called the Motel Mortier, pronounced like the French, *mour-tee-yay*. But this town has such a reputation for grand nights out that most refer to the motel as the Motel More-Tear, because more tears have been had there than anywhere else on the island.

I have had more than a few tears myself in the "Plywood Palace." (This motel has more nicknames than a minor-league baseball team.) Across the way is the legendary Beau Bois Pub. If you see me in a pub sometime, ask me why they call Thursdays "Dragger Night" at the Beau Bois. It's not what you might think, and I can't tell you here.

All this to say, Marystown is one of my fave nights out in all of Newfoundland and would be an excellent stop on your way to the Saint-Pierre ferry, which I can see clearly now as I have made it up all the way to the cemetery. I'm not sure why my "F—k Alan Doyle" avoidance has taken me up here, as I don't make a habit of visiting graveyards before shows. But this one is special. Well, special to me at least.

The first time I came to Saint-Pierre was when I was still in school in Petty Harbour. I couldn't have been more than thirteen or fourteen years old, and we came on a school trip for a day and a half. The bus ride down the Burin Peninsula was a hoot, as was watching classmates barf on the ferry. The French cars and croissants were fun to discover, but the thing that really told me I was in a whole new world was this graveyard.

I've come to learn it's a common thing in France, and indeed many European towns, not to bury the dead, but to lay them to rest in concrete or stone graves above ground. Some with small or stately mausoleums, but more with simple stacked concrete coffin enclosures, often with a viewing window to see the casket inside. I had never even heard of this until I walked, like I am walking this evening with dusk in the air, around the cemetery in Saint-Pierre.

I suppose it was a marker in my journey, in retrospect. A marker that told me there was so much more to see in this world than Petty Harbour or Newfoundland or Canada ever could show me. Long before we had the internet or cable TV with global travel shows, this place lit a fire in me and a curiosity that has never been quelled. In this place where the dead are honoured, I also give thanks for the birth of my wanderlust.

Oh, there goes one more "F—k Alan Doyle." This one has the last bit cut off, like someone has ripped the mic from whomever has been leading this chant intermittently for the past hour.

My set is scheduled to start in thirty-five minutes, so I figure I should take a deep breath and head to the site.

My long-time tour manager Gerry meets me at the back gate. I can't tell if he's red from laughing or fighting with people. He points to the stage. "Have you been hearing this?!"

"I have . . . all over town!" I sneak around sidestage to catch a glimpse of the band who've been cursing me all this time.

Gerry explains to me that four fellas from California in some kind of Zeppelin-esque tribute band somehow got this Rock and Rhum booking and set off to go to France. For some reason, not all of them made it. When I peek around the corner of the stage, I see a singer and a drummer. Whatever the configuration, they clearly got way too much into the *rhum* and were not really rocking at all.

The poor fellas had got onstage and immediately stunk the joint out. After a few poorly received tunes, the singer apparently tried one last effort to rally the crowd, shouting, "Are you here to rock with us today?"

When no one gave them the 1977 Zeppelin response he wanted, he'd shouted, "Nah, you ain't here to rock with us . . . you're all here just to see that Alan Doyle guy. Well . . .

"*F—k Alan Doyle.*"

I guess a few people laughed, and that was the biggest response they'd gotten so far, so he chucked in a few of them throughout the set.

It looks like the poor fella is finally giving up. He staggers off the stage and rages into his dressing room tent area, and the drummer . . . well, the drummer refuses to leave. I guess he's been promised a drum solo or something, so he starts wailing about as good as a fella might with a bottle of Saint-Pierre *rhum* in him, which is not very good at all.

Their set time is over, but he will not relent. The stage crew starts taking one piece of his drum kit away at a time. A cymbal, then a tom, then a bass drum, till the sad, sad sight of this drunken fella, with his drum stool being carted off, standing over his hi-hat cymbal, playing his last beat.

I am standing sidestage now, waiting for our crew to finish setting up. Darkness is fully fallen, and everywhere but the stage is dim. I'm wearing my in-ear headphones, so I don't hear the guy behind me till he taps me on the shoulder.

I turn around, and as I take my headphones out I realize it is the singer from the Zeppelin band. He is shit-faced. I think he wants to ask me for a smoke but can't really speak. And I guess he is also too drunk to recognize me from the face on the gig poster right over my head. I figure I should just say something.

"Rough gig up there, man. We've all had them."

"Yeah, man, this place sucks." He staggers but extends his hand with a "What's your name, man?"

"Me? I'm Alan Doyle." I grin a little as he goes as white as a sheet.

Then I shake his hand and say the only thing I can think of before hitting the stage.

"F—k me."

WELCOME TO NEWFOUNDLAND AND LABRADOR

N ewfoundland and Labrador. Welcome.
Might as well end with Welcome, as we started with Farewell.

There is an often-photographed road sign in Port aux Basques, on the southwest corner of the island, greeting travellers with a welcome.

Visiting or returning people post pics of it all the time as they roll off the ferry from Nova Scotia and finally step foot on the actual island of Newfoundland. You can only really see the sign as you exit the incoming ferry or if you make a crazy U-turn in the middle of a four-lane highway heading towards the outbound ferry, and who in their right mind would ever do that?

I have never seen the sign or photographed it myself because, I will somewhat sheepishly confess, I have never taken the ferry from Nova Scotia to Newfoundland. Not one time. Ever. I've taken it from Newfoundland to Nova Scotia twice, once from

Port aux Basques and once from Argentia, but never from North Sydney, Nova Scotia, to home.

So, I've never seen that famed sign. Truth be told, I've never truly seen Port aux Basques, even though I've been there twice. The first time, myself and Joanne drove from the highway right onto the ferry in the pitch black of night. Before the ferry sailed, we crashed in a sleeper room and I never even saw Port aux Basques as the ship pulled away. And the second time . . . well, the circumstances were whacky. I'll explain.

I bet it seemed like an excellent idea in the boardroom at the St. John's headquarters of a national brewery. Let's save everyone the red cheeks and call the brewery—I don't know—Smith.

So, I bet it seemed like an excellent idea at the headquarters of Smith Brewery in St. John's, back somewhere in the mid-1990s.

Great Big Sea had been playing for two or three years and were really taking off, especially at home. We got lots of gigs in the biggest bars because we filled the places with incredibly thirsty people. The breweries loved us for the same reason the bars did. That being, because we sold truckloads and truckloads of beer for them both.

The Smith Brewery set their eyes on a summer promotion that would really connect Smith beer and Great Big Sea, and we were more than happy to partner with them. The Smith marketing people thought up the idea of fans getting to see GBS in a really authentic and intimate way. And where better to hear us sing our shanties than on the water? So, late in the spring, Smith pitched us the idea for Rock the Boat—a contest where Smith drinkers could get to see a GBS gig on an actual boat.

To be fair, we loved the idea, too, and worked with them closely to conjure up this whole contest.

I say "contest," but I honestly can't recall how people "won" a ticket to the grand prize. I suspect, though, it wasn't a particularly hard nut to crack because very quickly, the number of "winners" grew and grew and grew. It became the game of the summer to get a berth for this gig. I honestly don't recall if we planned for a few dozen winners and ended up with hundreds and hundreds, but that's how many people had won or qualified to see us on a boat. It was the talk of the town.

The success of the marketing campaign was a big win for all concerned. We celebrated with the Smith gang and had almost finished patting ourselves on the back when someone far more sensible than me raised their hand and asked a very practical question:

"What boat has Smith Brewery booked for this?"

Silence till the sensible person spoke again.

"As a matter of fact, what boat is big enough to accommodate a professional concert stage and hundreds and hundreds of fans in front of it?"

Responses started with optimistic stuff like "There are a few options" and quickly melted away to "Holy shite, what are we gonna do?"

I can't say for sure how many phone calls were made to shipping outfits around St. John's, where we all lived, as did most of the contest winners. Nor can I say for sure how many times Smith got laughed at by an offshore supply vessel captain when asked if he would pause a shipping run to let five hundred drunk people on board to have a concert. But I do know calls were made and captains laughed.

Very soon, the options for the boat to be rocked were narrowed down to exactly one. The Port aux Basques ferry. It was the only boat big enough and willing to accommodate this whole deal.

Here's some fun facts for context. Firstly, Port aux Basques is over nine hundred kilometres from St. John's. It takes ten hours to drive it in a fast car with a couple of quick gas and pee breaks.

Secondly, the Port aux Basques ferry is not a cruise ship. It is not designed for concerts with hundreds and hundreds of people, and the only space aboard big enough for an event like this is the lower interior car deck.

But, as noted already, this was the one and only option.

So, on a hot summer day in the mid-1990s, hundreds and hundreds of people got put on school buses in St. John's at the crack of dawn and set out for a twelve-hour bus ride to Port aux Basques. And guess what else went on all those buses with the hundreds and hundreds of people? Even more hundreds and hundreds of cans of Smith Beer.

I'd ask you to pause reading for a sec and consider this scenario. Twelve hours on a school bus in the dead of summer with dozens and dozens of others who started drinking beer at 7 a.m. How would hour three look on that bus? How about hour six? How many pee stops do you think were politely requested, then shouted for in utter desperation, by the time they hit Gander—not even close to the halfway mark. You might ask yourself, too, if it's possible that any of those passengers discovered that drinking ever-warming canned beer on a moving school bus actually upsets their stomach.

I can't confirm first-hand, as me and the band took a flight west and jumped in a van as close as possible to the ferry. We nipped on to do the show. We were ushered into the belly of the ferry after it sailed out about five hundred metres into the harbour. It bobbed in the bay while we played.

I stood there onstage . . . well, I should say I *tried* to stand there onstage, as the boat tipped starboard and port. Sometimes a little and sometimes a lot, and it was hard to imagine which was harder for anyone who might get seasick, as lots and lots did. It is tough to say if it was the fumey, bobbing ferry or the twelve-hour warm-canned-beer bus ride or some twisted combo of them both that made people hurl, but hurl they did by the dozens.

I'll spare you the more gruesome details and just say this. We started our set for hundreds and hundreds of people in the fumey belly of that bobbing boat. We finished our set for dozens and dozens of people in the fumey belly of that bobbing boat. It wasn't till after our set that I learned the fate of the contest "winners." They were not staying in Port aux Basques for the night. They were to be boarded back on the school buses for a twelve-hour bus ride back to St. John's. Sweet Jesus.

We ran to the van as quickly as possible, and I hid in the windowless back seat. We were the first off the boat, and I wouldn't dare stick my head up by the windows. I didn't look up till we hit Corner Brook.

All this to say, though I have been to Port aux Basques twice, I have never actually seen it, or the famed "Welcome" sign. Let's remedy that together.

I rise around 6:30 and head to St. John's airport for a flight on Provincial Airlines, or PAL, as we call it. PAL's fleet of smaller planes used to fly pretty much only around Newfoundland and Labrador, but now operate on routes all around Atlantic Canada and even west as far as Montreal and Ottawa. Like any airline, lots of people whinge about this one for its small planes or its milk runs to Labrador West that stop in Gander, Deer Lake, St. Anthony, Wabush, and Churchill Falls along the way. But I am very happy to go on record and say that PAL is a godsend for this province and beyond.

It currently operates as the Air Canada partner in the region. If you want to fly anywhere around Atlantic Canada, you'll likely fly PAL. I find them to be very dependable, and while they don't have many frills and bells and whistles, they get you where you want to go safely and soundly.

I board the Dash 8 for a one-hour flight from St. John's to Deer Lake. It is a clear and cloudless day, so I get a good look at the wild interior of the island. I type two lines into the notes app on my phone. One reads, *Fresh water everywhere*, and the other *Lots and lots of room*. And while I don't know much about the wild and undeveloped parts of this place, I can tell you one thing with confidence. There are hectares upon hectares of land that could be really easily developed, with all kinds of access to highways and lakes and rivers and ocean. I am not talking about land that is way off, like in the Australian Outback or something. I mean land that is right next to the highway or the ocean. Loads of it. Practically everywhere.

If writing this book has taught me one thing, it most certainly is that I live on a massive island with very few people on it.

The plane touches down in Deer Lake and I quickly grab a rental car and head southwest. I am struck immediately by the contrast between where I am now and where I was about seventy minutes ago. Hardly the same world at all. And it's not just a simple matter of going from an urban environment to a rural one. The landscapes themselves are completely different. If you drive across the island, the transition from rocky and foggy to wooded and mountainous is somewhat gradual. But when you take a short flight from the Northeast Avalon Coast to the interior of the west of this island, the change is quick and radical. You could not be blamed for thinking you flew to a different country.

I am bound for Corner Brook, but not before stopping at the Deer Lake Irving Big Stop. It is kind of a ritual for travelling Newfoundlanders to visit the Big Stops to mark their journey across the island. These complexes, containing a gas station, a convenience store, and a restaurant, have become homogenized now, with many of them looking and feeling very similar, but they used to be more distinctive, and travelling folks often spoke of their favourites.

"You won't get a better baked bean than the breakfast at the Deer Lake Irving," people would say, or "The best Pepsi selection in the world is in Goobies." I always love to add, "How odd is it that one of the best views in Newfoundland is from the window over the urinals in the men's room at the Clarenville Irving Big Stop?"

The Deer Lake Big Stop is always a fascinating location for people-watching. This is the crossroads for the highway going southwest to Corner Brook and on, but also for the one headed north to the national park and Northern Peninsula, and south or east to various hunting and fishing grounds. There might be students or seniors. There could be one van headed to Marble Mountain with skis strapped to it, while next to it there is a vanload of hunters with guns strapped all over the place. There could be lumber trucks coming from the interior, or naturalists heading into the interior to save forests. It's as good as a concert.

I pop in, and the first thing that strikes me are the loud Texas accents. "AH NEVER THOUGHT WE WUZ EVER GUNNA GIT HERE!" one very tall fella wearing a vest embroidered with a salmon giving an enthusiastic thumbs-up shouted to his pals while loading cases of what he called "dangerously strong beer" onto the checkout counter. "PAY WITH THUH FUNNY MUNNEY, IT'S FREE!!" shouts back his pal in an orange baseball hat emblazoned with LUBBOCK in all-black caps. As I get my snacks, a lady next to me in a Tilley hat and holding a hiking trail map sighs, rolls her eyes, and shakes her head.

Deer Lake Big Stop. Don't miss it.

I pull out of the Big Stop and very shortly pass Deer Lake Hydro, one of the coolest buildings in the province. Built in 1925 to provide electricity primarily to the pulp and paper mill in Corner Brook, this plant graces the side of the highway through town. This long, low industrial—but fancy industrial—power plant grabs my attention every time I pass it and especially after dark, when twenty or more tall, round-top windows are lit from inside.

The other cool thing about this building is that it houses an air-raid siren that was repurposed as a work whistle when the plant was being constructed. It sounded, and apparently still sounds, every day but Sunday at 7 and 8 a.m., noon and 1 p.m., and 5 and 6 p.m.

"That's a lot of air raid siren," I dictate into my notes app.

If I needed any more reassurance that my "fresh water everywhere" comment is true, I am driving right past it. Deer Lake—the lake, not the town—is, well, enormous. I checked it on Google Earth once, and I measured it to be over twenty-six kilometres long and almost four kilometres wide. And if you just zoom out a little, you'll see that Grand Lake, just to the south, is at least twice as big as the one I'm driving past.

And all that water eventually dumps out into the mighty Humber River, snaking its way through the Humber Valley between Deer Lake and Corner Brook. This area is nothing short of magnificent, especially on a fall day like today with the hills covered in leafy trees turning red and yellow and orange along with the few stubborn evergreens.

The bottom of Deer Lake to the entrance to Corner Brook is only about fifteen kilometres. But what a fifteen kilometres it is. Along with the mighty river and the mountains lining the valley, I pass a hillside golf course, at least two resorts, and the best ski hill east of Quebec in Marble Mountain, which has an incredible lodge and quite a number of rental accommodations close by. It is just excellent. I have driven and hiked through the Swiss alps, resorts in Colorado and Vermont, and wondrous Western Canadian treasures like Banff and Whistler. The Humber Valley competes with those in every way—the scenery, nearby airport, the variety of summer and winter activities. Yet sadly, it remains a little off the radar.

It is a head-scratcher. This place should be a global destination. Spread the word!

A zig and a zag along the river's edge and under the awesome jagged cliffs that fall to the water make for a very cool drive onto the hills overlooking what is really Newfoundland's second city, Corner Brook.

Named for a tiny community with a water inlet, this city is another great example of amalgamation helping to pave the road forward. Settlement in this area goes way back to at least Captain James Cook's adventures in 1767, but it came to be the city it is now much more recently. Corner Brook is made up of four previously independent places: Curling, a fishing town; Humber West, a business area; Humber East or Humbermouth, which housed the railway operations; and Townsite, which was mapped and planned in the early 1920s to house what would become this company town's company, the Corner Brook Pulp and Paper Mill.

And it was in large part due to the early success of the paper mill that this gathering of settlements swelled to a city of around thirty-two thousand people. For much of my young life I knew that St. John's was the city on the east coast and Corner Brook was the city on the west. I knew both had fancy big-city stuff like street lights and universities. When the infamous Newfoundland Senior Hockey League was raging in the late '70s and early '80s, the big rivalry was between St. John's and Corner Brook.

It could be argued that these two cities are the headquarters for the centuries-old Townie-versus-Bayman conflict that pitted the urban crowd from "Town" in St. John's and the men from the Bay, "Baymen." Think Hamilton versus Toronto. Glasgow versus Edinburgh. Then you'll start to understand the relationship between Corner Brook and St. John's.

As I round the top of the highway, I get the full view of Corner Brook, nestled into the end of the Bay of Islands. It is surrounded by hills on three sides, and the water of the bay that eventually leads to the open ocean lines the fourth. I love hilly towns. I love that you can see every level, as opposed to flat places where the view's restricted to what's right in front of you.

Especially on a fall day like today, with the hills bursting with colour, Corner Brook is as pretty as a town can be with a hundred-year-old pulp and paper mill in the middle of it. But as noted already, it would be tough to imagine Corner Brook without the mill.

Don't get me wrong. Corner Brook is more than just a company town in the middle of random somewhere. It has marvellous vistas and hikes and drives out to Lark Harbour on the south side of the bay and Cox's Cove on the north. It is also the default hub service town for more than half of the land mass of the island. The hospital, the university, the college, and government services are all here. But even with all this going for it, Corner Brook was literally built around the one mill that dominates the shoreline and the skyline.

The history of the pulp and paper mill in Corner Brook dates back to 1925, when the Corner Brook Pulp and Paper Company was established. This venture marked a significant development in Newfoundland's industrial landscape, particularly in the context of its reliance on forestry resources. But this was not just a big deal for Newfoundland. This mill was a big deal globally. I've read that the Corner Brook mill was, at the time of its founding, the largest project ever in the history of papermaking. The world was hungry for paper, and the mill utilized the abundant softwood resources from the surrounding forests, primarily focused on producing newsprint. Remember newspapers? Before the internet, they were a pretty popular way of spreading information locally and internationally.

During the mid-twentieth century, the mill underwent various expansions and modernization efforts, especially after World War II, as demand for paper products surged. By the 1960s, Corner Brook Pulp and Paper had become one of the largest producers of newsprint in North America. The mill played a crucial role in the local economy, providing employment for thousands of residents. Corner Brook became a booming little city.

However, the industry faced challenges in the late twentieth and early twenty-first centuries, including fluctuating demand and environmental concerns. Newsprint is not as hot a commodity as it once was, but the mill goes on.

I park the rental car down in the town and scamper back up the wonderful Three Bear Mountain Trail, which winds its way through the trees. I walk out to a point overlooking the smokestacks that billow white smoke or steam up and out. I can detect the same scent, reminiscent of warm, flat beer that I remember from this and other mill towns. I can see into the yard, with acres of piled-up logs waiting to be processed. Trucks and utility vehicles run all over. Make no mistake, this mill is still very much a going concern.

There's much commercial and retail activity in the downtown, with bars and restaurants mostly on or near the main drag of Broadway. I have played here many times, and I can tell you, when the whistle blows in Corner Brook, there's a night and a half to be had.

But today I plan to visit three places in Corner Brook. One is old and one is new. And we'll walk between them on the third.

The mill really built this town and much of the infrastructure in it. By far the coolest addition to the city and the province is the Glynmill Inn. I am no architecture buff, but this Tudor-style hotel would still be remarkable in some centuries-old English hamlet where there might be dozens of other buildings in the same style.

Nestled here in the middle of downtown, hidden like a secret in the trees overlooking Glynmill Pond, the inn—the creation of architect Andrew Cobb—is just magnificent.

Early in the 1920s, the Armstrong-Whitworth Company of England were hard at work building the mill. They figured their senior staff would require comfy living quarters while supervising construction. When the mill became operational in 1924, the Glynmill Inn became a full-service hotel.

I stroll up a couple of the many one-way streets in Corner Brook (a traffic system Townies love to hate) and feast my eyes on this century-old hotel. It really feels like you've stepped out of modern-day Atlantic Canada and into a European village of long ago. The trees around the grounds have matured so much that you can't really enjoy the sight of the hotel till you are in the parking lot, which is kind of a shame, but what is not a shame at all is how separated you feel from the bustle of the city.

I take a quick wander around the lobby and dining rooms to remind myself what a time portal this place is. The beams from the Tudor construction decorate many corners of the inn. The round dining room is delightful. The cozy pub is a temptation, as it has hosted many a good time when I've stayed there.

But tonight, I want to check out a new place. And lucky for me, I can walk there on the Corner Brook Stream Trail.

On a fall day like today, I find myself surrounded by picturesque perfection en route to the middle of downtown. This multi-use trail meanders alongside the vibrant Corner Brook Stream, showcasing lush forests, diverse wildlife, and views of the surrounding hills. Walkers and joggers pass me and pause to take pics and make notes on the well-maintained pathways. I pause for a while at a rest stop with a lovely bench to sit and watch the ducks duke it out with the geese for the last of a little girl's bread crumbs. Just delightful in every way. My only critique of the Corner Brook Stream Trail is that I wish there was more of it, and apparently that will be addressed soon enough, as the city is constantly adding to it. Bravo.

I step out of the woods and round another one-way street and see my final Corner Brook destination, and indeed my accommodation for the evening: Hew and Draw. If the Glynmill Inn is the oldest hotel in town, this is surely the newest, and dare I say hippest.

The Hew and Draw is an independent, family-owned boutique hotel built into a wonderfully converted old retail building. The name is a reclaiming of what was once an insult to Canadians, often referred to as simple hewers of wood and drawers of water. The hotel describes itself as a celebration of the heritage of this part of the world, where folks made a living in the woods and on the water. And what a celebration it is.

The lobby is cool and casual, as are the staff, who are quick to point out the Best Coast Restaurant and Boomstick Brewing Company, which share the main floor. Both are hopping as I check in close to what must be happy hour. In an excellent mix of the past and present, the walls display artifacts and photos of the hew-and-draw culture, while the building itself is modern. They are going for something new in this place, but have certainly not let go of the past, as it is all around me.

Then, the coolest sound confirms that thought. It interrupts my investigation of the lounge area near the elevator. A distant sound, but one that feels significant enough for me to break stride. As the sound lingers, I start to recognize what it is. Robert at the front desk must have spotted my amusement, as he answers before I ask:

"Yes, that's the mill whistle. Still blows at the end of every shift."

I smile about it the whole night. In the excellent room, and while I had excellent food and drink, in my mind I could still hear the whistle blow as I said good night to an excellent day in Corner Brook.

I wake in the early morning like a man possessed with one notion.

"Today is the last day of travel for this book," I say to Joanne on the phone as I pull onto the highway heading southwest to Stephenville. "One pic of that 'Welcome' sign and we are done!"

"Stop talking on the phone while you're driving on the highway, please." Jo is always about safety first and knows I'm very easily distracted.

The drive between Corner Brook and Stephenville takes me between lakes and ponds beneath rising hills, again with the most magnificent colours of fall. I have undeniably struck it lucky with the weather, as everything shines as I make my way to the west coast's second city.

"The Friendly Invasion." The sign announcing the turnoff to Stephenville is confusing at first, but then I recall that this is the phrase used by folks in this town to describe and celebrate the storied partnership between the local populace and the American military.

Stephenville was a rural area with only a few hundred people before the US military started investing in the place in 1941 and established Ernest Harmon Air Force Base. Very, very quickly the place boomed, and by the early 1950s the population was well over five thousand. The Americans built not only the base and barracks and support buildings, but also a massive airport that lines the bay, as well as sidewalks and street lights and practically everything else.

From 1941 till the day the base closed in 1966, this place was, for all intents and purposes, American. One source actually refers to Stephenville having been a de facto enclave of US territory, first within the Dominion of Newfoundland and later within Canada.

Driving into Stephenville, it is difficult to imagine what it would have looked like without the base. Though they departed over half a century ago, the footprint of the mighty US armed forces literally defines the place. Half of the valley is covered by the old runway and airport and its industrial-looking support buildings. The houses I am driving around don't really look like houses, as I suppose they aren't. Rather, they are converted air force buildings and barracks, now used as apartments and homes as well as recreational buildings.

Past the base buildings into the commercial downtown, Stephenville has a look that strikes me as familiar, but at the same time oddly out of place. There's a single, long main street . . . and it is called Main Street. Not Water Street, as it is in St. John's or Harbour Grace—or even Halifax, for that matter. I see a couple of Stars and Stripes flying and a poster for a country music festival. Then it dawns on me. As I park the car, I am struck by a thought I cannot shake.

Stephenville looks . . . American. It's not just that it's been influenced heavily by the US occupation. It actually appears to be a small American town. It looks like one of the places I have played in the Midwest, like Kansas or Missouri. I can't believe how much this street reminds me of many of them. Perhaps I should not be so surprised, as this place was really drawn up and built by Americans.

I have a quick bite of breakfast at Hartery's Family Restaurant. Go there. Thank me later. Then I get a pastry at Danny's Bakery. Go there, too. Thank me later.

I really want to go to my fave restaurant in Stephenville, but it is a little too early for pizza. And not only does Stephenville have great pizza, but it has a great pizza story. The Domino Pizza House and the Estoppey family have been making superb food in Stephenville for more than half a century. Their pizza and sandwiches are legendary in this area. I have had many of their subs, and I would devour one now if it wasn't before opening hours.

You are probably thinking, how cool is it that this town had such an early franchise of the globally known pizza chain. But that's where this pizza story gets interesting.

When they named their pizza joint in the early 1960s, the Estoppeys had never even heard of that other Domino's Pizza— because the Michigan-founded franchise that went on to become a global success story wasn't trademarked until 1965. When they eventually found out about the common name, the family likely figured it would be nothing to worry about. Surely this international entity didn't care what they were doing in their teeny family shop in small-town Newfoundland. But then the big company sued the family business for trademark infringement in a case that became famous in Stephenville as *Domino's v. Domino's*.

The town swept to the defence of the local biz till the suit was dropped when the Estoppeys produced receipts proving their pizzas predated the chain by a couple of years.

So you can get Domino's pizza almost anywhere in the world. But you can only get the original Domino's pizza in Stephenville.

As I roll west out of Stephenville and through the neighbouring town of Kippens, the road signs slowly go from English to French. I pass Gaudon's Lane and then Doucette's Lane as I approach a treasured part of this province, the Port au Port Peninsula.

The peninsula is connected to the main island by the narrowest causeway, and when I cross it, I am immediately aware that I have effectively left one island and driven onto another. The landscape, and certainly the road signage, changes instantly.

This area is commonly said to be Francophone, as it contains the highest proportion of French-speaking families of any settlement on the island. In truth, it is a wonderful melting pot of cultures with a history that includes everything from Basque to Mi'kmaq, Acadian, and English settlers, all in the wonderful mix that gives us such varied place names as Boswarlos, Aguathuna, Lourdes, and Piccadilly.

I turn up the hill towards Boswarlos to start a drive around the perimeter of the peninsula. I intend to check out some quaint little towns, but I nearly put the car off the road when a towering cathedral comes into view. I immediately pull off the road into the parking lot, where I am dwarfed by an enormous white wooden church with a bell tower rising to the heavens. To the best of my knowledge, I am not even in a town yet, but on the road somewhere between Port au Port West and Aguathuna, there is a church in front of me that must be able to hold at least a thousand people.

Our Lady of Mercy Church is the tallest wooden Catholic church in the province, standing over 115 feet. It was built entirely with volunteer labour between 1914 and 1925. A hydraulic lift and a pile of paint cans tell me someone is preserving this incredible structure, and as luck would have it, a work crew steps around the corner and lets me inside.

If the outside of this wooden treasure is impressive, the inside is truly divine, and not just because it is a church. All handmade wooden features, including the pews, columns, and indeed the altar itself. But the real eye-catcher is the ceiling.

"It looks like the belly of a ship turned upside down!" I say to one of the workers.

"H'off course. The carpenters, d'ey were h'all boatbuilders." The gent's Franglais accent is wonderful.

I wander the church, and it is so singular and impressive that I could have left Port au Port satisfied without exploring another kilometre. But I press on, past the beaches in Boswarlos that look across the water to the mountains behind Point au Mal. I have an inspired walk around a religious grotto in Lourdes, where they have fashioned fishing nets and markers into giant rosary beads. I drive up the steep hills between Mainland and Cape St. George, where you can survey so much of the peninsula. I am constantly blown away by view after view from the best oceanside drive in the whole province. The cliffs by Felix Cove are as dramatic as I've seen anywhere, and the sun shining on the water near Boutte du Cap Park fuelled me for the drive down the Humber Valley to the southwest coast and our final Welcome.

When I pass the Flat Bay exit heading south, I know that I am effectively in what is new territory for me. As noted earlier, I have driven down here twice before, but once in the dark and once hiding in a van, so I've never really seen the Humber Valley. Again, shame on me. The drive almost always has an ocean on one side or a mountain range on the other, and often both. I have heard this touted as the most fertile and agriculture-friendly part of the province, and I can see why. Large farm fields roll down valleys and up hills that look to be covered in deep topsoil. It is a botanical garden . . . till it isn't.

Much like driving to Cape Spear Lighthouse, the drive to Rose Blanche Lighthouse on the southwest coast has a moment where the treeline just suddenly stops. One second you are surrounded by tall trees and vegetation, then almost randomly, Mother Nature decides that's it for the trees and you are down to mossy rocks and stubborn shrubs.

I have heard that the lighthouse in Rose Blanche is not just any old lighthouse, but a very special one and a must-see for anyone in the area. I have also taken you and me both to traditional lighthouses in Cape Spear, Bonavista, and southern Labrador, so it feels right to check this one out, too.

The route to Rose Blanche takes you past Isles aux Morts, Burnt Islands, and Harbour le Cou to what is really and truly the end of the road. The only way to continue travelling along the southwest coast is to board the ferry for La Poile, and we don't have time for that till the next book.

I round the turn into Rose Blanche, and way, way off in the distance I see what looks to be the silhouette of a small stone castle. It casts a very peculiar shadow for this part of the world, but I'm not here to see that, so I keep looking for a lighthouse.

Road signs indicate that it's out by that castle-looking building, but I still don't see a tower or anything resembling a traditional lighthouse. I finally can't drive anymore. I have reached a dirt parking lot with signage that points to a lighthouse walking trail. I walk up over a few hundred metres of trail, then it rises out of the ocean and rocks like a set from *Game of Thrones*.

Turns out the small castle *is* the lighthouse. I can see now that the turret is the light tower. As I get closer, it's clear that it is made not of steel or concrete in a tall column, but with large cubic stones that form a kind of square house with the light turret on top. It is surreal. Built between 1871 and 1873, apparently, with rock quarried from nearby, it is the last remaining granite lighthouse in the province.

I could linger all day, but I'm losing light and have to meet a fella in Port aux Basques.

Much like where I grew up in Petty Harbour, Channel-Port aux Basques clings to the rocks, and for centuries has made a living off the water. At around five thousand people, it is larger than average for a rural Newfoundland town, mostly due to the jobs and infrastructure created around the ferry.

I have a quick tour around with local Scott Strickland, a retired teacher who was born and raised here and knows the place like the back of his hand. I learn quickly that Channel-Port aux Basques does not refer to the channel leading to the town Port aux Basques, as I—and I'd bet 95 percent of people from our province—assume. Rather, this place is another winning example of amalgamation, as the towns of Channel and Port aux Basques joined forces in 1945. Scott is a wealth of local knowledge and is mighty proud of the staying power of this stubborn place in the face of centuries of winds and storms. One of the worst of those was the deadly Hurricane Fiona, which ripped through here in September 2022. She carried off a dozen or more whole houses, including Scott's, but still the people here hang on and hold fast. I find his pride in the place uplifting, to say the least.

I shake Scott's hand, and he drops me at the hotel overlooking the bay and the ferry terminal. Then, in the last of the dusk light, I see it round the bend. The unmistakable sight of the ferry coming from North Sydney. The vessel and route that have been our railway and highway for a hundred years or more.

As it nears the dock, I feel my pilgrimage around this province is complete. For now, anyway. I'm weary from the travel and eager for a bed. I turn to head in as the ferry spins in place at the dock.

"Jesus, the sign!" I scare a half dozen others who have been watching the boat like I am. I probably should explain myself, but it is getting dark, and very soon a few hundred vehicles will get off that boat.

I jump in the car and drive onto the highway towards the terminal. When the coast is clear, I make a crazy U-turn in the middle of a four-lane highway and spin around. I can finally see it. I pull the car off the curb and run out for a poorly advised but long-awaited selfie.

I am not sure if it is the sign or the notion that I may be at the end of a long journey home, but as I snap a pic, I do something that maybe Sir Cavendish Boyle used to do all the time.

I feel my feet on this land, and I smile.

Newfoundland and Labrador.

Welcome.

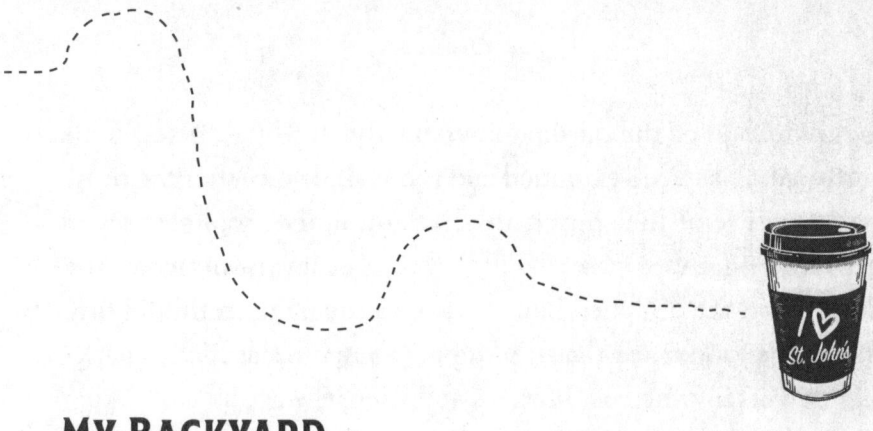

MY BACKYARD

"**D**on't miss The Gut!" I shout as I type at the island in the kitchen. "What a wicked way to end the St. John's bit!"

I wait for Joanne or Henry to congratulate me, but they both have headphones on, involved in their own things. How dare they?! All I hear is the grumpy exhale of Spencer. He's been sleeping on the floor beside me and is not impressed that I've woken him without having a wiener ready. The audacity!

I decide I will reward myself for completing the hometown parts of the new book with a walk, as the midafternoon sun finally seems to be getting the better of the fog. Our house sits on the east side of downtown, and my favourite coffee shop, The Parlour, is a very pleasant five-to-seven-minute walk from our place. And what makes the walk so pleasant is that it takes me right next to, or actually through, four beautiful St. John's landmarks.

St. Thomas's Anglican Church is a very impressive wooden structure with a tall bell tower all wrapped in traditional rough-side-out clapboard painted in jellybean blue. It was built in 1836 and has been extended and renovated since, but the original structure of the church still lives on in the front section of the building. As I pass through the breezeway between the church and the attached hall, I wave to the gang in the Johnny and Mae's food truck that sits all year round in the church parking lot, serving the best burgers and fries in St. John's.

Such deliciously devilish food for such holy ground. That's St. John's for you. A place where the divine and the debaucherous have danced together for centuries.

I make my way past another nineteenth-century wooden building and gem of the downtown core. The Commissariat House was built between 1818 and 1820 as the house and offices for the commissary general of the British forces. I'm dying for that coffee, so I don't linger and peek inside at the exhibitions or the interpreters in period costume. Lucky for me, the most direct route from my place to the coffee shop passes the church and Commissariat House and heads directly through the most impressive property in the province.

Government House is a National Historic Site and serves as the home of the lieutenant-governor of Newfoundland and Labrador, who is effectively the British monarch's local representative. This stone palace was also built in the late 1820s, and it is as close to regal as we get here on a rock in the middle of the ocean. The building is a sight to behold and stands as a reminder of a time when we were very much a colony, subjects of the Crown and all its elegance and authority.

As I stroll through the massive gardens lined with ceremonial statues and trees, I turn my head to see one of the Royal Newfoundland Constabulary horses cantering back into what must be the best equine accommodations in eastern Canada.

A few strides later, and I am in the lee of the house itself, and although I am not a monarchist of any kind, I give my usual bow of the head to the guards and staff and sometimes to the lieutenant-governor him- or herself.

I can almost taste the coffee, I'm so close, but I have one more landmark to pass before I can sip my americano in full view of Bannerman Park through the spacious windows of The Parlour.

The Colonial Building was the home of the colonial and eventually the provincial government, and it has recently undergone a massive restoration. Its limestone was imported from Cork, and its impressive front steps lead up to a main entrance supported by tall decorative columns. If Government House looks regal, this place looks *important*. More history has gone on within those walls than my caffeine-hungry brain can comprehend at this moment. Elections and riots and votes to leave Britain and become Canadians. So much of it all happened in that building, but all I can dwell on today is how lovely it looks with the sun shining through the stained glass in the cupola that crowns the place like a jewel.

The gals in The Parlour see me coming and they know what I want before I get to the counter. A few hellos and thank yous later and I'm sitting in the window overlooking the park and the mighty steps to the Colonial Building. I am about to sip my victory coffee—and then it dawns on me. After weeks of searching and discovering and describing so many wonderful people and places in this province, I figured I had covered much of it. Not all by a stretch, but a nice cross-section to help guide a trip or two to this province.

But now I realize that I've taken you on what I thought was an extensive journey around my home and almost overlooked these national and provincial sites that are literally in my backyard.

I can't help but think that this province is a treasure trove that keeps on giving. Just when you think you've uncovered all its jewels, the wind stops and the sun shines on a whole new batch of gems on the beach. And in a moment's pause, you might even realize you've overlooked a bunch that have been staring at you this whole time.

I scratch my head and finally take a sip as the coffee shop and the sidewalks have become instantly busier. I love watching the city I love come to life. St. John's does that whenever the sun shines, and I love that it does. Especially in this, the springtime of the year, when most of the city has been wet or cold or both since Halloween. I love that I live in a place where sunshine is not a given, and when it shows up we are grateful for it.

I watch young parents wheel prams into Bannerman Park, and toddlers emerge from the snowsuits they've been trapped in since the first fall of snow in November and run to the playground to embrace the jungle gym like a returning friend at the airport. Two university students remove a blanket from a knapsack, and in a quick minute there's textbooks and sandwiches and a study date. Two gents with briefcases grab coffee and walk across to the steps of the Colonial Building and start what looks to be a business meeting al fresco. All hands taking advantage of a moment in the sun.

Is this why I love this place so much? Is it because I live in a place where we have no expectations that the sun will automatically shine? That, instead of feeling low and jilted when it is foggy, we feel high and grateful when it is not?

Does this notion extend to life in general? We are preconditioned to expect that things can be hard, and when they very occasionally are easy, we celebrate. Are we programmed, after generations on the frozen coast and island, to just accept that we might have it a little harder than most, and when the clouds finally lift, we should smile because they did?

What's better than a nice day? A nice day in a place that doesn't always get them.

Everywhere I look.

Grins as bright as the sun.

And maybe, just maybe, that's what makes Newfoundland and Labrador the Smiling Land.

Acknowledgements

Joanne and Henry made the biggest sacrifice for this project. Together we logged thousands of kilometres and close to a hundred hours in the van for this book, and I'll be forever grateful to them for suffering me in close quarters for that long. I could not have done it without them. In truth, I would not have even wanted to.

In many of these places, I relied heavily on folks for local knowledge and help in the writing of and the editing and fact-checking of this book. Thanks to each of them in no particular order: Zita Cobb, Steve Sheppard, Wayne and Annette Parsons, Peter Bull, Brenda O'Reilly and Craig Flynn, Michael Rubinoff, Scott Strickland, and Allan Hawco.

Many thanks to Tim Rostron and to Ward Hawkes and Scott Sellers at Doubleday Canada for their patience and encouragement with all of this.

Thanks to my manager, Louis Thomas, and all at Sonic Entertainment for looking out for me for thirty-plus years.

Grateful to Michael Levine for insisting that this was a good idea.

My touring bandmates and crew have suffered through over two years of my annoying clicks and clacks on the tour bus as I hammered out this book while we rolled through sun and snow. We made it. Special thanks to Modelo Negra, Basil Hayden, and Old Milwaukee.

And, as ever, thanks to you all for reading this book and all of the others, and for listening to the tunes, and coming to concerts, and laughing at musicals, and watching the TV shows and movies, and all the other crazy stuff I ask of you all the time.

Thanks for all of it.

Cheers,
A